SADLIER'S
Coming to Faith Program

COMING TO
GOD'S LIFE

Dr. Gerard F. Baumbach

Dr. Eleanor Ann Brownell

Moya Gullage

Joan B. Collins

Helen Hemmer, I. H. M.

Gloria Hutchinson

Dr. Norman F. Josaitis

Rev. Michael J. Lanning, O. F. M.

Dr. Marie Murphy

Karen Ryan

Joseph F. Sweeney

The Ad Hoc Committee
to Oversee the Use of the Catechism,
National Conference of Catholic Bishops,
has found this catechetical text to be
in conformity with the
Catechism of the Catholic Church.

with

Dr. Thomas H. Groome
Boston College

Official Theological Consultant
   The Most Rev. Edward K. Braxton, Ph. D., S. T. D.

Scriptural Consultant
   Rev. Donald Senior, C. P., Ph. D., S. T. D.

Catechetical and Liturgical Consultants
   Dr. Gerard F. Baumbach
   Dr. Eleanor Ann Brownell

Pastoral Consultants
   Rev. Msgr. John F. Barry
   Rev. Virgilio P. Elizondo, Ph.D., S. T. D.

Catechetical Assessment Consultant
   Dr. George Elford

William H. Sadlier, Inc.
9 Pine Street
New York, New York 10005-1002

Nihil Obstat
✠ Most Reverend George O. Wirz
Censor Librorum

Imprimatur
✠ Most Reverend William H. Bullock
Bishop of Madison
May 9, 1997

The *Nihil Obstat* and *Imprimatur* are official
declarations that a book or pamphlet is free of
doctrinal or moral error. No implication is contained
therein that those who have granted the *Nihil Obstat*
and *Imprimatur* agree with the contents, opinions, or
statements expressed.

Printed in the United States of America.

Credits appear on page 304.

Home Office:
9 Pine Street
New York, NY 10005–1002

ISBN: 0-8215-4305-9
123456789/987

DEAR YOUNG PEOPLE,

This book, **Coming to God's Life**, was written to help you understand more about the sacraments—the special ways we share in God's life and love.

In the sacraments, the Church recalls and carries on the work of Jesus Christ. You will learn that, through the sacraments, we are to become signs of God's love by welcoming, forgiving, healing, and serving others. We are to live as Jesus' disciples, sharing his good news with others.

When you use this book, ask the Holy Spirit to help you to:

- share more fully in the life and mission of the Church, especially in the celebration of the sacraments;
- celebrate the sacrament of the Eucharist weekly and Reconciliation regularly;
- discover ways that you can be a sign of God's love for your family, your friends, and your neighbors;
- learn to be like Jesus in his healing, forgiving service to everyone;
- imagine how Jesus wants you to continue his work and be a person of justice and peace.

All of us hope that you will enjoy learning about sharing God's life and love this year. Our prayer is that you will continue to grow as disciples of Jesus.

All of Us in the Sadlier Family

CONTENTS

Jesus the Good Shepherd
Life in all its fullness
   John 10:7–15

Faith Alive at Home and in the Parish

Unit 1   Jesus Christ Blesses Our Lives   page

Doctrine: Catholic Teaching

Jesus Christ, human and divine
God's love in our lives
   John 10:11; 11:1–44; Matthew 8:23–27;
   1 John 4:8

Our Catholic Identity: Church art, an aid
   to prayer

Faith Alive at Home and in the Parish

The kingdom of God
The good news of God's love
   Luke 4:16–22; 7:18–22;
   Matthew 6:10; 22:34–40

Our Catholic Identity: Catholic migrant ministry;
   Saint Teresa of Avila

Faith Alive at Home and in the Parish

Jesus welcomed all people
Jesus forgave and healed
   Matthew 8:5–11; Luke 5:17–26;
   23:34; John 13:1–7

Our Catholic Identity: Washing of feet on
   Holy Thursday

Faith Alive at Home and in the Parish

A welcoming and serving Church
A healing and forgiving Church
   Acts 2:1–13; Matthew 20:28;
   John 13:31–35; 1 Corinthians 12:26;
   Acts 3:1–10; Acts 4:34

Our Catholic Identity: Parish communities;
   joining a parish

Faith Alive at Home and in the Parish

Jesus, the sacrament of God
Seven effective signs
   Luke 12:54–56; Colossians 1:15;
   Matthew 1:19; Psalm 103:8, 11, 13

Our Catholic Identity: The Catholic family;
   Saint Joseph

Faith Alive at Home and in the Parish

The good news of God's forgiveness
Examining our conscience
   John 20:19–23

Faith Alive at Home and in the Parish

Jesus, our Bread of Life
Eucharist, meal and sacrifice
   2 Kings 4:1–7; 1 Corinthians 10:16–17;
   11:24; John 6:35

Faith Alive at Home and in the Parish

Unit 1 Review and Unit 1 Test—see page 260

Unit 4   A Community of Faith, Hope, and Love   page

Doctrine: Catholic Teaching

OPENING PRAYER SERVICE

Leader: We gather at the beginning of our year together to ask for God's help and to dedicate ourselves to be stronger disciples of Jesus Christ. Let us listen to the words of Saint Paul about God's love that comes to us in Jesus.

Reader 1: What will separate us from the love of Christ? Will anguish, or distress, or persecution, or famine, or nakedness, or peril, or the sword? . . . No, in all these things we conquer overwhelmingly through him who loved us. For I am convinced that neither death, nor life, nor angels, nor principalities, nor present things, nor future things, nor powers, nor height, nor depth, nor any other creature will be able to separate us from the love of God in Christ Jesus our Lord.
Romans 8:35, 37–39

Leader: What wonderful good news to share among ourselves and with others! But before we pray together, let us listen to a challenge that Saint Paul puts before us as members of the Church.

Reader 2: For the scripture says, "'Everyone who calls on the name of the Lord will be saved.' But how can they call on him in whom they have not believed? And how can they believe in him of whom they have not heard? And how can they hear without someone to preach? And how can people preach unless they are sent? As it is written, 'How beautiful are the feet of those who bring [the] good news!'"
Romans 10:13–15

Leader: We are these messengers. I now invite each of you to come forward and ask God the Holy Spirit to strengthen you so you may grow as disciples of Jesus.

(Each one comes forward, stands before the teacher and says the following:)

"I, _____, ask for God's help to

_____

_____ ."

(Then the teacher traces the sign of the cross on the forehead of each one and says the following:)

"May God help you and strengthen you."

(Sing a favorite hymn as a closing prayer.)

Called to Life

Jesus, we come to you as we begin this new year together. Help us to grow as your disciples

Our Life

Have you ever thought about your future? What kind of life do you want to have?

Take a few minutes now to write some key words that describe what your hopes are for your life.

Then write at least three qualities you have that will help you reach that goal.

Sharing Life

Join with a partner and share your ideas. Begin by making sure you know each other's name.

Listen carefully to each other. Maybe you can add to your partner's list of gifts and abilities. Sometimes people see gifts in us that we do not recognize in ourselves.

Then ask one another: What are God's hopes for your life?

Life in Its Fullness

Jesus once told this parable. His listeners did not understand it. Maybe you will.

I am the gate for the sheep. . . . Whoever comes in by me will be saved. . . . The thief comes only to . . . destroy. I came so that they might have life and have it more abundantly.

I am the good shepherd. A good shepherd lays down his life for the sheep. A hired man, who is not a shepherd . . . sees a wolf coming and . . . runs away, and the wolf catches and scatters them. I am the good shepherd, I know mine and mine know me.

John 10:7–14

What does this parable say about Jesus' love for us?

Jesus, our Good Shepherd, wants us to "have life." He was willing even to die that we might have fullness of life.

This year we will explore together the life that Jesus Christ came to give us. We will learn how this life can be nourished and grow through the life-giving sacraments of the Church.

We will share the life of faith among ourselves and find ways to reach out to others so they, too, may have "life in all its fullness."

We will identify and fight against all those things that threaten Christ's life in us—the "thieves" and "wolves" of falsehood, abuse, violence, indifference, and irresponsibility.

Take a few minutes now to look through your new book *Coming to God's Life*. Share together what lesson you are most looking forward to studying this year.

COMING TO FAITH

Play a word association game. Take turns saying what words or pictures come to mind when you hear the word *life*. Have someone write the ideas on newsprint or the board as they are given.

Choose the word or picture that says best what life means to you. In the space above, create a personal symbol or logo that illustrates it.

During the year, you might want to look back occasionally at this page to see whether your thoughts about life have changed.

PRACTICING FAITH

With your friends in a prayer circle, hold your *Coming to God's Life* book. Go around the circle, each one saying: "My name is .... This year I hope to grow in God's life by...."

† Close by praying the Our Father together.

Talk with your teacher about ways you and your family might use the "Faith Alive" pages together. You might especially want to do the Good Shepherd activity with a family member.

REVIEW

Jesus, the Good Shepherd

Think about what a good shepherd is like.
Then tell how Jesus is our Good Shepherd.

A good shepherd	Jesus
● cares for his sheep	_____
	_____
● feeds his sheep	_____
	_____
● would die for his sheep	_____
	_____
● will go looking for any sheep that is lost	_____
	_____

FAITH ALIVE AT HOME AND IN THE PARISH

This year your son or daughter will explore what Jesus meant when he said that he had come "so that they might have life and have it more abundantly" (John 10:10). He or she will learn how as Catholics we are called to live a sacramental life, a life ever alert to a special awareness of God's presence in the ordinary things and events of life. The basis for the seven sacraments is the life of Jesus, who lives today in and through the Church and who continues his saving action in the sacraments. The sacraments are encounters with Jesus Christ.

In the seven sacraments, the Church recalls and carries on the work of Jesus Christ in our world.

Your child will learn how we are to become life-giving signs ourselves—signs of God's life by becoming people who welcome, forgive, heal, and serve others. You can participate in this sacramental formation by talking with your child about these things and by growing with your child in God's life.

Learn by heart **Faith Summary**

- Jesus Christ is our Good Shepherd.
- Jesus came to bring us life—life in all its fullness.

1 Jesus Christ Reveals God

Jesus, thank you for showing us that "God is love."

Our Life

Someone once said that "a picture is worth a thousand words." See how well you can "read" the pictures on this page. What do they tell you about the ways God is with us in our world today?

What does God mean to you?

Sharing Life

Help one another remember what you know about Jesus that shows

- He is divine—God's own Son;
- He is human—as we are.

Imagine some things that Jesus can teach you about yourself.

Jesus was human and Divine

Work in small groups to share favorite Scripture stories about Jesus. Choose one story and prepare a dramatization or a role-play to present to the whole group.

See whether your classmates can find in the story what Jesus is teaching us about living as his disciples.

This week we will discover more about the ways Jesus reveals God to us.

We Will Learn

- Jesus Christ is both human and divine.
- Jesus shows us who God is.
- We can find many signs of God's love in our lives.

OUR CATHOLIC FAITH

- Jesus, you are the way and the truth and the life.
- How do you think Jesus was like us? unlike us?

Jesus Is Human

We first learned about Jesus as small children when someone told us the Christmas story. We know that Jesus was born in a stable at Bethlehem because there was no room for Mary and Joseph in the inn.

As we got older we learned from other gospel stories how much Jesus was like us. Jesus got tired. He felt thirsty and hungry. Jesus loved and obeyed his parents. He enjoyed doing things with his friends. He prayed and worshiped in the synagogue. Jesus was like us in every way except one—he never sinned. He was tempted, but he always said no to sin.

This story helps us remember how human Jesus was.

Among Jesus' closest friends were a man named Lazarus and his two sisters, Martha and Mary. One day Lazarus became sick and was dying. Martha and Mary sent for Jesus, but by the time Jesus arrived, Lazarus had died.

When Jesus saw Mary and Martha crying, he felt very sad and began to cry, too. He felt as we do when a loved one dies.

Based on John 11:1–44

Jesus also faced death as all people do. In his suffering and death, Jesus was truly one of us.

Jesus Is Divine

Jesus is one of us, but he is also the Son of God. This is what we mean when we say that Jesus is divine.

In the Creed at Mass, we say that Jesus is "one in Being with the Father." This means "Jesus is true God." Here is one of the stories from the gospels that tells how the disciples began to learn that Jesus was God's own Son.

One day Jesus was in a boat on the lake of Galilee with his disciples. Jesus was sleeping when a fierce storm suddenly started. The disciples were so scared that they woke Jesus, yelling, "Lord, save us! We are perishing!"

"Why are you terrified, O you of little faith?" Jesus answered. Then he got up and commanded the winds and the waves to stop, and there was a great calm. The disciples were amazed. Jesus had done something only God can do.

Based on Matthew 8:23–27

Like the disciples in the boat, we turn in prayer to Jesus for help. Because Jesus is really one of us, we know that he always understands how we feel. Because he is the Son of God, he can always help us.

Incarnation

The Son of God became one of us. This is called the incarnation. The word incarnation means "became flesh." The incarnation is the mystery of God becoming one of us in Jesus Christ. Jesus is a divine Person with two natures: a human nature and a divine nature. The incarnation, then, is the mystery of the wonderful union of the divine and human natures in one Person.

Describe some of the ways Jesus was like us.

Jesus was kind, he sinned, he died on the cross, he preached the Gospel. He cried, he also had friends

Name some things Jesus did that showed he was fully human and fully divine.

When do you most need to turn to Jesus in prayer? Will you?

OUR CATHOLIC FAITH

- My Lord and my God.
- Name some times when Jesus really influences your life.

Jesus Shows Us God

People have always wondered what God is really like. God chose to reveal himself to the Israelites. We learn what they believed about God in the Old Testament of the Bible.

God reveals who he is in a special way to us in Jesus. Jesus showed us who God is more clearly than anyone had ever done before. John, one of Jesus' closest friends, used three words to tell what he had learned about God from Jesus. He wrote, "God is love" (1 John 4:8).

We learn about God by looking at Jesus. Jesus showed us that God is love. Jesus cared for the rich and the poor, the healthy and the sick, saints and sinners. He showed us how to work for justice and peace. Jesus still works through us and through others to show God's love in the world.

A **disciple** is one who learns from and follows Jesus Christ.

Jesus often told stories to his disciples about God's love. In one story Jesus compared his own love and God's love for us to the way a shepherd cares for sheep.

A shepherd works hard to care for the sheep. To find grazing pastures to feed the sheep, a shepherd walks many miles in good weather and in bad.

The shepherd watches closely to keep the sheep together because they wander away and get lost. At night a shepherd huddles together with the sheep to protect them from other animals. A really "good shepherd" is even willing to die to save the sheep.

Jesus said, "I am the good shepherd. A good shepherd lays down his life for the sheep" (John 10:11).

Jesus cares for us like a good shepherd. He keeps us close to God. He protects us from the evil of sin. Jesus died to save and free us from our sins. If we think of Jesus as the Good Shepherd, we know how much God loves and cares for us.

We follow the Good Shepherd. We show God's love to our family, friends, and neighbors by following Jesus' example of caring for people.

What do you learn about God from Jesus?

How will you show God's love to someone in your life this week?

OUR CATHOLIC FAITH

■ Jesus, Good Shepherd, care for all those in your flock.

■ How can you tell when a person really loves you? when you really love someone?

God's Love in Our Lives

Because Jesus was God's Son, he brought God's love in a special way to everything and to everyone he met. Jesus lived his whole life aware of God's loving presence.

Jesus wants us to know that God loves us like a good shepherd.

God works through other people to help us live as his children. God works through our parents and families to provide us with food, shelter, and clothing. He also works through teachers to pass on knowledge, and wisdom, and through our friends to help us become loving persons.

Most importantly, God works through these people to give us the love that we need. Their love shows us that we are very special to God. Even when other people fail to love us, we know that his love for us will never end.

We can help others to know God's love for them through very simple, everyday actions. We show God's love, for example:

• by a kind word to someone with hurt feelings;

• by a cheerful smile to a sad friend;

• by reaching out to someone who is lonely;

• by trying to bring peace to an argument;

• by being just and fair in our dealings with everyone.

Family Portraits of Jesus

No one today knows what Jesus really looked like when he walked the earth. But Catholic churches around the world display "family portraits" of him. These works of art help us to understand in a deeper way that Jesus is both human and divine.

What "family portraits" of Jesus do you recall from your parish church? Perhaps you have seen the following:

- the infant Jesus with the Blessed Virgin Mary
- a crucifix
- a statue of Jesus as a boy or as the risen Lord
- stained-glass windows displaying scenes from the gospels
- the fourteen stations of the cross showing how Jesus suffered and died for us.

Make a visit to church on your own. Choose one work of art that tells you about Jesus. Spend a few minutes looking at it prayerfully. Thank Jesus for revealing God's love to you.

A Child Artist

One day a famous artist was traveling in the countryside near Florence, Italy. He saw a shepherd boy drawing a sheep. The boy's "brush" was a pointed stone. His "canvas" was a stone slab. His sheep was so well done that the famous artist took the boy with him as his pupil.

The boy's name was Giotto di Bondone. It was the thirteenth century, and he was about to change Christian art forever. God had given Giotto the gift of drawing biblical scenes that seemed to come to life for people. They made Jesus look as real and familiar as someone in your family.

Giotto's paintings help Catholics to appreciate that Jesus is both human and divine. We can be grateful for the gift of Christian artists whose works deepen our faith by turning our hearts and minds to God.

Faith Summary

- Jesus Christ is both human and divine.
- Jesus showed us that "God is love" by the things he said and did.
- God works through us and others to show God's love in the world.

Noli me tangere,
School of Giotto, (13th century)

Coming To Faith

How would you explain to a friend that Jesus is both human and divine?

Complete the following sentences.

Because Jesus wept when his friend Lazarus died, I know that....

Because Jesus calmed the storm at sea, I know that....

Because Jesus' love for us will never end, I know that God....

Because Jesus worked for justice and peace, we should....

Practicing Faith

Gather quietly in a circle. Imagine that Jesus is with you in the center of the circle. After a minute, read aloud each of the following situations. Take turns going to the center of the circle and responding to each situation the way you think Jesus would want.

● I have a lot of trouble getting along with my brother or sister. Jesus says....

● It really bothers me that I am not good at sports (or schoolwork). Jesus says....

● Sometimes I feel sad and alone. Jesus says....

● Some people think the best way to solve problems is through fighting. Jesus says....

● I feel a friend has really betrayed me. Jesus says....

† Pray together: Jesus, help us to be more like you. Help us to show God's love to others so that all will know that we are your disciples.

Talk with your teacher about ways you and your family might use the "Faith Alive" section. Tell a family member the gospel account of Jesus and Lazarus.

22

REVIEW ∎ TEST

Complete the sentences.

1. One who follows Jesus' way of life is called a _Christian_.

2. The mystery of God becoming one of us in Jesus Christ is called the
incarnation.

3. Jesus was like us in every way except _for miracals_.

4. The incarnation means that Jesus is both human and
divine.

5. What will you do to grow closer to Jesus Christ?
I will help other if help is needed.

FAITH ALIVE AT HOME AND IN THE PARISH

This chapter deepened your fifth grader's understanding that Jesus is both human and divine. That the divine nature and a human nature exist together in the one Person of Jesus Christ is a central doctrine of the Christian faith. It is called the incarnation.

Believing that Jesus is one of us helps us to turn to him more readily and to try to live as he did. Believing that he is truly God gives us confidence in his ability to help us. Jesus, the Son of God and our brother, came to bring us God's love. You can lead your son or daughter to an appreciation of God's love by providing an experience of a family trying to live as disciples of Jesus.

Jesus, Human and Divine

Jesus Christ is true God and true Man. Because of the unity of his two natures in one divine Person, he is the one and only mediator between God and us. There can be no other.

2 Jesus Christ and the Kingdom of God

Jesus, help us to be messengers of your life to others—life in all its fullness.

OUR LIFE

GOOD NEWS BULLETINS

Join us after 8 A.M. Mass. We need helpers to make sandwiches for our "special guests," the homeless.

Environment Guardians: Meet at 9 A.M. Saturday for beach and street cleanup. Bring plastic bags!

Thanks to all the fifth and sixth graders who visited the nursing home last week. Everyone wants you to come back!

Can you add a bulletin about something you have done or might do to bring good news to others?

SHARING LIFE

Share your ideas about what might be the very best "good news" our human family could hear.

Make a list of your ideas and try to come to agreement about the best "good news" of all. Talk about what you can do to make it happen.

Now that you and your friends have chosen what "good news" you will share this year, make your ideas specific by completing this plan together.

 **OUR GOOD NEWS PROJECT**

Describe the Project:

_____

How often will the group do this?

_____

Details:

- Whom will we need to contact?   _____

- Will transportation be required?   _____

- Other   _____

Evaluation:

How will we check on our project during and after it?

_____

_____

_____

This week we will be exploring how we are to be messengers of the gospel, the good news of Jesus.

We Will Learn

- Jesus announced the good news of God's love.
- Jesus showed us how to live for the kingdom, or reign, of God.
- We live for the reign of God by living the Law of Love.

OUR CATHOLIC FAITH

- Jesus, help us to know you and love you.
- In what ways is the teaching of Jesus good news to you? Explain.

Jesus Brings the Good News

The best news we can hear is that God loves us and cares deeply about us—no matter what. God gave us Jesus to show us that God loves us and will always love us. This is the very best "good news" that Jesus came to share with us.

When Jesus was about thirty years old, he began his ministry of preaching the good news of God's love. One Sabbath he went to the synagogue in Nazareth to pray with others in the Jewish community. He was asked to read from the Bible.

Jesus stood up and unrolled the scroll on which the Scriptures were written. With everyone's eyes fixed upon him, Jesus searched for and read these words from the prophet Isaiah.

"The Spirit of the Lord is upon me, because he has anointed me to bring glad tidings to the poor. He has sent me to proclaim liberty to captives and recovery of sight to the blind, to let the oppressed go free, and to proclaim a year acceptable to the Lord."

Rolling up the Scriptures, Jesus said, "Today this scripture passage is fulfilled in your hearing."
Based on Luke 4:16–22

What a surprise! Jesus was announcing the good news that the prophecy of Isaiah was fulfilled in him that very day. God the Father had sent Jesus to show people his love and to help them do his will. Jesus had come to free them from all forms of sin and oppression.

God's Promises

The people of Israel knew that God made a covenant, or special agreement, to love and care for them always. The Israelites in return promised to love God and to love one another by obeying the Ten Commandments. When the people of Israel kept the covenant, they lived as God's own people.

Sometimes, however, they, like us, found it very hard to live the Ten Commandments. Sometimes they disobeyed one or more of the commandments. They sinned and broke their agreement with God.

The **kingdom**, or **reign, of God** is the saving power of God's life and love in the world.

But God continued to keep the promises of the covenant. He promised to send a Messiah, or Savior, who would show people how to live for the kingdom, or reign, of God.

For many, many years, the Jewish people waited for the promised Messiah. Finally, the time had come. Jesus, the carpenter's son, announced that God's promise was fulfilled in him.

Jesus came to show God's love for all people. He came to bring about a new covenant between God and all people. He came to teach us how we are to live for the reign of God by loving him and one another. Jesus Christ is our Messiah and Savior.

- Tell in your own words the good news that Jesus came to announce.
- How will the good news that God always loves you help you to live for the reign of God? Give examples.

27

OUR CATHOLIC FAITH

- Jesus, you are the Son of God and our Savior.
- How do you think Jesus brought about the kingdom of God?

The Kingdom of God

The people saw the things that Jesus was doing. He showed great compassion for all. He healed the sick. He helped the poor, fed the hungry, and forgave sinners. The people began to realize that Jesus was someone very special.

Just about the time Jesus began his work among the people, a prophet was telling everyone that the Messiah, or Savior, was coming soon. The prophet's name was John the Baptist.

One day some of John's followers came to see Jesus and asked whether he was the Promised One, the Messiah.

In response, Jesus pointed out the special things he was doing: "The blind regain their sight, the lame walk, lepers are cleansed, the deaf hear, the dead are raised, the poor have the good news proclaimed to them."

Based on Luke 7:18–22

Jesus was saying that his words and actions were the very things the Messiah, the Promised One of God, would say and do. Jesus Christ was the Messiah. He lived his whole life for the kingdom, or reign, of God.

Living the Good News

Jesus invites all people to live for the kingdom of God. In the Our Father Jesus taught us to pray "Your kingdom come, your will be done, on earth as in heaven" (Matthew 6:10).

In the Our Father we ask God to help us to share in Jesus' work of bringing about God's kingdom, or reign, on earth.

There are times when we do not live the good news of God's love. We fail to love others as we should. We fail to do the things that bring God's justice and peace. These things keep us from living for God's reign. Because of our sins, the reign of God is not yet complete.

There are many ways that we can live for God's reign. These include carrying an elderly person's bundles, cleaning up a messy room without being asked, or saying no to cheating. All these are ways of doing God's loving will for us.

We build the reign of God every time we try to be just, or treat others fairly, and work to be peacemakers. Living in God's reign also means helping everyone to know and share in God's life and love.

Choose a beatitude from the list on page 293. Then write three things you can do to live this beatitude.

1. _____

_____

2. _____

_____

3. _____

_____

Explain how you can live for the reign of God?

What one thing will you try to do better so that God may reign in your life today?

OUR CATHOLIC FAITH

But that is what disciples of Jesus are asked to do. We cannot leave anyone out. Jesus told us that our neighbor is every human being.

■ Pray the Our Father together.

■ What are some ways that you help to bring about the reign of God every day?

The Law of Love

Sometimes people wonder what God really wants them to do. One day a leader of the Jewish people asked Jesus about this. He said, "Teacher, which commandment in the law is the greatest?"

Jesus answered, "Love the Lord, your God, with all your heart, with all your soul, and with all your mind.... Love your neighbor as yourself."

Based on Matthew 22:34–40

We often call this greatest of all commandments the Law of Love. We live the Law of Love by trying to live at peace with others and by treating others justly. We try to put the needs of others before our own. We try to serve people in need and treat all people with compassion.

Living the Law of Love is sometimes difficult. We need the support of our parents, teachers, and others to help us live the Law of Love. We need to ask the Holy Spirit to help us, too.

It can be very hard to be kind to someone we don't like, or to someone who is mean to us. Sometimes it is difficult to speak out for people whom others make fun of.

We sometimes forget how important we are in God's eyes. Some young people choose to use drugs or alcohol. Others don't work hard in school. They do harm to their minds and bodies. They are forgetting an important part of the Law of Love: God wants us to love ourselves always because he loves us.

The Law of Love may be difficult to live. But God promises happiness to those who try to live for his reign.

Kingdom Builders

As people travel around the United States, they often see migrant workers in the fields during harvest time. Migrant workers move from place to place, picking other farmers' crops. They are often paid little and work long hours. Sometimes they are treated unjustly, and their children are forced to move from school to school. The shelters in which they live are frequently poor and rundown.

The Catholic Church is very concerned about the needs of migrant workers and their families. That is why dioceses in which there are migrant workers provide spiritual and social services to help them. There are many priests, religious and lay people involved in this important ministry. This is another example of people in the Church who show us what it means to be kingdom builders.

What are your dreams for the kingdom of God?

Words from a Great Teacher

Over four hundred years ago in Spain, there lived a great kingdom builder. Today we know her as Saint Teresa of Avila. She reminds us that living for God's kingdom involves more than doing activities. She knew from experience how important it is to live a life of prayer.

Teresa's favorite prayer was the Our Father. She said that it was better to pray one Our Father with loving attention than to rush through twenty without thinking. She taught that one way to pray with "loving attention" is to remember that Jesus is always there with us "like a friend in a dark room." Above all, Teresa said, speak to God simply from the heart with love.

Sometime today, pray the Our Father using Saint Teresa's suggestions.

Learn by heart **Faith Summary**

- Jesus announced the good news of the kingdom, or reign, of God. The good news is that God loves us and will always love us.
- The reign of God is the saving power of God's life and love in the world.
- Jesus lived his whole life for the reign of God and calls us to do the same.

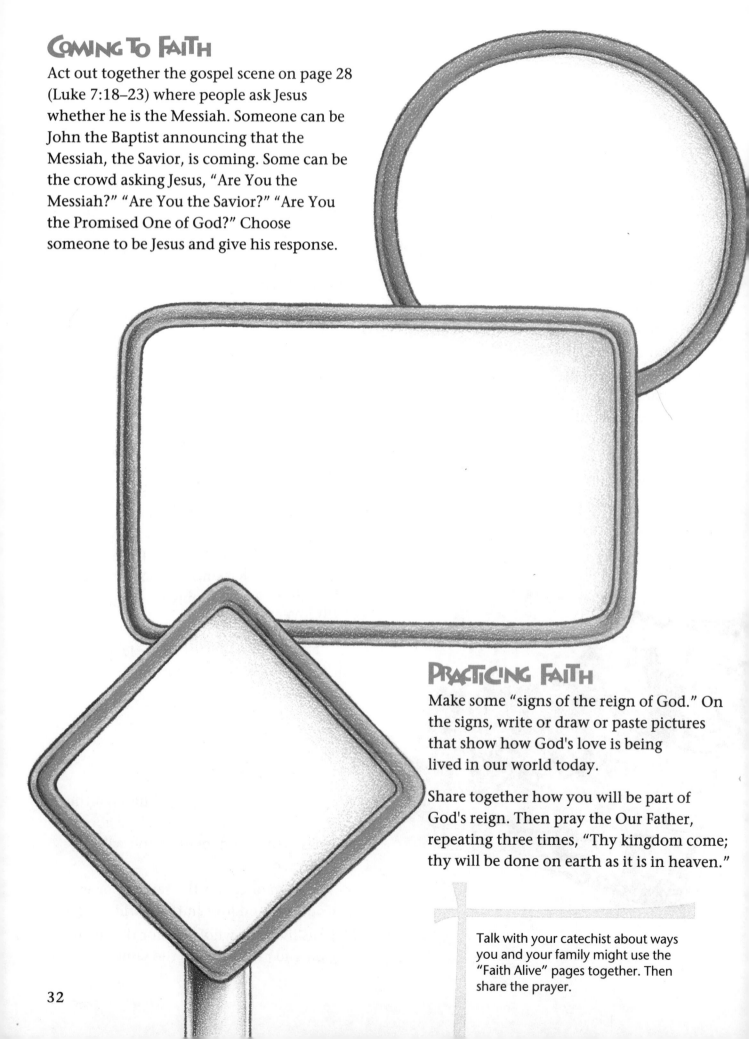

COMING TO FAITH

Act out together the gospel scene on page 28 (Luke 7:18–23) where people ask Jesus whether he is the Messiah. Someone can be John the Baptist announcing that the Messiah, the Savior, is coming. Some can be the crowd asking Jesus, "Are You the Messiah?" "Are You the Savior?" "Are You the Promised One of God?" Choose someone to be Jesus and give his response.

PRACTICING FAITH

Make some "signs of the reign of God." On the signs, write or draw or paste pictures that show how God's love is being lived in our world today.

Share together how you will be part of God's reign. Then pray the Our Father, repeating three times, "Thy kingdom come; thy will be done on earth as it is in heaven."

Talk with your catechist about ways you and your family might use the "Faith Alive" pages together. Then share the prayer.

32

REVIEW ▪ TEST

Circle the correct answer.

1. The people of Israel knew that God made a (covenant, *creed*)
   to care for them always.

2. Jesus announced the (*good news*, commandment) that God
   always loves us.

3. We ask God to help us to share in Jesus' work when we pray
   the (Creed, *Our Father*).

4. (John the Baptist, *Jesus*) said, "The spirit of the Lord is
   upon me."

5. Explain one way you can live for the reign of God.
   Be specific.

   I will always be helpful
   to others.

FAITH ALIVE AT HOME AND IN THE PARISH

In this chapter, your fifth grader continued to learn more about the reign of God. Although the kingdom has already come in Jesus, it is also a future reality that will only be completed at the end of time. As the Lord's Prayer teaches, it begins on earth and is completed in heaven. Jesus founded the Church to proclaim the good news of the reign of God. From its beginning, the Church contained the seed of the kingdom of God (Based on Luke 12:32).

The Church is an instrument of the kingdom and helps us to live for it. Your fifth grader has learned that to live for the reign of God includes trying each day as hard as we can to love God, our neighbors, and ourselves. This includes living justly and being peacemakers. To help your family understand this, talk about the great commandment, the Law of Love.

† Praying about the Reign of God

We can take a small passage from a prayer and think about or explore its meaning. In the Our Father we pray: "Thy kingdom come; thy will be done on earth as it is in heaven."

Closing our eyes, we can imagine what God wants the reign of God to be and how he wants us to live. This kind of prayer is called meditation. Try it together as a family.

3 | Jesus Christ Blesses Our Lives

Lord Jesus,
make us
instruments of
your peace.

OUR LIFE

Dana and Michael were helping their mother clean the attic. In the chest of drawers they found a diary. "That was mine," their mother laughed. "I kept that diary when I was about your age. You twins can look at it if you want."

They opened the diary to a page that said:
October 14: A bad day. Lisa, Carla, Anne, and I had planned to go shopping at the mall today. When I went to meet them, they had left without me. I feel.... sad

Fill in how you think the diary entry might end. Have you ever felt left out? How did you handle it?

Another entry in the diary said:
Mom and I had a real fight about what I wanted to wear to school. She's so out of it! But I know I upset her. I'll.... say I'm sorry

Complete the entry. What do you usually do to make up?

SHARING LIFE

Share together:

● why we should make people feel welcome and included in a group.

● how we can solve problems that separate us without hurting one another.

34

Let's do a brainstorming activity to illustrate our discussion. On the board or on a large piece of newsprint, have one person draw two mountains with a huge gap between them. Brainstorm feelings or actions that separate us from family or friends. Write each suggestion in the "gap" between the mountains.

Now for each idea or phrase you have come up with, see whether you and your friends can suggest what could be done to close the gap. Each time you suggest a solution, color over the problem word. See if you can color in the whole gap.

Talk about your finished product and display it during the week as we learn more about Jesus and the healing and forgiveness he brings to us.

We Will Learn

- Jesus invited everyone to live for the reign of God.
- Jesus healed and forgave others.
- Jesus served other people in need and asked us to do the same.

35

Holy Spirit, guide us in following Jesus' way.

Is it difficult to join a new group? move into a new neighborhood or school? Why or why not?

An Invitation to All

None of us likes to be left out. We enjoy being part of a group. It makes us feel wanted. We know we belong.

Jesus chose disciples from among people left out by other people in society. His friends included women, tax collectors, poor people, and sinners. This may not seem strange to us, but in Jesus' time it was unusual.

Jesus was most interested in the people society ignored. He worked to change unjust or unfair attitudes and practices.

Here is a Bible story of Jesus reaching out to one of the Jewish people's greatest enemies, their Roman conquerors.

Jesus and the Roman Officer

One day a Roman soldier, hoping and trusting that Jesus would help him, came up to Jesus and said, "Lord, my servant is lying at home paralyzed, suffering dreadfully."

Jesus said immediately, "I will come and cure him."

Kingdom of heaven is another way of saying kingdom of God in Matthew's Gospel.

Surprised that Jesus would actually go to his house, the officer blurted out, "I do not deserve to have you come into my house. Just give the order, and my servant will get well."

Amazed by this Roman's faith, Jesus turned to the Jewish people watching Him and said, "I tell you, I have never found anyone in Israel with faith like this. I assure you that many will come from the east and the west and sit down at the feast in the kingdom of heaven."

Based on Matthew 8:5–11

By healing the Roman officer's servant, Jesus showed that all people are welcome in the reign of God.

We, too, must try to live the Law of Love by living justly and peacefully with others. We must try to follow Jesus' example and share that love, peace, and justice with all people.

Whether it be a new student in school, a new family in our parish, or new neighbors next door, we are called to make them feel that they belong in our community. We cannot allow anything to blind us from seeing each person as someone loved by God.

- What does the story of the Roman soldier teach you about the reign of God?
- What will you do to help another person feel more welcome?

■ Lord Jesus, say but the word, and we shall be healed.

■ How do you feel when someone you love is very sick? What do you try to do?

Jesus, Forgiver and Healer

None of us likes being sick. It keeps us from doing the things we enjoy. Jesus understood how it feels to be sick. No matter where he was or how tired he felt, he always took time to help sick people. This was another way Jesus showed God's great compassion and love for us.

People who were sick flocked to Jesus. They saw how he healed others, and they believed that he would heal them, too. Some believed that just by touching Jesus' clothes they would be cured. Here is a story of one person who really went out of his way to be healed by Jesus.

One day Jesus was in a house teaching the good news and healing the sick. A man who had been paralyzed his whole life was carried by his friends on a stretcher to the house. The crowd was so large that they could not get near Jesus.

His friends had a great idea. Lifting the paralyzed man up onto the roof of the house, they lowered the stretcher down until the paralyzed man lay right in front of Jesus.

Jesus saw how much trouble the paralyzed man and his friends had gone through to reach him.

Moved by their faith, Jesus said to the man, "Your sins are forgiven."

This shocked the crowd. How could Jesus forgive sins? Only God could forgive sins!

Then Jesus spoke to the unbelieving crowd, saying, "But that you may know that the Son of Man has authority on earth to forgive sins"— he said to the man who was paralyzed, "I say to you, rise, . . . and go home!" At once the man stood up, strong and healthy, in front of them all. The people were amazed.

Based on Luke 5:17–26

Forgiving Is Healing

Besides physical healing, there is another kind of healing, a spiritual healing. It is called forgiveness. Forgiveness heals the separation from God and from others that sin causes.

For Jesus, forgiveness of sins was even more important than physical healing. Jesus, our Savior, reached out to heal the separation brought about by sin. He forgave sinners and reconciled them with God.

Jesus forgave people to the very last moment of his life. Even as he was dying on the cross, Jesus forgave those who crucified him. He said, "Father, forgive them, they know not what they do." (Luke 23:34).

Like Jesus, we try to forgive those who hurt us, no matter how great the hurt. When we have been the ones who have hurt another person, we must try to tell that person that we were wrong and ask for forgiveness.

Jesus will help us to be friends again. He wants us to live in peace with all people. This is how we do God's loving will for us and live for the reign of God.

Why was healing and forgiveness so important to Jesus?

How will you forgive someone who has hurt you?

39

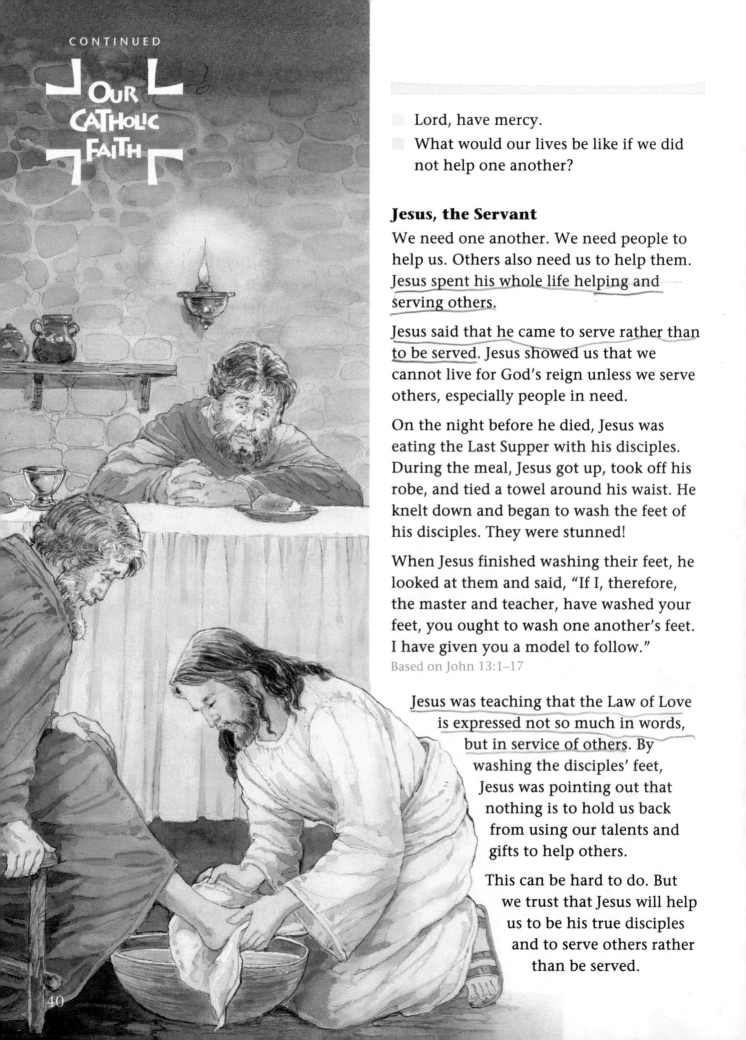

Our Catholic Faith

■ Lord, have mercy.

■ What would our lives be like if we did not help one another?

Jesus, the Servant

We need one another. We need people to help us. Others also need us to help them. Jesus spent his whole life helping and serving others.

Jesus said that he came to serve rather than to be served. Jesus showed us that we cannot live for God's reign unless we serve others, especially people in need.

On the night before he died, Jesus was eating the Last Supper with his disciples. During the meal, Jesus got up, took off his robe, and tied a towel around his waist. He knelt down and began to wash the feet of his disciples. They were stunned!

When Jesus finished washing their feet, he looked at them and said, "If I, therefore, the master and teacher, have washed your feet, you ought to wash one another's feet. I have given you a model to follow."
Based on John 13:1–17

Jesus was teaching that the Law of Love is expressed not so much in words, but in service of others. By washing the disciples' feet, Jesus was pointing out that nothing is to hold us back from using our talents and gifts to help others.

This can be hard to do. But we trust that Jesus will help us to be his true disciples and to serve others rather than be served.

Servants of the Lord

On Holy Thursday, the Church celebrates the Evening Mass of the Lord's Supper. Catholics are often surprised that the gospel reading used at this Mass is not the full account of the Last Supper. In fact, the gospel reading is Saint John's account of Jesus washing the feet of his disciples. Why do you think Jesus did this?

Jesus lived in a dry and dusty country surrounded by deserts. People walked long distances in their sandals. When they came to someone's home, the head of the household would have towels and water brought to them to wash their feet. This was a sign of hospitality.

At the Last Supper, Jesus took this custom and gave it new meaning. Jesus not only provided the water and towels, but he knelt down and personally washed the feet of his disciples. Jesus, the Son of God, was showing himself to be the servant of all. He was serving rather than being served. This is the way he wanted his disciples to live.

Today in many parishes, the ritual of the washing of the feet takes place during the Mass on Holy Thursday. Twelve parishioners come forward, reminding us of the twelve apostles. The priest then kneels before them and washes their feet, drying them with a towel. He does this as a reminder of the beautiful and challenging example Jesus gave to all of his disciples.

How can fifth graders follow the example of Jesus, who became the servant of all?

Learn by heart **Faith Summary**

- Jesus invited everyone to live for the reign of God.
- Forgiveness heals the separation from God and from others that sin causes.
- Like Jesus, we try to forgive those who hurt us, no matter how great the hurt.

41

Coming To Faith

Here are some role-playing situations to do with your friends to help you understand welcoming, healing, forgiveness, and reconciliation. Divide into groups and act out what might be said and done.

● Mike is coming back to school after a battle with cancer. He is anxious about it because he looks so different. His hair has not grown back yet and he is very thin. How will people react to him?

● Meg and Brittany have been arguing and fighting together. They say they hate each other. Friends decide to bring them together and try to solve the problem.

● A new boy has just joined your class. He seems to want to be by himself and be unfriendly.

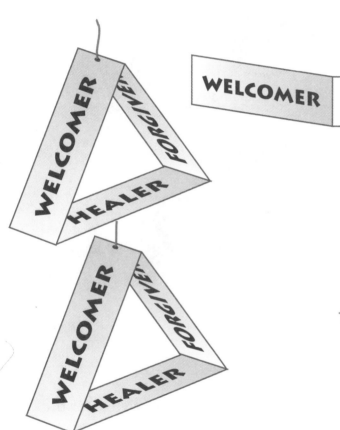

WELCOMER   HEALER   FORGIVER

Talk with your teacher about ways you and your family might use the "Faith Alive" section. Ask your family to help you make up the "Help Needed" list.

Practicing Faith

Take a strip of paper (10" x 2"). On one side write one of these words: welcomer, healer, or forgiver. On the back put one thing you will do this week to be the kind of person who lives for the reign of God.

†Now gather in a prayer circle. Quietly link your strip of paper with those of the people on either side. When the chain is complete, pray as follows:

● *The "welcomers" pray*: Jesus, your love and care went out to everyone. Help us to be welcomers in your name.

● *The "healers" pray*: Jesus, help us to be healers by speaking and acting kindly.

● *The "forgivers" pray*: Jesus, you forgave even those who put you to death. Teach us how to mend the things that separate us.

All hold the chain up high and pray the Prayer of Saint Francis (page 290).

REVIEW ■ TEST

Circle the letter beside the correct answer.

1. The Sermon on the Mount is a summary of the
  a. Ten Commandments.
  b. teachings of Jesus.
  c. Acts of the Apostles.
  d. Laws of the Church.

2. For Jesus, forgiveness of sins was
  a. central to his message.
  b. given only to the Roman officer.
  c. expensive.
  d. given only to sick people.

3. For a Christian being a servant means
  a. doing your own thing.
  b. working for pay.
  c. helping those in need.
  d. being unimportant.

4. Forgiveness is a kind of
  a. spiritual healing.
  b. separation.
  c. physical healing.
  d. magical act.

5. How will you follow Jesus' example this week? Be specific.

I can help by getting the mail and trash. I can help vacuum.

FAITH ALIVE AT HOME AND IN THE PARISH

In this chapter your fifth grader has learned more about the ways Jesus showed us to live for the reign of God. Jesus welcomed everyone, helped the poor, healed the sick, and showed us how to forgive.

To know Jesus Christ is to recognize how central to his ministry are the works of hospitality, healing, forgiveness, and reconciliation. Jesus constantly extended his friendship to sinners, to the poor, to the outcasts. As his disciples, we are called to continue his mission of healing and reconciliation.

The Sermon on the Mount contains a summary of many of Jesus' teachings about living for the reign of God. You may wish to read together part of the Sermon on the Mount (Matthew 5:1—7:29).

Love and Service

To imitate Jesus' life of service, have each family member tell one another how they need help to do something around the house. Make a "Help Needed" list. Tape it in a spot where everyone can see it everyday. Help each other to get things done.

4 The Church Carries on Jesus' Mission

Jesus, help us to help one another bring about the reign of God.

OUR LIFE

While Jesus was on earth, he had many disciples. Let's see how some of them might be described.

Peter—a rough, uneducated fisherman. He was good-hearted but often boastful. Jesus saw special qualities in Peter. He made Peter the leader.

Martha—sometimes worried too much about everyday cares. But she was one of the first disciples to recognize Jesus as the Messiah and Son of God.

Thomas—often called "Doubting" Thomas, because for him only "seeing was believing." He wouldn't accept Jesus' resurrection until he could actually touch him.

Mary Magdalene—described in the gospels as a helper of Jesus. With other women disciples, she stood at the foot of Jesus' cross and was one of the first to hear the good news of his resurrection.

These are just some of the disciples of Jesus. Why do you think they followed him?

How would you describe yourself as a disciple of Jesus?

SHARING LIFE

Discuss together: Why is it sometimes difficult to work with other people? When is it easy?

Are there things in our Church or society that sometimes make it difficult for people to work together?

Imagine that you are a casting director for a movie about the disciples of Jesus. Work together to discuss who should play each of the disciples described and why. Try to reach a consensus.

Choose a partner and role-play one of the characters interacting with Jesus. Make up your own dialogue, but be sure to stay in character! Then share what you felt about your character.

This week we will discover more about the Church and the ways we carry on Jesus' mission.

We Will Learn

● The Church is helped by the Holy Spirit to carry on the mission of Jesus.
● The Church tries to bring healing and forgiveness to all people, as Jesus did.
● Each one of us has a part to play in carrying on the mission of Jesus.

45

- Lord Jesus, help us to be your strong disciples.
- When you find it difficult to do something, do you ask for help? Why or why not?

The Church Welcomes

When we are very small children, our parents have to do everything for us. But as we grow older and learn to do things, our parents and others ask us to become more and more responsible for our actions and our lives.

At the Last Supper, Jesus asked his disciples to be more responsible for building up the reign of God. Jesus said that he was giving them a new commandment. He told them, "As I have loved you, so you also should love one another."

Based on John 13:31-35

Jesus gave this new commandment to the disciples because he would soon be returning to God his Father in heaven. The disciples would have the responsibility to bring God's love to other people by loving the way Jesus had loved. They would do this in the community that Jesus founded, the Church.

Jesus knew his disciples would need help to build up his Church. He promised to send them the Holy Spirit. God the Holy Spirit is the third Person of the Blessed Trinity. After Jesus' ascension into heaven, the disciples were praying together with Mary. Suddenly they heard a strong wind.

Then they saw what looked like tongues of fire settling over the heads of each one. They were filled with the Holy Spirit, as Jesus had promised. This happened on Pentecost, the day the Church celebrates the coming of the Holy Spirit.

The disciples, who were once afraid, were now full of courage. The Holy Spirit helped them to come out from behind locked doors and to preach the good news of Jesus to everyone.

Based on Acts 2:1–13

The disciples invited and welcomed all people into the community of Jesus' followers, the Church.

46

They could speak all languages

FAITH WORD

The **ascension** is the event in which Jesus Christ was taken into heaven after the resurrection.

· 40 days after thursaday

The Catholic Church

Today the mission of the Church is to teach Jesus' good news and way of life to all. The good news is that Jesus came to save us from sin. The Church teaches this good news to all because the Church is catholic. It is a universal, worldwide community of faith.

catholic with small c means univers

We need to help our relatives, friends, and classmates see this good news in what we say and do. We can bring this good news to others by loving as Jesus loved.

As Catholics we teach the good news when we welcome those who are pushed aside or treated unfairly by society. We must bring to them the compassion, justice, and peace that Jesus taught us.

God the Holy Spirit, our Helper, gives us the courage to accept this responsibility to welcome and care for all, as Jesus did.

Describe in your own words what happened at Pentecost.

How will you try to share the good news of Jesus today? with whom?

OUR CATHOLIC FAITH

- O God, help us to proclaim your praises throughout the earth.
- Have you been healed in some way? Tell how it made you feel.

The Church Heals and Forgives

The Holy Spirit helped the disciples to carry on Jesus' mission of healing and forgiving. The New Testament has many stories about the disciples healing and caring for people's bodies, encouraging people to turn away from sin and be forgiven by God. They brought God's forgiveness and peace to all in Jesus' name.

In the Acts of the Apostles, for example, we read about Saint Peter healing a paralyzed man. One day Peter and John went to the Temple at a special time for prayer. There at the gate, they met a beggar who had been crippled all his life. Every day his friends carried him to the same spot where he would beg for money from those going into the Temple.

Peter went up to the man and said, "Look at us…. I have neither silver nor gold, but what I do have I give you: in the name of Jesus Christ the Nazorean, [rise and] walk."

Peter reached down and took the man's right hand. The man stood on his feet. Jumping in the air with joy and praising God, he started walking into the Temple with Peter and John.

Based on Acts 3:1–10

The disciples did more than heal and care for people's bodies. They encouraged people to turn away from their sins and be forgiven by God. They brought God's forgiveness and peace to all.

The Body of Christ

Today the Church carries on the mission that Jesus gave to his first disciples to heal and forgive. Many people around us need the healing and forgiveness of Jesus Christ. All of us at times need to be healed or forgiven.

scit Jesus head we members

We can be sick in body or in spirit. When we are sick in body, the Church prays for us that we may get well again. When our spirits are sick from sin, the Church forgives us in the name of Jesus.

When the Church, by the power of the Holy Spirit, brings healing and forgiveness to one person in the name of Jesus, the whole Church shares in that joy. Saint Paul said that we are all connected like the parts of a body. "If [one] part suffers, all the parts suffer with it; if one part is honored, all the parts share its joy" (1 Corinthians 12:26). Jesus is the head of his body, the Church, and we are its members.

When one person is sick or in sin, the whole body of Christ is affected. We are to care for the well-being of everyone. We are called to be signs of Jesus' healing and forgiving love in our families, our schools, and our communities.

Explain in your own words what Saint Paul meant by the body of Christ.

What will you do to try to be a peacemaker among your friends?

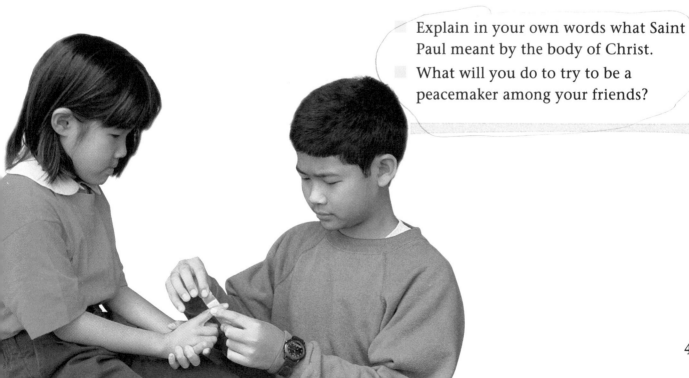

OUR CATHOLIC FAITH

■ Holy Spirit, guide the Church in carrying on Jesus' mission.

■ Name different things our Church does to help others. Which would you enjoy doing the most? Why?

The Church Serves

The first Christians never forgot that Jesus "did not come to be served but to serve" (Matthew 20:28). They also remembered his commandment, "As I have loved you, so you also should love one another" (John 13:34).

Jesus' disciples took special care of people who were in need, such as widows, orphans, and the poor. They knew that every baptized Christian was to take part in this work of justice and mercy.

But the needs were so great that they also set aside special people to see to it that the community served people in need. These people were called *deacons*, a word that means "servants."

The Acts of the Apostles says that "there was no needy person among them" (Acts 4:34). Because the Christians shared their talents and possessions with one another, others said, "See how those Christians love one another."

Whether it was teaching the good news, welcoming new people, or bringing

healing and forgiveness, the Church served others as Jesus did.

The Church continues to serve all people. Like Jesus, each member of the Church can give something to others. For example, we can give a special talent, a piece of clothing, or some food. The best gift we can give is the gift of ourselves and our time.

By Baptism we become members of Christ's body, the Church. As we work together, everyone's gifts are important. This means that each of us is a very important member of the body of Christ. Everyone has a part to play in carrying on the mission of Jesus. We must work together in this great mission.

We do not have to travel around the world to share our gifts. We do not have to wait until we are older. We can serve others with compassion, as Jesus did right here, right now.

Our Parish Family

Each and every day we carry out the mission of Jesus in our parish. A parish is a community of Catholics who come together under the leadership of a pastor. The pastor is appointed by the bishop of the diocese to care for the needs of the parish family.

We come together each week as a parish to celebrate the Eucharist, the high point of parish life. In the parish we also celebrate the other sacraments, hear the word of God, and come to know the teachings of the Church.

The parish is so important in Catholic life that many Catholics identify themselves simply by the name of their parish: "I'm from Saint Monica's Parish; I'm from Our Lady of Angels' Parish."

Every parish has something special about it. What sets your parish apart as it carries on the mission of Jesus?

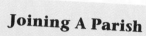
Joining A Parish

Every Catholic should belong to a parish. How do we go about becoming a member of a parish? The first thing is to register. We can do this by going to the parish office or rectory and introducing ourselves to the parish staff. The priest or another staff member will ask about our family, our sacramental history (Baptism, Confirmation, First Holy Communion, and so forth), and what needs we may have.

Once we get to know all about our parish family, it will be time to join in the life and work of that parish. We do this by being active in parish activities and organizations.

All the members of the parish should use their gifts and talents for the good of the whole parish community. What talents or gifts can you bring to your parish?

Welcome to Our Parish

Learn by heart Faith Summary

- The Holy Spirit helps the Church carry on the mission of Jesus to all people.
- Jesus is the head of the Church, his body, and we are its members.
- Like Jesus, the Church serves people and brings them Jesus' healing and forgiveness.

COMING TO FAITH

Describe the ways in which the early Church carried on Jesus' mission.

Talk together about your parish. How does it:

- welcome?
- heal?
- forgive?

- serve?
- act justly?
- bring peace?

Choose one of the above. What can fifth graders do to help out?

PRACTICING FAITH

Talk over these ideas about ways to serve your parish:

- welcome the newly baptized.
- form a "cleanup" group for the church and grounds.
- distribute or sort food and clothing for parish outreach.
- write a letter to a local newspaper about an issue of justice and peace.
- serve as ushers, gift bearers, or choir members at a parish liturgy.
- Other: _____

After you decide what your group will do, ask yourselves questions like these:

- Whom should we talk to in our parish?
- What adults do we need to help us?
- When will we do this service?

† Form a prayer circle. After a moment of quiet, pray together:

Jesus, we come to you with all our gifts and with our faults, too. We want to follow you as your disciples. Help us as we place ourselves at the service of others in your name. Amen.

Talk with your teacher about ways you and your family might use the "Faith Alive" section. Encourage family members to choose a way of loving and serving others.

REVIEW ∎ TEST

Complete the sentences.

1. _____ is the head of the Church, his body.

2. The work of the Church is to welcome, heal, forgive

   and _____.

3. The event in which Jesus was taken into heaven after the resurrection is

   called the _____.

4. The Church received the Holy Spirit on _____.

5. How can a fifth grader help build the reign of God? What will *you* do?

   _____

   _____

   _____

5 The Sacraments and the Church

Our Life

Kate loves her grandmother. They talk to each other on the phone several times a week. Kate feels that she can tell her grandmother everything and her grandmother really listens! She doesn't criticize, but she gives Kate good advice. Kate loves the way her grandmother talks to her. "She treats me like a person," Kate says.

How do Kate and her grandmother show each other love and respect?

How do you show respect to others?

Darryl was upset after soccer practice. "Coach Tate just doesn't like me," he complained to his friend Sam. "You're crazy," Sam replied. "Whatever made you come up with that idea? Has he told you that?"

"It's not what he says; it's how he acts," said Darryl. "He never puts me in the game. And he turns away when I come near him."

What signs made Darryl think the coach didn't like him?

Explain how actions can sometimes "speak louder than words."

What signs do you give people to let them know how you feel about them?

Sharing Life

People give us many signs of caring or not caring about us. Discuss together what some of these signs might be.

Imagine some of the signs that Jesus wants us to give to other people.

Now think about signs that you might give other people and what the signs "say."

Sign	What It Says
Frowning	not happy at what your doing
Smiling at someone	I'm happy
Whispering behind someone's back	talking about you
A "high five"	a job well done

Share your ideas. Why do you think that both words and actions are signs? This week we will explore the special signs of the Church called sacraments.

We Will Learn

- There are many signs of God's love in our lives.
- The Church is the sign of Jesus Christ.
- The Church celebrates the sacraments of initiation, healing, and service.

■ Thank you, O God. Your love for us never ends.

■ Why do you think welcoming, forgiving, healing, and serving others are signs of God's love?

Signs of God's Love

Signs of God's love are everywhere if we are willing to notice them. A *sign* is something visible that tells us about something invisible.

We see God's love for us in the beauty of the world God created. Every sunrise is a promise that God, whom we cannot see, is with us. God gives us a new chance each day. Each sunset reminds us that he will care for us during the dark times of our lives.

People can also be visible signs of God's love. A friend greets us with a warm smile or a friendly hug. A teacher listens to what we have to say and treats us with respect. Our friends treat us fairly. Our parents take care of us when we are sick.

Jesus used many signs to show God's love. For example, he reminded farmers that they looked at signs in nature to predict the weather. He said, "When you see [a] cloud rising in the west you say immediately that it is going to rain—and so it does; and when you notice that the

Christ Savior, **Titian,** **(16th century)**

wind is blowing from the south you say that it is going to be hot—and so it is." Jesus went on to say that we should look for signs of God's love just as much as we look for signs of the weather.
Based on Luke 12:54–56

Jesus, Sign of God's Love

We find the greatest signs of God's love in Jesus' words and actions. Jesus is the perfect sign of God to us. Saint Paul called Jesus "the image of the invisible God" (Colossians 1:15). Paul meant that in Jesus we meet the Son of God made flesh.

The Son of God became one of us and shared our everyday lives. Because Jesus is God, he is the perfect sign of God's love for all humankind. In Jesus we meet God himself. This is why we say that Jesus is the Sacrament of God to us.

FAITH WORD

A **sacrament** is an effective sign through which Jesus Christ shares God's life and love with us.

The Last Supper, Salvador Dalí, 1955

A sacrament is the most effective kind of sign. It causes to happen the very thing for which it stands. Jesus is the greatest Sacrament of God because he is God with us.

God asks each of us to be a sign of God's love to others by what we do and what we say. We can make someone feel welcome. We can help to make peace. We can say "I forgive you" to another person. We can show respect to people who are different from us. Then other people will see and know God's love in us.

As disciples of Jesus, we try to live as signs of God's love. When we live our faith like this, we help make God's love visible and real in the lives of others.

- Explain why Jesus is the most perfect sign, or sacrament, of God's love.
- How will you live your faith as a sign of God's love today?

OUR CATHOLIC FAITH

Mr. Beach

BAPTISM

CONFIRMATION

EUCHARIST

■ Jesus, you are God with us.

■ Why do you think the Church is called a sign, or sacrament, of Jesus?

The Church, A Sacrament of Jesus

After Jesus ascended into heaven and after the coming of the Holy Spirit, Jesus' disciples began to carry on his mission. The early Christians loved others and worked for the reign of God, as Jesus had taught them. In this way, the Church was an effective sign of the risen Christ's continuing presence in our world.

Jesus had died and risen from the dead on Easter. But now Jews and Gentiles, men and women, rich and poor could see in the lives of his disciples the love of Jesus. Many of them were also able to believe that Jesus truly was the Son of God. By the way they lived, Jesus' friends showed others how to live for the reign of God.

The Church is also a sign, or sacrament, of Jesus for us. We meet Jesus each time our Church welcomes, forgives, teaches, serves, and works for justice and peace.

But the Church is not always a perfect sign of Jesus Christ because it is made up of many imperfect people, including ourselves. As each of us becomes a better sign, the whole body of Christ, the Church, becomes a more effective sign, or sacrament, of Jesus.

Seven Special Signs

The seven sacraments—Baptism, Confirmation, Eucharist, Reconciliation, Anointing of the Sick, Matrimony, and Holy Orders—are effective signs of Jesus' presence with us.

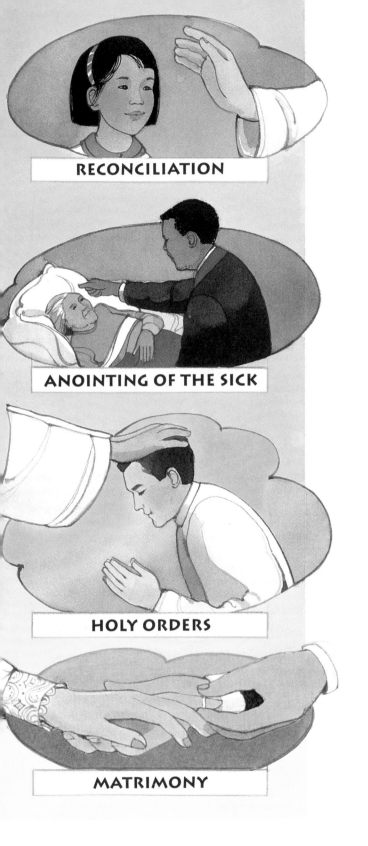

RECONCILIATION

ANOINTING OF THE SICK

HOLY ORDERS

MATRIMONY

In the sacraments, Jesus shares God's life with the Church by the power of the Holy Spirit. He calls us to respond by living as his disciples. In the seven sacraments, Jesus Christ, the Son of God, really and truly comes to us in our lives today. Jesus shares God's life and love with us in a very special way.

God's life and love in us is called grace. Grace is a sharing in the divine life, in God's very life and love. We receive his grace in the sacraments. Grace helps us to be living signs of God's life and love in our world. His grace is a gift that blesses our entire lives.

Living the Sacraments

By celebrating the sacraments, the Church worships and praises God. As Catholics, we praise God for the loving gift of Jesus Christ and God's grace that Jesus shares with us.

We try to live the sacraments by welcoming, healing, forgiving, and serving others. With the help of the Holy Spirit, we try to do God's loving will and live for the kingdom of God.

We try to respond to God's love by loving one another and by working for justice and peace. We share God's life of grace, which we receive in the sacraments, with all those whom we meet.

In this way the Church becomes a powerful sign of Jesus' presence and God's reign in our world.

These seven sacraments are called effective signs because they do more than ordinary signs. Through the power of the Holy Spirit, they actually bring about what they promise. The sacraments are the most effective signs of Jesus' presence with us.

▢ Name the seven sacraments celebrated by the Catholic Church.

▢ How will you be a sign of Jesus' presence to others?

- Holy Spirit, help us to be signs of love each day.
- What would your life as a Christian be like without the sacraments?

Welcoming, Healing, Serving

The Church carries on Jesus' mission of welcoming members into the body of Christ when we celebrate Baptism, Confirmation, and Eucharist. We call these the sacraments of initiation.

At Baptism we begin a new life with Jesus. We become members of the Church, the body of Christ, and receive the grace to live and love as Jesus did.

At Confirmation we are sealed with the Gift of the Holy Spirit to help us work for the reign of God in our world.

In the Eucharist we receive the Body and Blood of Christ. The Eucharist gives us the grace to work and live together as the body of Christ and to live as Jesus' disciples.

The Church forgives and heals as Jesus did by celebrating Reconciliation and Anointing of the Sick. We call these the sacraments of healing.

The sacrament of Reconciliation brings us God's forgiveness for sins. We become signs of God's forgiving love by bringing forgiveness and peace to others.

In the sacrament of the Anointing of the Sick the grace of God strengthens us to live with faith and trust in God's love when we are seriously sick.

The Church serves others and is a special sign of God's love by celebrating and living the sacraments of Matrimony and Holy Orders. We call these the sacraments of service.

In the sacrament of Matrimony a man and a woman promise to love and serve each other, their family, the Church and all those around them. The married couple's love becomes a sign of God's love for all of us.

In the sacrament of Holy Orders a man leads a life of service as an ordained bishop, priest, or deacon. Those who are ordained carry on in a special way Jesus Christ's priestly ministry of worship and service.

A Way of Loving

Love that does not show itself in action is as useless as a book written in invisible ink. One way Catholics make their love visible is by celebrating the sacraments and following the way of Jesus.

The best place to see this way of loving in action is in the Catholic family. Parents show their love right from the start by their willingness to have children, to have them baptized, and to teach them to pray.

Catholic parents respect children as a gift from God. They provide for their children's religious education. They show by example that their faith is a treasure to be lived and shared.

We can support parents and guardians in this unselfish way of loving by showing that we, too, value and live our Catholic faith.

A Loving Foster Parent

In today's world, many children have a foster parent. We sometimes forget that the Holy Family in which Jesus grew up included a foster parent, too.

Although Jesus was first of all the Son of God, he was also the foster son of Saint Joseph. Joseph was the husband of Mary and the provider for the Holy Family. He is described in the Bible as "a righteous man" (Matthew 1:19).

Joseph protected Jesus and Mary from the evil King Herod. He made sure that Jesus learned and practiced the Jewish faith. He was a skilled carpenter who taught his foster son how to work with wood and earn a living. He was the loving protector of Mary and Jesus.

Catholics honor Saint Joseph as the patron of the universal Church. We thank God for the example he gives to our families.

Learn by heart   Faith Summary

- A sacrament is an effective sign through which Jesus Christ shares God's life and love with us.
- There are seven sacraments: Baptism, Confirmation, Eucharist, Reconciliation, Anointing of the Sick, Matrimony, and Holy Orders.
- We receive God's grace in the sacraments.

61

Coming To Faith

How is Jesus a sign, or sacrament, of God's love for you?

How can you be a sign of God's love to others today?

Practicing Faith

Form seven small groups, one for each sacrament. As your group is named, step forward. At the end the groups should be in a single circle.

Leader: Baptism! (Group 1 steps forward.)

Group 1: We thank you, O God, for the gift of new life with which you have blessed us.

Leader: Confirmation!

Group 2: We bless you, O God, and thank you for the Holy Spirit, who strengthens us for service in your Church and in the world.

Leader: Eucharist!

Group 3: Our lives are nourished with the Body and Blood of Christ.

Leader: Reconciliation!

Group 4: Blessed are we, O God, with your forgiveness and mercy and peace.

Leader: Anointing of the Sick!

Group 5: You bless us, O God, with this healing sacrament. You comfort, console, and give us peace.

Leader: Holy Orders!

Group 6: Continue to bless your Church, O God, with the gift of this sacrament of ministry and service.

Leader: Matrimony!

Group 7: Thank you, O God, for this sacrament that blesses our lives with married love and families.

All: (stretching hands out to center of circle, palms down) For all these signs of your love and grace that bless our lives, thank you, God! Amen.

Talk with your teacher about ways you and your family might use the "Faith Alive" section. You might want to use the blessing prayer on this page at a meal during the week.

REVIEW ▪ TEST

Match.

1. sacraments

_____ sacraments of service

2. Baptism, Confirmation, Eucharist

_____ sacraments of healing

3. Reconciliation, Anointing of the Sick

_____ effective signs through which Jesus Christ shares God's life and love with us

4. Matrimony, Holy Orders

_____ sacraments of life

_____ sacraments of initiation

5. What can you do this week to be a sign of God's love?

_____

_____

FAITH ALIVE AT HOME AND IN THE PARISH

Your fifth grader has been introduced in a deeper way to the seven sacraments. She or he has been taught that Jesus is the perfect sign, or sacrament, of God and that the Church is the sacrament of Jesus. Each of us, as a member of the Church, is called to carry on Jesus' mission of welcoming, healing, forgiving, and serving. Talk about some things your family can do to be signs of God's compassionate love.

† **Family Prayer**

Merciful and gracious is the LORD,
   slow to anger, abounding in kindness.
As the heavens tower over the earth,
   so God's love towers over the faithful.
As a father has compassion on his children,
   so the LORD has compassion on the faithful.

Psalm 103:8, 11, 13

6 | Celebrating Reconciliation

Jesus, help us to forgive others as you forgive us.

OUR LIFE

In East Africa there is a fascinating tribe called the Masai. They are very tall, beautiful people who live gently and calmly in harmony with themselves and the natural world around them. This harmony is so important to the Masai that if one family offends another the whole tribe is upset. The whole tribe works to bring the separated families together so there can be peace and reconciliation.

The tribe members encourage the two families to prepare special foods, which they then bring to the center of the village. Everyone encourages them and cheers them on. The two families then exchange their food with each other and sit down to eat. This is the sign of forgiveness. The whole tribe then celebrates the return of peace and harmony.

What do you think about the Masai sign of forgiveness?

How do you show signs of forgiveness?

SHARING LIFE

What can we learn from the Masai for our lives?

Talk together about the best ways to show forgiveness in our culture.

Work in small groups. See whether your group can suggest a simple sign of forgiveness that might be appropriate for today. Consider these situations:

- a family in your town is being harassed by others because of their race
- children of divorced parents feel that they are torn between the father and mother
- cliques and "in-groups" in school are causing hurt to people

Share with the whole group the simple sign that your group would suggest. It is a way of preparing for what we will learn about the forgiveness of Christ in the sacrament of Reconciliation.

We Will Learn

- Jesus teaches us that God always forgives our sins.
- The Church carries on Jesus' mission of forgiveness in the sacrament of Reconciliation.
- We prepare for Reconciliation.

OUR CATHOLIC FAITH

Good News of Forgiveness

God the Father sent Jesus to show us that he is always waiting to forgive our sins, no matter how bad they are. Jesus taught us that God always forgives us when we are sorry for our sins and ask his forgiveness.

Jesus understood that living as his disciples and doing God's loving will are not always easy. He knew that his followers might sin and need God's forgiveness.

Here is a gospel story in which Jesus tells the disciples to forgive sins in his name.

Late the first Easter Sunday evening, Jesus' disciples were hiding in a locked room. They were afraid that the people who crucified Jesus would kill them, too.

Jesus came and said, "Peace be with you."

After looking at the wounds in Jesus' hands and side, they were amazed and filled with joy. They knew it was Jesus.

Jesus said to them again, "Peace be with you. As the Father has sent me, so I send you.... Whose sins you forgive are forgiven them."

Based on John 20:19–23 *1st Easter*

jesus started the sacrament of reconciliation

Our Church Forgives

Today our Church continues Jesus' mission of forgiveness in the sacrament of Reconciliation. We prepare ourselves to celebrate Reconciliation by examining our conscience and by becoming aware of our sins.

We think about our sins or the things that showed we did not follow the way of Jesus. We are sorry for what we have done that is wrong. We remember that God is always ready to forgive us if we are sorry. We can think about the story of the prodigal son and his forgiving father (Luke 15:11–24).

When we examine our conscience, we may ask ourselves questions like these:

● Do I show that I love God?

● Does God come first in my life, or are other things more important to me?

● Have I used God's name with respect, or have I sometimes said God's name in anger?

● Do I take part in Mass on Sundays and on holy days of obligation, or have I missed Mass for no serious reason?

● Do I obey my parents or guardians or have I disobeyed them?

● Do I show that I love other people as I love myself?

● Have I tried to act lovingly to others, or have I hurt anyone by my words or deeds?

● Have I shared my things with others, or have I been selfish or taken others' things without permission?

● Have I been truthful and fair, or have I lied and cheated?

● Have I cared about the poor, the hungry, and those who are oppressed?

● Do I try to be a peacemaker and treat everyone with justice?

● Do I try to live like Jesus?

After we have examined our conscience and are sorry for our sins, we are ready to continue with the celebration of the sacrament of Reconciliation.

COMING TO FAITH

Take a minute to look again at the examination of conscience. Then work in groups or with a partner to change each question into several "we can..." statements. For example:

Do I show that I love God? We can show we love God by being more patient with those who annoy us.

Share all your "we can..." statements with your group.

67

Practicing Faith

A Prayer Service of Forgiveness

Opening Hymn

Theme

We praise and give thanks for God's love and forgiveness.

Greeting

Leader: Jesus brings us God's forgiveness. May the peace and mercy of Jesus be with you.

All: And also with you.

Leader: Jesus, we have come to celebrate God's forgiveness. Hear us as we ask for this forgiveness and peace.

All: Amen.

First Reading

God is always ready to forgive us. A reading from the Book of Joel. (Read Joel 2:13.)

Responsorial Psalm

Leader: Teach me, O God, what you want me to do, and I will obey you faithfully.

All: Great is your love for us, O God.

Leader: You, O God, are a merciful and loving God, always patient, always kind, and always faithful. Turn to me and have mercy on me.

All: Great is your love for us, O God.

Gospel

The group may act out the gospel story about the prodigal son (Luke 15:11–24) or several readers may take different parts and read it together.

Examination of Conscience

A member of the group reads the examination of conscience questions on page 66. After each question is read, pause for quiet reflection. Then pray:

Leader: Jesus, forgive us our sins.

All: Lord, hear our prayer.

Leader: Jesus, help us to love one another.

All: Lord, have mercy on us.

Leader: Jesus, give us the courage to turn away from sin and to change our lives.

All: Lord, forgive us our sins.

Leader: Jesus, free us from our sins and lead us to the freedom enjoyed by your faithful disciples.

All: (Pray the Our Father together.)

A Prayer of Praise

Select a psalm as a prayer of praise, for example, Psalm 136:1–9 or Psalm 145:1–13.

Sign of Peace

Share with one another a greeting of peace.

Closing Hymn

REVIEW • TEST

Answer true (**T**) or False (**F**).
If the answer is false, correct it.

1. God is always ready to forgive our sins if we are sorry.   **T**   **F**

   _____

2. The Church continues Jesus' mission of forgiveness in the sacrament of Confirmation.   **T**   **F**

   _____

3. After celebrating Reconciliation we should make an examination of conscience.   **T**   **F**

   _____

4. Jesus gave His disciples the power to forgive sins in God's name on Easter evening.   **T**   **F**

   _____

5. How does it make you feel to know you are forgiven?

   ~~great~~ It makes me
   feel great

FAITH ALIVE AT HOME AND IN THE PARISH

This liturgical lesson provided your fifth grader with a further development of the meaning and grace of the sacrament of Reconciliation and a deepened awareness of the meaning of forgiveness. The ability and desire to forgive others and to ask forgiveness of others is one of the greatest virtues we can develop in our children. Forgiveness is a mature virtue, but it can be modeled and encouraged from your child's earliest years. When children witness and experience forgiveness in their homes, they more readily practice it themselves.

The sacrament of Reconciliation emphasizes the role of the Church community in our celebration of this sacrament. Since our sins take from the holiness of the community, it is most fitting that our sacramental reconciliation with God should be through the ministry of the Church.

Learn by heart Faith Summary

- God is always ready to forgive our sins.
- Jesus gave His disciples the power to forgive sins.
- Reconciliation is the sacrament in which we are forgiven by God through the ministry of the Church.

7 Celebrating Eucharist

Jesus, help us who share the Bread of Life to become one in mind and heart.

Our Life

In the Old Testament we read about a man named Elisha, who lived long ago. Elisha helped those who were sick or poor.

One time a woman explained to him that her husband had just died and that a man to whom her husband owed money had come to her demanding to be paid. The woman was very poor, and her family no longer even had food to eat. All that was left in her home was a small jar of olive oil.

Elisha instructed her to go home and borrow as many empty jars as she could. He told her to start pouring the olive oil from the small jar that she had into all the other jars her sons could bring to her.

Elisha smiled when the woman returned and told him that she had a house filled with jars of olive oil. He said to her, "Go and sell the oil to pay off your creditors; with what remains, you and your children can live."

Based on 2 Kings 4:1–7

What did you learn from this story?

Who gives you what you need for life?

Sharing Life

Imagine you could ask Elisha for a certain food or drink that would never run out. What would you ask for? Why?

Did Jesus give us any special food?

What is it? How does it help us?

Think quietly for a moment about the Eucharist and the privilege of receiving Jesus in Holy Communion.

Express your thoughts in a cinquain. A cinquain has five lines. Line 1 has one word that *names* what your subject is. Line 2 has two words *describing* it. Line 3 has three words of *action* about it. Line 4 has four words *telling your feelings* about it. Line 5 has one word *renaming* the subject. Here's an example:

Christ,
Our Bread,
Food for life.
Filling, energizing, making holy,
Eucharist!

Share your cinquains. You might print them on large newsprint and display them in the room.

We Will Learn

- We celebrate that Jesus is our Bread of Life.
- The Eucharist is the most important sign of our unity as the body of Christ.
- The Eucharist is the Church's greatest prayer of praise and thanksgiving.

Food That Lasts Forever

The early Christians frequently shared the special meal Jesus gave us. They followed the instruction that Jesus gave to his disciples at the Last Supper, "Do this in remenbrance of me" (1 Corinthians 11:24).

They came together to celebrate the Eucharist. They sang songs; remembered Jesus' teachings; and recalled his life, death, and resurrection. They took bread and wine and did what Jesus did at the Last Supper. Then they shared in the Body and Blood of Christ together.

Jesus himself is the Bread of Life, the food that we receive in the Eucharist. Jesus is really present with us in the Eucharist to nourish and strengthen us to live for the reign of God.

One time Jesus told the people, "I am the bread of life; whoever comes to me will never hunger, and whoever believes in me will never thirst" (John 6:35).

One with Jesus and Others

Celebrating the Eucharist together as the Church is the most powerful sign of our unity with Jesus Christ and with one another.

Teaching about the Eucharist as a sign of our unity with Jesus and one another, Saint Paul wrote:

"The cup of blessing that we bless, is it not a participation in the blood of Christ? The bread that we break, is it not a participation in the body of Christ?… We, though many, are one body, for we all partake of the one loaf."

1 Corinthians 10:16–17

We come together as the community of Jesus' followers to share in his life and love. In our eucharistic assembly, we unite ourselves with Jesus and the Church all over the world. We are the sign of Jesus' life and love in the world.

Our Thanksgiving Prayer

The Eucharist is both a meal and a sacrifice. At Mass we celebrate the Eucharist. It is the Christian community's greatest prayer of praise and thanksgiving to God.

In the *Introductory Rites* we prepare for our celebration. We remember that we are the community of Jesus' disciples.

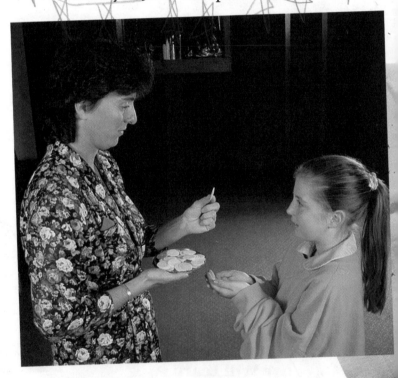

The Scripture readings in the *Liturgy of the Word* recall how we are to live as the people of God, the body of Christ. We listen carefully, because God speaks to us through the Scripture readings. We learn how to live for the reign of God, as Jesus taught.

In the *Liturgy of the Eucharist* we praise and thank God for Jesus, God's own Son. Jesus gave himself for us. We give thanks that through Jesus we are made one again with God and one another.

The priest breaks the Bread because we who are many are one in the sharing of the one Bread. We receive the gift of Jesus, our Bread of Life, in Holy Communion. We give thanks to Jesus for coming to us.

We pray and receive God's blessing in the *Concluding Rite*. We go forth and try to show our family, our neighbors, and even strangers that we are the body of Christ in the world today. We try to live as disciples of Jesus.

COMING TO FAITH

What food do we receive in the sacrament of the Eucharist?

We recieve the body and blood of Jesus.

Why is the Mass the most important sign of our unity with Jesus and the Church?

We come together as one body.

How will you show that you are thankful for the gift of Jesus in Holy Communion?

by telling god himself.

73

Practicing Faith

Planning a Celebration of the Eucharist
Plan your Mass celebration together in small groups.

Theme: Look at the readings for the Mass of the day. Read the Opening Prayer. What is the prayer about? Write it here.

_____

_____

_____

_____

Hymn: Choose an opening hymn for your Mass. Write the title here.

_____

Readings: Name the readings for the Mass of the day. You can find these readings in a book called the Lectionary. List the readings and who will read them.

_____

_____

_____

_____

Prayer of the Faithful: Write several petitions that express your thanks and the thanksgiving of your group to God. Write them here.

_____

_____

_____

_____

Presentation of the Gifts: Decide who will present the gifts of bread and wine and write their names here.

Gift	Presenter
_____	_____
_____	_____

Hymn: Choose a closing hymn. Write the title here.

_____

_____

Share your ideas with the whole group and create a single plan.

REVIEW ■ TEST

Circle the letter beside the correct answer.

1. At the Last Supper Jesus said, "Do this
   a. often."
   b. in memory of me."
   c. at every Passover."

2. Jesus called himself "the
   a. Wine of Life."
   b. Food for all peoples."
   c. Bread of Life."

3. Paul said that those who share the body of Christ are
   a. united as one.
   b. free from suffering.
   c. his apostles.

4. Which of the following is NOT part of the Mass?
   a. Liturgy of the Word.
   b. Liturgy of the Eucharist.
   c. Liturgy of the Hours.

5. How can you show your love for Jesus in the Eucharist?

_____

_____

_____

FAITH ALIVE AT HOME AND IN THE PARISH

In this liturgical lesson the fifth graders are drawn into a deeper understanding of the Eucharist.

For Catholics, the Eucharist is both a meal and a sacrifice. It is the source and summit of our Christian life. In the Eucharist, we are fed by the Lord with his Body and Blood; Jesus' death and resurrection are made present to us. During the celebration, we hear the word of God proclaimed in the readings. We respond with words of thanksgiving and praise. We receive Christ in Holy Communion and are strengthened for our life of faith.

Learn by heart

Faith Summary

- At Mass we celebrate the Eucharist, our greatest prayer of thanksgiving and praise.

- In the Liturgy of the Word we listen as God speaks to us in the readings.

- In the Liturgy of the Eucharist we praise and thank God through Jesus, whom we receive in Holy Communion.

8 Jesus Christ Brings Us Life
(Baptism)

Come, Holy Spirit, help us be signs of your life to others.

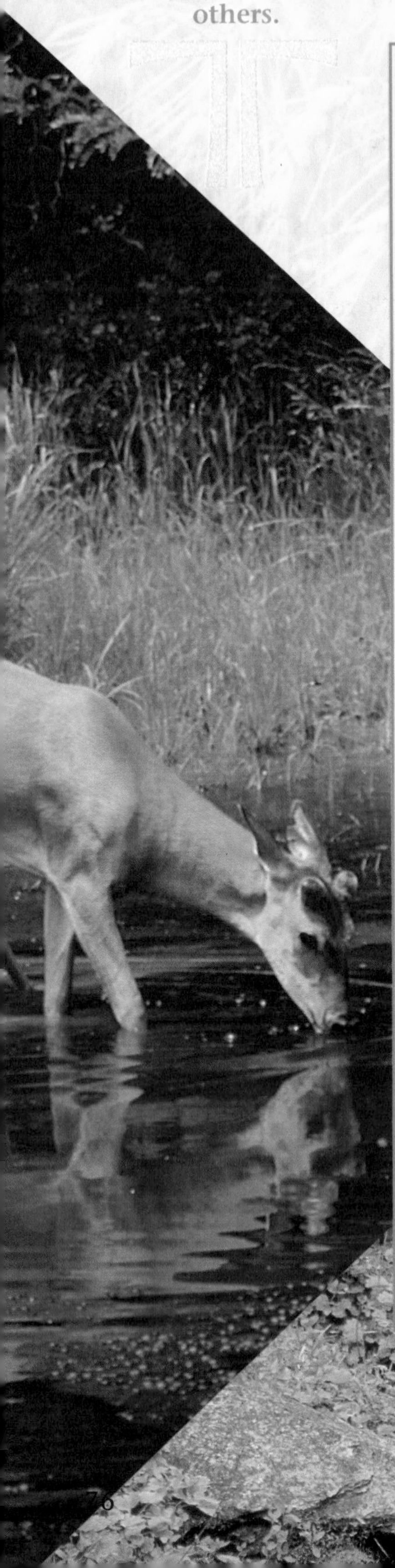

Our Life

Finish the story.

Angie went out on the tractor with her father as he plowed the field. She breathed in the wonderful smell of the earth as it was turned over to receive the new seed. In the spring days that followed, the gentle rains and warm sunshine made it a perfect growing season. Then one morning Angie saw the first green shoots of wheat covering the field. She ran out into the fields. Stooping down, she touched the new wheat shoots and whispered,

"______________________________"

What does life mean to you?

Each of us has dreams about our life. What are some of your dreams about life for yourself? for others? for our world?

Sharing Life

Discuss together.

Give some reasons why you believe that life is God's greatest gift to us.

What do you imagine God wants us to do with the gift of life?

Come up with some good reasons why you think water is used as a sign of new life in the sacrament of Baptism.

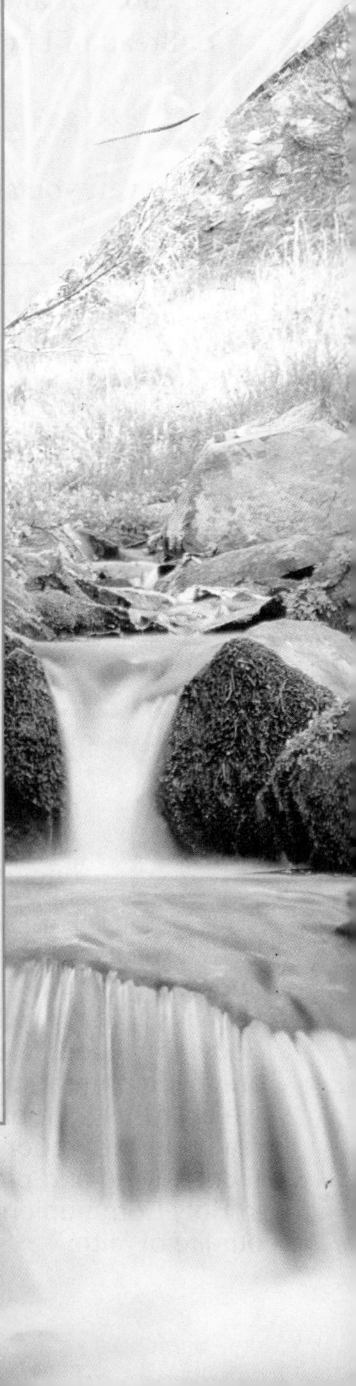

Reflect for a moment on the ideas you have just discussed. Then create a haiku, telling what God's gift of new life means to you as a Christian.

A haiku is an unrhymed, 3-line verse.
Line 1 has 5 syllables.
Line 2 has 7 syllables.
Line 3 has 5 syllables.

Here is an idea to get you started.

> **All is bare and dry.** (5 syllables)
> **Then from above flow**
> **springs of** (7 syllables)
> **Living water. Life!** (5 syllables)

Share your haikus. Explain why you wrote what you did. You might illustrate your haikus with art or photographs. Display them in the room as a way of introducing this week's work.

We Will Learn

- We share God's new life of grace in the sacrament of Baptism.
- By Baptism we become members of the Church, the body of Christ.
- We are to live our Baptism.

■ O God, your gift of water brings us life.

■ Tell what difference water makes to your daily life. Why?

New Life at Baptism

Water does many things. It helps animals and plants grow. It makes people feel alive again.

Water was especially important to the people of Palestine, the land where Jesus lived and the Bible was written. Palestine was a hot, dry land surrounded by desert. The people of the Bible valued water as a great gift of God, and as a sign of God's new life and compassionate care for them.

Water is also a sign of life in the Church. Water is used in Baptism as a sign that God is giving the person being baptized a new life in Jesus. At Baptism we are joined to Jesus and initiated into the community of the Church, the body of Christ. We commit ourselves to live the way of Jesus.

That is why Jesus spoke of "being born of water and Spirit." (John 3:5)

Jesus and Nicodemus

A Jewish leader named Nicodemus had heard many wonderful stories about all that Jesus did for others. He wanted to ask Jesus how he might find eternal life. But Nicodemus was afraid because of what some other Jewish leaders might think.

Finally, Nicodemus got up enough courage to come to Jesus by night under the cover of darkness. He said to Jesus, "No one can do these signs that you are doing unless God is with him."

78

Jesus answered, "No one can see the kingdom of God without being born . . . from above."

Nicodemus was confused. He wondered how a grown-up could be born again. Jesus explained, "No one can enter the kingdom of God without being born of water and Spirit."
Based on John 3:1–21

In Baptism we are born again through water and the Holy Spirit. This sharing in God's new life is called grace.

It is by God's grace that we can live for the reign of God as Jesus showed us. In Baptism, we begin our life of faith.

We are initiated into this new life that Jesus spoke about to Nicodemus at Baptism. The new life of Baptism is for people of every color, race, religion, and sex. Jesus wants everyone to be baptized and initiated into the Church, the body of Christ.

Original Sin

When Adam and Eve, our first parents, chose to turn away from God, they sinned. Because of this sin, they lost the original holiness given to them by God for themselves and all their descendants. We call this loss original sin. All human beings are born with original sin and suffer from its effects. By Baptism we are set free from original sin but are still left weakened by it. That is why we have a tendency to sin and need God's grace.

- In your own words tell the story of Nicodemus. What do you learn from it?
- How will you try to live your new life of Baptism today?

OUR CATHOLIC FAITH

Thank you, God, for the gift of new life in Baptism.

What do you think happened on the day of your Baptism? What difference has it made in your life?

Baptism, A Sacrament of Initiation

When we are born, we become members of families. Then there is another important family that we are invited to join—the Church. By Baptism we join or begin our initiation into the Church, the body of Christ. We are freed from the power of original sin and become children of God.

By Baptism we are united with Jesus in his death and resurrection. We die to sin and rise to new life as Jesus did. Baptism enables us to live as God's own people with new life for doing his loving will.

Celebrating Baptism

Many parishes celebrate Baptism during a Sunday Mass. This reminds all present of their own Baptism and of their responsibility to help new members to live their faith.

During the celebration of Baptism a priest or deacon blesses the water that will be used as a sign of rebirth. The celebrant prays, "We ask you, Father, with your Son to send the Holy Spirit upon the water of this font. May all who are buried with Christ in the death of baptism rise also with him to newness of life."

The priest or deacon pours the water on the heads of the people being baptized, or immerses them, saying,

"(Name), I baptize you in the name of the Father, and of the Son, and of the Holy Spirit." The water and these words are the signs of the sacrament of Baptism.

At this moment they are reborn of water and the Holy Spirit. They receive new life. They are reborn into the divine life of God's grace, become members of the Church, the body of Christ, and receive the responsibility to live for God's reign.

The newly baptized are next anointed with holy oil, as Christ was anointed priest, prophet, and king. This shows that they share in Jesus' work of bringing about God's justice and peace.

Baptism is the sacrament of our new life with God and the beginning of our initiation into the Church.

The newly baptized are also given a white garment and a candle. The white garment shows that they have put on the new life of the risen Christ. A candle, lit from the Easter candle, is held. This is a sign that the baptized are to keep the light of Christ burning brightly by following Jesus Christ always.

The newly baptized are called children of God, for indeed they are. The whole Church prays with them the Our Father.

Each time a person is baptized, Jesus' last command to his disciples before he ascended into heaven is fulfilled. Jesus said, "Go, therefore, and make disciples of all nations, baptizing them in the name of the Father, and of the Son, and of the holy Spirit, teaching them to observe all that I have commanded you" (Matthew 28:19–20).

Priest, Prophet, King

Jesus was a priest, a prophet, and a king. He was a priest by offering his life to God, a prophet by calling us to live God's loving will, and a king by showing us how to let God reign in our lives.

In the sacrament of Baptism of what is water a sign?

What will you do to become a better member of the Church?

OUR CATHOLIC FAITH

■ Lord Jesus, let your light shine through us.

■ Think of a special time when you acted like a baptized person by living God's new life. What did you do? Why?

Living Our Baptism

Most of us were probably very young when we were baptized. At that time our parents and godparents promised to help us live our new life as Christians. When we are old enough, we must also make this choice and renew our baptismal promises for ourselves.

No one can live our Baptism for us. We receive God's grace and the support of others. We have the Holy Spirit to help us live our new life as disciples of Jesus. Our parents, friends, and the whole Christian community give us support. But we must choose now to live the way of Jesus.

know three or two of these

Here are some signs that show you are trying to keep your baptismal promises:

● On waking, you thank God for another day and ask God to help you live the new life of Baptism.

● You decide who in your family needs a laugh, a hug, or a little help. You give it.

● You try to help those in need and to be a peacemaker between angry friends.

● You cooperate with your catechist so that you learn and grow in living your Catholic faith.

● On your way to and from school and on weekends, you see whether there are people in your neighborhood you can help.

● In your family or parish, you help teach younger children their prayers.

● You celebrate the sacrament of Reconciliation regularly. You listen carefully as the priest advises you how to live each day well.

● With your family, you take part in Mass on Sunday or Saturday evening. If they do not go, you try to go to Mass with others and ask God to help and bless your family.

● Each night you thank God for the day. You ask God to help you to become a peacemaker and to be fair and loving to all.

A Record of Baptism

Just as the record of our birth is kept by the city and state, the record of our new birth in Baptism is kept by the Church.

When a person is baptized—either an infant or an adult—the priest or deacon of the parish writes that person's name into a large book called the *baptismal register*. Next to the person's name is written the date of birth, the date of Baptism, the names of the parents and godparents, as well as the name of the priest or deacon who performed the Baptism.

All this information is kept forever in the parish church where the Baptism took place. The baptismal record always stays in the same parish. In this way, the important information of our Baptism will never be lost. We can always call that parish and get a copy of our baptismal record whenever we need to do so.

Extra

Other Important Records

The Catholic Church also keeps records of other important information. As time goes on, the information is added to our baptismal record. This happens when we are confirmed, married in the Catholic Church, ordained, or take religious vows. Wherever these events take place in the world, the information is always sent back to the original church of Baptism to be added in the baptismal register.

Where were you baptized? Have you ever seen a copy of your baptismal record? Tell about it.

Learn by heart Faith Summary

- We receive new life at Baptism when we are reborn of water and the Holy Spirit.
- At Baptism we are initiated into, or begin to become members of, the Church, the body of Christ.
- Our Baptism calls us to decide to live for the reign of God.

COMING TO FAITH

Work together to create a collage or a mural of the signs of Baptism. Call it "Signs of New Life." Illustrate with drawings or pictures of water, a candle, a white garment, and holy oil. Then explain briefly what each signifies.

PRACTICING FAITH

Talk together about ways your group might be of service to people in your parish preparing for Baptism. If possible, invite your pastor to discuss with you ways you might contribute.

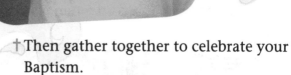

† Then gather together to celebrate your Baptism.

Leader: Through Baptism we have become your beloved sons and daughters.

All: Blessed be God.

Leader: We have been born again of water and the Holy Spirit.

All: Blessed be God.

Leader: Help us to be faithful disciples of Jesus Christ and his witnesses.

All: Blessed be God.

End your prayer by making the sign of the cross together.

Talk with your teacher about ways you and your family might use the "Faith Alive" section together. Invite your family to do the "Signs of Baptism" activity. Close by praying the baptismal blessing with your teacher and friends.

REVIEW ▪ TEST

Circle the letter beside the correct answer.

1. Baptism is a sacrament of _____
   a. initiation.
   b. healing.
   c. service.

2. _____ is a sharing in God's life and love.
   a. Membership
   b. Church
   c. Grace

3. Signs used in Baptism include a white garment, a candle, and _____
   a. incense.
   b. water.
   c. bread.

4. Jesus Christ is _____, prophet, and king.
   a. priest
   b. brother
   c. healer

5. How can you live your Baptism each day?

By

_____

_____

_____

9 Jesus Christ Strengthens Us
(Confirmation)

Come, Holy
Spirit,
strengthen us
to be Christ's
witnesses.

OUR LIFE

The early missionaries to North America
faced many dangers. One day in 1642
Father Isaac Jogues was ambushed by the
Iroquois, the enemies of the Hurons, and
tortured as a hostage for one year.

Instead of returning home after being
ransomed, Father Jogues assumed the role of
a peacemaker between the Hurons and the
Iroquois. Once again, he was taken hostage.
This time he and seven other French
missionaries were killed.

In 1930 the Church canonized these martyrs
as saints. They are called the North
American Martyrs. The word *martyr* means
witness.

Why do you think Father Jogues stayed in
North America?

Tell some of the ways that you give witness
to your Christian faith today.
Who helps you?

SHARING LIFE

Talk together about the following questions.

What are some of the things that make it
difficult for you to be a Christian?

What in our society makes it difficult for
anyone to be a good Christian?

How do you imagine you could be a better
witness to your Christian faith?

Work with a partner. List your best responses to the questions on this chart.

What makes it difficult for me to be a Christian?

_____

_____

_____

_____

What in society makes it difficult to be a Christian?

_____

_____

_____

_____

How can we be better Christians?

_____

_____

_____

_____

Share your responses with the group.

This week we will be exploring how the Holy Spirit helps us to be Christ's witnesses.

We Will Learn

● God sends the Holy Spirit to help us live our faith.

● At Confirmation we are called to become witnesses to the good news of Jesus.

● We try to be witnesses to the good news in many ways.

Our Catholic Faith

Come, Holy Spirit, fill the hearts of your faithful.

Why do you think God will help you when you are afraid or ashamed? when you find it difficult to do the right thing?

Sending of the Holy Spirit

God made human beings to depend on one another. When we are babies, we need parents in a special way. As we grow up and go to school, we need our friends and teachers. As adults we will still need the help of others to live our lives.

It should be no surprise, then, that we also need the help of others to live as good Christians. We get this help from other members of the Church.

Jesus also promised us a special Helper, the Holy Spirit. God the Holy Spirit is the third Person of the Blessed Trinity.

The Holy Spirit comes to us first at Baptism and guides us to live our initiation into the Christian life. In the sacrament of Confirmation, we are sealed with the Gift of the Holy Spirit. We also are filled with the gifts we need to live our baptismal promises and to witness to our faith throughout our lives.

The Pentecost Story

It is not always easy to be a Christian and a witness to our faith. We need God's special help.

At the Last Supper on the night before he died, Jesus knew that his disciples would be afraid and feel lost without him. Jesus tried to give them courage by promising, "I will ask the Father, and he will give you another Advocate to be with you always" (John 14:16).

After Jesus ascended into heaven, his disciples became frightened and locked themselves in an upper room. They were afraid of being found and arrested.

Ten days later, while they were still huddled there, God the Holy Spirit came. Each disciple was blessed with the fullness of the Holy Spirit and received the gifts that we receive in the sacrament of Confirmation. Jesus had kept his promise to send the Holy Spirit.

Now they became fearless and ready to give witness to their faith in Jesus. They ran into the streets and began to preach the good news of Jesus to everyone they met.
See Acts 1:7–14; 2:1–13

88

Our Church calls this day Pentecost. On that day God the Holy Spirit came upon the first Christian disciples. They now had the courage to invite others to believe in and to follow Jesus.

The Holy Spirit is with us today and guides us to be witnesses to our Catholic faith. The gifts of the Holy Spirit give us the courage to announce the good news of Jesus by living as Jesus did.

GIFTS OF THE SPIRIT

The Holy Spirit helps us to live our faith by giving us these seven gifts.

Gift	Helps us to
wisdom	know the right things to do.
understanding	explain our faith and know how to make good decisions.
right judgment	guide others in their faith because we live our own.
courage	practice courageously the faith we believe.
knowledge	learn about our Catholic faith from the Bible and from the Catholic tradition.
reverence	live the good news willingly and pray for ourselves and others.
wonder and awe	show respect for God, God's people, and God's world.

Act out the story of Pentecost. Tell what you learned from the story for your life.

What will your class do to show that the Holy Spirit helps you to practice your faith openly?

What will you do?

Pentacoste, Barnaba da Modena, circa 1370

OUR CATHOLIC FAITH

- Holy Spirit, fill us with your gifts.
- How do you get help to meet your responsibilities at home? as a member of a group or team?

Confirmation, A Sacrament of Initiation

In Confirmation we receive the sign, or seal, of the Holy Spirit. This seal is not visible, but it marks us as followers and witnesses of Christ.

When we were baptized, we began our initiation into the Church. Confirmation is one more step in this initiation into the body of Christ. Now we are called to give public witness to the good news to our family, our neighbors, and even strangers. We are sealed with the Gift of the Holy Spirit and strengthened to live out our baptismal promises.

Celebrating Confirmation

step 1 Confirmation is celebrated during Mass with a bishop or his representative presiding. As a sign of our greater responsibilities, the bishop asks us to renew the promises of Baptism.

This shows that we accept the responsibility to live these promises with the help of the Holy Spirit.

step 2 When we are confirmed, we may choose another name in addition to the one we were given at Baptism. We may select the name of a saint whose life we have read about and whom we admire. This is a sign of our new commitment to live our faith.

A high point of the celebration of Confirmation is the "laying on of hands." The bishop extends his hands over those to be confirmed, praying to God the Father,

"Send your Holy Spirit upon them
to be their Helper and Guide.
Give them the spirit of wisdom and
    understanding,
the spirit of right judgment and courage,
the spirit of knowledge and reverence.
Fill them with the spirit of wonder and awe
    in your presence."

Then the bishop dips his thumb into blessed oil, called holy chrism. He makes the sign of the cross on their foreheads and anoints them, saying,

"(*Name*), be sealed with the Gift of the Holy Spirit."

This anointing is the most important sign of the sacrament of Confirmation.

Confirmation is the sacrament in which we are sealed with the Gift of the Holy Spirit and are strengthened to give witness to the good news of Jesus.

The bishop asks God to continue the work of the Holy Spirit in our hearts. Together we pray, "Our Father...."

Our parents probably did much to help us live our faith when we were younger. Once we are confirmed, we promise to accept more responsibility ourselves to carry on Jesus' mission of spreading the good news and working for the reign of God.

Confirmation helps us to practice our faith openly and bravely, no matter who makes fun of us or how difficult it may be.

Describe ways you see the gifts of the Holy Spirit at work in your school, your parish, or at home.

_____

_____

_____

_____

_____

_____

_____

_____

_____

- By what actions are we sealed with the Holy Spirit at Confirmation? Explain.
- Think of things to do today to show that your faith is becoming more active and responsible.

OUR CATHOLIC FAITH

Holy Spirit, help us to be strong witnesses to Christ.

Think of someone you like who is a happy witness to the good news of Jesus. What will you do to follow this person's example?

Witnessing Today

As confirmed Catholics, God calls us to be witnesses to Jesus and his Church. We show others that we have been initiated into the Church by living as Jesus did. As confirmed Catholics we can witness to our faith today by:

● encouraging friends to join us at Sunday or Saturday evening Mass;

● not being ashamed to let others know we pray and receive Holy Communion and Reconciliation frequently;

● standing up for and being a friend to a classmate who is treated unfairly;

● helping adults in the parish who teach other children our faith;

● visiting and doing things for someone who is lonely, sick, or elderly;

● asking adults to do something for those being treated unfairly;

● being a peacemaker in our families and praying for peace in our world.

The Holy Spirit helps us so that other people will see the good news of Jesus alive in us. They will know by our actions that God loves every human being.

When we live our Confirmation, we become witnesses to the reign of God in the world today.

know three of these

92

The Fruits of the Holy Spirit

We know how important the Holy Spirit is in our lives. It is the Holy Spirit who guides the Church. It is by the power of the Holy Spirit that we follow Jesus and celebrate the seven sacraments.

How can we tell whether or not we are responding to the guidance of the Spirit in our lives? The Catholic Church teaches us that the Holy Spirit develops in us certain qualities, or virtues. We call these qualities the twelve fruits of the Holy Spirit. The usual naming of these twelve fruits is as follows: charity, joy, peace, patience, kindness, goodness, generosity, gentleness, faithfulness, modesty, self-control, and chastity.

You may be familiar with most of these qualities. However, two may be new to you: modesty and chastity.

Men and women who are modest have deep respect for the human person. One way they do this is by showing in word and action the dignity the body deserves.

Chastity is another important fruit of the Holy Spirit. People who live the virtue of chastity know how to love unselfishly, responsibly, and faithfully. Chastity calls us to have deep respect for human sexuality—in the ways we act, in what we read, and in what we look at.

Which fruits of the Holy Spirit do you think our world needs most today? Will you pray for them?

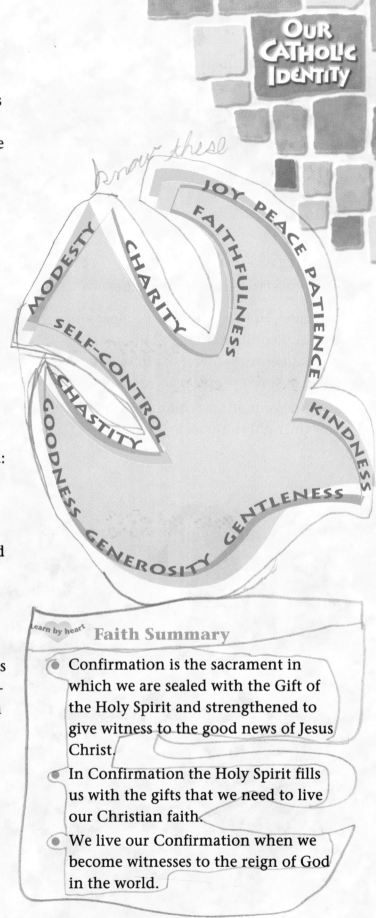

pray these

JOY PEACE PATIENCE
FAITHFULNESS
CHARITY
MODESTY
SELF-CONTROL
CHASTITY
KINDNESS
GOODNESS
GENEROSITY
GENTLENESS

Learn by heart · **Faith Summary**

- Confirmation is the sacrament in which we are sealed with the Gift of the Holy Spirit and strengthened to give witness to the good news of Jesus Christ.

- In Confirmation the Holy Spirit fills us with the gifts that we need to live our Christian faith.

- We live our Confirmation when we become witnesses to the reign of God in the world.

COMING TO FAITH

After your Confirmation, what would you tell others about:

- the promises Jesus gave his disciples;
- the coming of the Holy Spirit;
- the important signs used at Confirmation;
- how you can be a better Christian witness to others?

PRACTICING FAITH

†Gather in a circle and pray together.

All: Come, Holy Spirit, be our Helper and Guide. (Repeat after each petition.) (All hold out arms to center of circle, palms down as seven people read.)

1. Give us your gift of wisdom so we may know the right thing to do. (All)

2. Give us your gift of understanding so our faith will be real and deep. (All)

3. Give us your gift of right judgment so that we may help others in their faith. (All)

4. Give us your gift of courage so we may practice what we believe with courage. (All)

5. Give us your gift of knowledge so that we may desire to learn all we can about our faith. (All)

6. Give us your gift of reverence so that we may be people of prayer and worship. (All)

7. Give us your gift of wonder and awe so that we may treat all people and all creation with respect and wonder. (All)

Close by singing
"Come, Holy Spirit."

Talk with your teacher about ways you and your family might use the "Faith Alive" section. You might especially want to pray together the prayer to the Holy Spirit.

REVIEW ▪ TEST

Match the gifts of the Spirit to how they help us.

Gift

1. courage

2. wisdom

3. right judgment

4. wonder and awe

Helps us to . . .

___3.___ guide others in their faith

___4.___ show respect for God, others, and the world

_____ explain our faith to others

___1.___ courageously practice our faith

___2.___ know the right thing to do

5. How can you be a more active and responsible Catholic?

_____

_____

FAITH ALIVE AT HOME AND IN THE PARISH

In this chapter your fifth grader has learned more about the sacrament of Confirmation. In this sacrament of initiation, the baptized are sealed with the Gift of the Holy Spirit. The Holy Spirit helps us live our Christian faith by giving us special gifts. These gifts are wisdom, understanding, right judgment, courage, knowledge, reverence, wonder and awe.

Fruits of the Spirit

The fruits of the Holy Spirit are the good results people can see in us when we use the gifts of the Holy Spirit. These fruits are charity, joy, peace, patience, kindness, goodness, generosity, gentleness, faithfulness, modesty, self-control, and chastity.

Discuss with your fifth grader ways you see the gifts and fruits of the Spirit at home or in your parish.

✝ **Family Prayer**

Holy Spirit, come to us. Make us courageous witnesses to our faith. Amen.

10 Jesus Christ Feeds Us
(Eucharist) communion

Jesus, Living
Bread, fill us
with your life.

OUR LIFE

Once the people asked Jesus what miracle
he would do so that they might believe
in him. Jesus said, "I am the bread of life;
whoever comes to me will never hunger, and
whoever believes in me will never thirst."

The people started grumbling. They said, "Is
this not Jesus, the son of Joseph?"

Jesus answered, "Stop murmuring among
yourselves. I am the living bread that came
down from heaven; whoever eats this bread
will live forever; and the bread that I will give
is my flesh for the life of the world."

At this an angry argument began. "How can
this man give us [his] flesh to eat?" they
asked. But Jesus quietly repeated what he
had said. Many of his followers who heard
him said, "This saying is hard ; who can
accept it?" They turned away and walked
with him no more.

Based on John 6:35, 41–43, 51–53, 60, 66

What do you hear Jesus saying in this
Scripture story?

SHARING LIFE

Why do you think Jesus compared himself
to bread?

Discuss together: Why are there so many
hungry people in our world?

What do you think Jesus wants us to do for
people who are hungry?

Together talk about possible projects you might do as disciples of Jesus to respond to the needs of the hungry. List your ideas in a place where all can see them. Keep your own list in the space below.

HELPING

HUNGRY PEOPLE

Decide on one thing you will do together to help hungry people. Ask for any adult assistance you need. Then do it!

This week we will be discovering more about Jesus, our Bread of Life, and the ways he wants us to care for others.

We Will Learn

- Jesus is our Bread of Life.
- Jesus gives us his own Body and Blood.
- We thank God for the Eucharist.

■ Jesus, you are the Bread of Life.

■ Talk about a time when you were really hungry. What did your experience tell you about people who are hungry all the time?

Jesus, Our Bread of Life

We all need food to live. Without food we slowly weaken and die. Jesus knew that we need food. Jesus knew what it was like to be hungry because he was one of us. Jesus felt hungry and cared for the hungry people around him.

Jesus Feeds Five Thousand

One day almost five thousand people followed Jesus to hear his words. As the day went on, they became very hungry. Jesus knew how hungry they were. He was very concerned because they were far from the markets and had no food.

Jesus asked his disciple Philip, "Where can we buy enough food for them to eat?" Philip was shocked! It would take two hundred days of work to make enough money to feed so many people.

Andrew, Peter's brother, spoke up, "There is a boy here who has five barley loaves and two fish; but what good are these for so many?"

The Miracle of the Loaves and Fishes, **carved ivory, (6th century)**

FAITH WORD

The **Eucharist** is the sacrament of Jesus' Body and Blood. Jesus is really present in the Eucharist.

Multiplication of Loaves and Fishes, Limbourg Brothers, (15th century)

Jesus, knowing what he would do, replied, "Have the people recline." Taking the bread and fish from the boy, Jesus looked up to heaven and thanked God. He then asked his disciples to pass out the food. Everyone was amazed. All five thousand had enough to eat.

After everyone had eaten, Jesus said to his disciples, "Gather the fragments left over, so that nothing will be wasted." They went through the crowds and collected enough bread and fish to fill twelve baskets.

The people came back to Jesus the next day, hoping to get more food and to see another miracle. Instead, Jesus promised to give them another kind of food and drink that would last forever.

Jesus said, "I am the living bread that came down from heaven; whoever eats this bread will live forever; and the bread that I will give is my flesh for the life of the world.... My flesh is true food, and my blood is true drink.... Whoever eats this bread will live forever."
Based on John 6:1–13, 22–58

The Bread of Life that Jesus promised to give us was his own Body and Blood. Today Jesus gives us that Bread of Life in the Eucharist.

Jesus is really present in Holy Communion. In Holy Communion, we receive Jesus himself. He is our Bread of Life.

Today Holy Communion nourishes us so that we, too, can live as Jesus' disciples. Receiving Jesus in Holy Communion strengthens us to live the responsibilities of being members of the Church, the body of Christ.

- Tell what Jesus meant when he said, "I am the bread of life" (John 6:48). What do his words mean to you?
- How will you thank Jesus for giving us himself as our Bread of Life?

OUR CATHOLIC FAITH

Lord Jesus, may we become a living sacrifice of praise.

Talk about special meals in your family. What makes them so special?

The Eucharist, A Sacrament of Initiation

Sometimes we share a meal not only because we are hungry, but also because we are celebrating a special event like Thanksgiving or a birthday.

At Passover the Jewish people celebrate an important meal to remember that God brought them from slavery in Egypt to freedom in the Promised Land. During Passover, on the night before he died, Jesus ate a very special meal with his friends. This meal is called the Last Supper.

At the Last Supper Jesus gave us the gift of himself, his own Body and Blood. Jesus' disciples never forgot this meal. They told everyone about it. This food that is Jesus himself helps us to live free from the slavery of sin and free for doing God's will.

Saint Paul was not at the Last Supper, but he learned about it from the other friends of Jesus. Paul then wrote down what he had learned so no one would forget the great gift Jesus gave us. This is what happened.

"The Lord Jesus, on the night he was handed over, took bread, and, after he had given thanks, broke it and said, 'This is my body that is for you. Do this in remembrance of me.' In the same way also the cup, after supper, saying, 'This cup is the new covenant in my blood. Do this, as often as you drink it, in remembrance of me.'"

1 Corinthians 11:23–25

At the Last Supper Jesus gave thanks to God. Ordinary bread and wine became his own Body and Blood. Then Jesus asked his disciples to do the same in memory of him. We call this the *Eucharist*, a word that means "to give thanks."

The Eucharist, Sacrifice and Meal

The Eucharist is both a sacrifice and a meal. In the Eucharist we share in the one sacrifice of Christ. We give thanks and celebrate Jesus' death and resurrection. In this sacrifice of praise to God, we remember all that Jesus did for us. In the Eucharist we offer ourselves with Jesus to God. When we celebrate the Eucharist, we pray to the Father, through the Son, in the unity of the Holy Spirit.

The sacrament of the Eucharist is also a community meal. In this sacrament we receive the gift of Jesus, who gave himself to us as our food. Jesus is really present in the Eucharist. Sharing in the Eucharist makes us one with God and with one another in the Church, the body of Christ.

We assemble as Jesus' community of disciples to celebrate the Eucharist at Mass. We remember that Jesus loved us so much that he sacrificed himself for us and died on the cross to save us from our sins. Through the Eucharist we become a living sacrifice of praise.

We remember that Jesus rose from the dead and now remains with us in the Eucharist. We give thanks to Jesus for the gift of himself by living as his disciples.

Blessed Sacrament

The Blessed Sacrament is another name for the Eucharist. Jesus is really present in the Blessed Sacrament. The Blessed Sacrament is kept in the tabernacle in a special place in the church for bringing Holy Communion to the sick and for worshiping Jesus.

- Imagine you and your friends were at the Last Supper. Act it out. Talk about what you learned.
- Make up a brief "eucharist," or thanksgiving, prayer to God for the gift of Jesus. Will you say it each time you receive Holy Communion?

OUR CATHOLIC FAITH

■ Thank you, God, for the gift of the Eucharist.

■ Did you ever receive a gift you really needed? How did you show you were thankful?

Thanking God for Jesus

At Mass our gifts of bread and wine become the Body and Blood of Christ. This happens through the power of the Holy Spirit. Jesus is really present under the appearances of bread and wine.

Our participation in Mass is a sign of our full initiation into the Church, the body of Christ. The Eucharist nourishes us to give thanks to God by living as God's own people. In Holy Communion we receive Jesus himself. He is our Bread of Life. We can also visit our parish church and pray to Jesus, who is present in the Blessed Sacrament.

Saint Augustine once said, "Because we receive the Body of Christ in Holy Communion, we must live as the body of Christ in the world." We can share Jesus, our Bread of Life, by:

- caring for the hungry by organizing food collections in our parish.
- sharing Jesus' joy by visiting a lonely or elderly person.
- welcoming a newcomer into our group or neighborhood.
- being kind to someone whom others treat badly.
- being careful not to waste food or drink when many other people are so hungry.
- being kind and patient with our family and friends.

Special Gifts of Bread and Wine

Whenever we come together to celebrate the Eucharist, we offer the gifts of bread and wine that will become the Body and Blood of Christ.

The Catholic Church knows how important these gifts of bread and wine are. That is why they must be made in a special way.

The wine must be made from grapes, the fruit of the vine. It should be pure and have nothing else added to it.

The bread that we use is very different from the ordinary bread we have in our homes each day. The bread for the Eucharist is called *unleavened bread*. This means that nothing has been added to the bread dough to make it rise before it is baked. That is why the bread is flat. This unleavened bread is made only from wheat. We use this kind of bread because we want to follow the example of Jesus at the Last Supper.

The Church also requires that the bread prepared for the Eucharist be made in such a way that it can be broken into parts, since it will be distributed to the people.

Finally, the bread and wine should be as fresh and well made as possible. After all, the bread and wine will become the Body and Blood of Christ.

When you see the gifts of bread and wine being carried to the altar, remember that they represent you, too. What does it mean for you to offer yourself to God?

learn by heart **Faith Summary**

- The Eucharist is the sacrament of the Body and Blood of Christ.
- Jesus is the Bread of Life. The food that Jesus gives us is his own Body and Blood.
- We respond to the gift of the Eucharist by living for the reign of God.

TIHSEIBNRME EAMDOORFYL OIFFMEE

I AM

_____

COMING TO FAITH

Decode the message from Jesus about the Eucharist. Beginning with the first letter in the lines of letters, circle every other letter to find the message. Then write the message.

Discuss together the best way to explain the sacrament of the Eucharist to a young person who is not a Catholic.

PRACTICING FAITH

How can you show that you *really* believe that Jesus is present in the Eucharist? Remember, belief is expressed in action. Some ideas are listed on page 102. Your group might come up with your own. Make a group plan about how and when you will share Jesus, our Bread of Life, this week. Write your plan.

Close by praying the prayer on page 96.

Talk with your teacher about ways you and your family might use the "Faith Alive" section. You might invite your family to do the "Giving Thanks" activity.

REVIEW ■ TEST

Answer each question.

1. Define the Eucharist.

_____

_____

2. Why do we say that the Eucharist is a meal?

_____

_____

3. Why do we say that the Eucharist is a sacrifice?

_____

_____

4. What happens to our gifts of bread and wine at Mass?

_____

_____

5. How is Jesus the Bread of Life to you?

_____

_____

FAITH ALIVE AT HOME AND IN THE PARISH

This chapter on the Eucharist is an opportunity to deepen your understanding of why this sacrament is central to our Catholic faith. Saint Thomas Aquinas called the Eucharist "the sacrament of sacraments"—the greatest sacrament of all! Read with your family the words of Jesus in which he describes himself as the Bread of Life (John 6:35–61). Discuss what the words of Jesus might mean for your family today.

The Blessed Sacrament is another name for the Eucharist. After Mass, the Blessed Sacrament is usually kept, or reserved, in the tabernacle in a special place in the church. This is done so that Holy Communion may be brought to the sick of our parish, and so that we may worship Jesus truly present in the Blessed Sacrament.

Giving Thanks

The word *Eucharist* means "giving thanks." Take a few minutes together this week to "count" your family blessings. Think of all the good people and good things in your life and offer thanks for them at a family meal and at the Eucharist this week.

11 Our Church Celebrates the Eucharist
(The Mass)

Lamb of God, you take away the sins of the world, grant us peace.

Our Life

The parish is having a big farewell party for Mr. Sandro. He has been a catechist in the parish for five years, and now he is leaving to work as a lay missionary in Central America.

The fifth graders are sad. Mr. Sandro has been their catechist for two years. He has also been their friend. Two years is a long time. They wonder whether he will forget them.

Mr. Sandro says goodbye. He tells them that sharing faith with them was wonderful for him. He says, "I'll always remember you—each one of you!"

Is there someone who has been a special person in your life? Who? How?

How would you say goodbye to that person? How would you remember that person?

Sharing Life

Discuss together.

Do you have memories of someone important to you to whom you had to say goodbye?

Tell how the memory of that person makes a difference in your life.

How does remembering Jesus make a difference in your life now?

What do you think is the best way to remember Jesus?

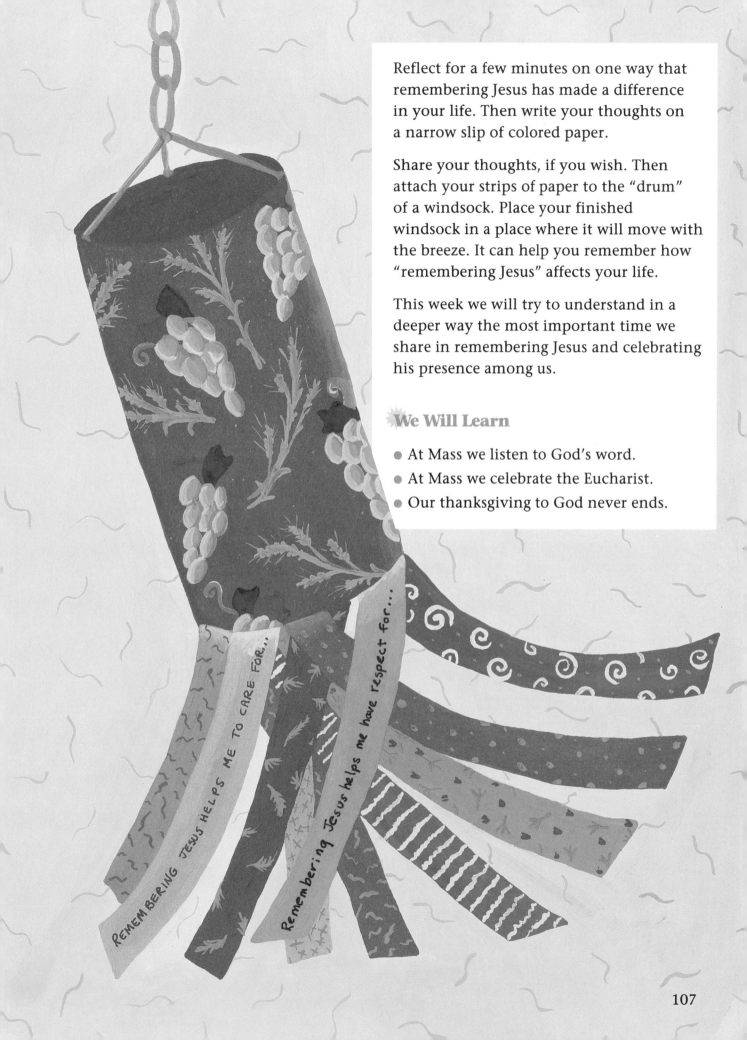

Reflect for a few minutes on one way that remembering Jesus has made a difference in your life. Then write your thoughts on a narrow slip of colored paper.

Share your thoughts, if you wish. Then attach your strips of paper to the "drum" of a windsock. Place your finished windsock in a place where it will move with the breeze. It can help you remember how "remembering Jesus" affects your life.

This week we will try to understand in a deeper way the most important time we share in remembering Jesus and celebrating his presence among us.

✸We Will Learn

- At Mass we listen to God's word.
- At Mass we celebrate the Eucharist.
- Our thanksgiving to God never ends.

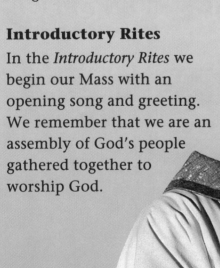

OUR CATHOLIC FAITH

We give you thanks, O God.

Share what memories you have that have made a difference in your life.

Celebrating Mass

The Mass is our celebration of the Eucharist. Every Sunday or Saturday evening, the Catholic community gathers together as a worshiping assembly. We do this to remember the life, death, and resurrection of Jesus. At Mass we praise and honor God.

The two major parts of the Mass are the Liturgy of the Word and the Liturgy of the Eucharist. We listen and respond to God's word from the Bible. We offer and receive gifts from God. We thank God for all his gifts in our lives.

Introductory Rites

In the *Introductory Rites* we begin our Mass with an opening song and greeting. We remember that we are an assembly of God's people gathered together to worship God.

After asking God and one another for forgiveness in the Penitential Rite, we praise God and pray for the strength to live for God's reign.

Liturgy of the Word

God speaks to us in the *Liturgy of the Word*. Selections from the Old and New Testaments are read aloud from the Bible by the reader, deacon, or priest.

The first reading is usually from the Old Testament. The Old Testament reading tells us about God's covenant, or agreement, with the people of Israel. Like ourselves, the Israelites sometimes responded well and sometimes poorly to God.

The Responsorial Psalm follows the first reading. We praise and thank God for his faithful love for us. Praying this psalm response helps us to make a connection between our lives and the Old Testament story.

The first New Testament reading is from one of the letters, also called epistles, or from the Acts of the Apostles or the Book of Revelation. These readings help us, as they helped the first Christians, to believe in Jesus and to live his way of love and compassion.

We prepare for the gospel proclamation by standing and singing the Alleluia. *Alleluia* is a Hebrew word meaning "praise to God." We remember the resurrection of Jesus and get ready to listen to Jesus, who speaks to us in the gospel. Standing shows our respect for the Word of God, Jesus Christ.

The deacon or priest then proclaims the good news of Jesus from one of the four gospels: Matthew, Mark, Luke, or John. We listen to the teachings of Jesus. We hear how Jesus lived, died, and rose from the dead to save us.

After the gospel the priest or deacon gives a homily, or sermon, about the readings. This helps us to live God's word in our world today. After the homily we profess our faith by saying the Creed together.

Liturgy is the official public worship of the Church. The Liturgy includes the ways we celebrate the Mass and other sacraments.

The Liturgy of the Word concludes with the Prayer of the Faithful. We pray for our own needs, the needs of others, the needs of the Church, and the needs of the whole world.

The New Testament at Mass

New Testament readings at Mass are from:

the *gospels,* which teach the meaning of the events of Jesus' life, death, and resurrection;

the Acts of the Apostles, which describes the early Church;

letters, or epistles, which were written by Saint Paul and other Church leaders to Christian communities they founded;

the Book of Revelation, which was written to give Christians hope in difficult times.

Write the title of your favorite New Testament story. Share it with your class.

_____

_____

_____

_____

- Name and explain the parts of the Liturgy of the Word.
- How will you try to live this Sunday's gospel reading?

OUR CATHOLIC FAITH

- Christ has died, Christ is risen, Christ will come again.
- Tell the story of the Last Supper in your own words. What does it mean to you today?

Liturgy of the Eucharist

The Liturgy of the Eucharist begins with the Preparation of the Gifts. Members of the assembly bring our gifts of bread and wine to the altar. These gifts are signs that we are returning to God the gift of our lives. They are also signs of our efforts to care for one another and all of God's creation.

The priest then praises God for all his gifts. He prays that the bread and wine will become our Bread of Life and spiritual drink.

We stand as the priest invites us to join in the Eucharistic Prayer. This is our Church's great prayer of praise and thanks to God for all creation and our salvation. We respond with the "Holy, holy, holy Lord" prayer.

We then kneel in reverence as the priest says and does what Jesus did at the Last Supper. Taking the bread, the priest prays,

"Take this, all of you, and eat it:
this is my body which will be given up
   for you."
Taking the chalice, he continues:
"Take this, all of you, and drink from it:
this is the cup of my blood,
the blood of the new and everlasting
   covenant.
It will be shed for you and for all
so that sins may be forgiven.
Do this in memory of me."

Through the power of the Holy Spirit and the words and actions of the priest, the bread and wine become Jesus' own Body and Blood. We call this the consecration.

You will see the priest raise up the consecrated Host and chalice of consecrated Wine for all to worship. The whole community responds by proclaiming its faith in Jesus.

We then pray for the pope, the bishops, and for our own needs. We pray also for our whole Church, for all of humankind, and for all who have died. We conclude the Eucharistic Prayer by saying or singing "Amen."

After proclaiming the mystery of faith and the Great Amen, we prepare for Holy Communion by saying or singing the Our Father. We pray for God's forgiveness and then share a sign of peace with those around us.

While praying the Lamb of God prayer, the priest breaks the consecrated Host. This is a sign that we share in the one Bread of Life, the Body of Christ broken for us.

The priest receives Holy Communion. The members of the community next share Jesus' Body and Blood. We may receive the Host in our hand or on our tongue. We may also be invited to receive Communion from the chalice.

The priest or eucharistic minister says to us, "The body of Christ," and if we receive from the chalice, "The blood of Christ." We respond "Amen." Our Amen means that we believe Jesus is really present with us in the Eucharist and in our lives. We believe Jesus strengthens us to live for the reign of God.

To receive Communion worthily, we must be in the state of grace. A person who has commited a mortal sin must receive absolution in the sacrament of Reconciliation before going to Communion.

At the end of the Communion Rite, the priest prays that we will live the way of Jesus in our world.

Concluding Rite

In the Concluding Rite the priest blesses us. He or the deacon sends us forth, and says, "Go in peace to love and serve the Lord."

Through the Mass, we receive the grace to live as true members of the Church, the body of Christ. We are nourished to be the sacrament of God's reign in the world.

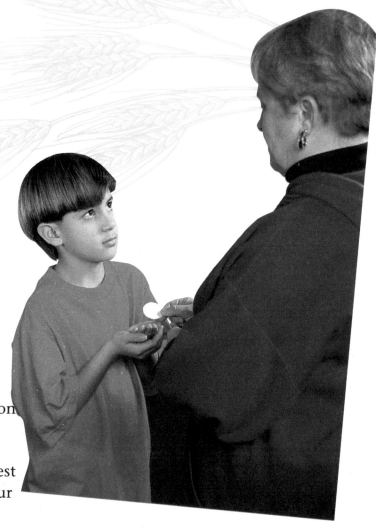

- What does the priest say and do at Mass that Jesus said and did at the Last Supper?
- This week how will you live the words "Go in peace to love and serve the Lord"?

OUR CATHOLIC FAITH

■ Jesus, help us to live in your peace.

■ Why do you think the Church requires Catholics to celebrate Mass on Sunday or Saturday evening, and on other important holy days?

Our Thanksgiving Never Ends

The Mass is our greatest celebration and sign that we are the body of Christ in the world. We are sharing in the Body and Blood of Christ, Saint Paul said, "Because the loaf of bread is one, we, though many, are one body, for we all partake of the one loaf."

1 Corinthians 10:16–17

As Catholics we know that the Laws of the Church require us to participate in the Mass on Sunday or Saturday evening and on certain other holy days during the year.

Our First Holy Communion a few years ago was a very important step in our initiation as members of the Church. Every time we receive Holy Communion, we are made one with Jesus and with one another.

We are to live as the body of Christ in the world. We are to make alive in our actions all that the Mass means to us.

We can try to live the Mass by:

● forgiving those who hurt us, whether they say they are sorry or not;

● asking for forgiveness when we do something wrong;

● serving or helping out in our parish church;

● trying to be welcoming, even when we feel cranky or tired;

● working for justice and peace every chance we get;

● thinking and praying about what we will do to serve God and God's Church now and when we grow up.

Communion Under Both Kinds

At the celebration of the Mass, the priest consecrates both bread and wine. These gifts become the Body and Blood of Christ. By the power of the Holy Spirit, Christ is fully and really present both in the Host and in the Precious Blood.

Often when Catholics celebrate the Eucharist, they receive Holy Communion by taking only the Host. At other times, however, we enjoy the privilege of receiving Communion under both kinds, the Host and the Precious Blood from the chalice.

The bishops of the Church have guidelines for us to follow in receiving Holy Communion under both kinds. It is a wonderful privilege as we celebrate the Eucharist together.

Receiving Communion Reverently

From time to time, we need to remind ourselves of the proper way to receive Holy Communion. When we approach the priest, deacon, or eucharistic minister, we do so reverently. After hearing the words "the body of Christ" or "the blood of Christ" we respond "Amen."

For those receiving the Host in their hands, the proper way is to place one open palm on top of the other. In this way, the Host can be placed on our palm, and we can put the Host into our mouth with the other hand. We never take or grab the Host.

The next time you go to receive Holy Communion, let your reverent example remind others of the importance the Eucharist has in your life.

Learn by heart ## Faith Summary

- The two major parts of the Mass are the Liturgy of the Word and the Liturgy of the Eucharist.
- During the Liturgy of the Word, we listen to God's word from the Bible.
- During the Liturgy of the Eucharist, our gifts of bread and wine become the Body and Blood of Christ.

COMING TO FAITH

Explain why the Mass is the greatest celebration for God's people.

Put a "W" for the parts of the Mass in the Liturgy of the Word. Put an "E" for the parts of the Mass in the Liturgy of the Eucharist. Then number each part in the order in which it occurs.

Letter	Number	
_____	_____	Sign of Peace
_____	_____	Gospel
_____	_____	"This is my body."
_____	_____	"This is the cup of my blood."
_____	_____	Homily/Sermon
_____	_____	Epistle/Letter
_____	_____	Consecration
_____	_____	Lord's Prayer

PRACTICING FAITH

Talk together about ways you can live as the body of Christ in the world. For example:

- serve, be a helper, in your parish
- find ways to help the poor, the homeless
- be aware of and respond to injustices
- be peacemakers at home, in your parish, in your neighborhood

Plan what your group will try to do this week. Then pray the prayer of Saint Francis together (page 290).

Talk with your teacher about ways you and your family might use the "Faith Alive" section. You might go over the readings for Mass together.

REVIEW · TEST

Circle the correct answer.

1. At Mass the bread and wine become the Body and Blood of Jesus.
We call this the

homily.   consecration.

2. When the priest or eucharistic minister says to us, "The body of Christ,"
we respond

"Alleluia."   "Amen."

3. The Liturgy of the Eucharist begins with the

homily.   Preparation of the Gifts.

4. Our Church's great prayer of thanks and praise is the

Eucharistic Prayer.   Creed.

5. How will you try to live the Eucharist this week by being "bread" for others?

_____

_____

FAITH ALIVE AT HOME AND IN THE PARISH

In this chapter your fifth grader has explored how the Mass is our greatest celebration and sign that we are the body of Christ in the world. Saint Paul wrote that we are sharing in the Body and Blood of Christ. "Because the loaf of bread is one, we, though many, are one body, for we all partake in one loaf" (1 Corinthians 10:17).

The Laws of the Church require Catholics to participate in the Mass on Sunday or Saturday evening and on certain other holy days of obligation. This is a serious responsibility, as well as a great privilege. Talk together as a family about what you will do to share more fully and responsively in the Mass.

Preparing for Mass

Look up and read together in a missalette the readings for next Sunday's Mass. Share what messages you find.

Be sure to discuss the reasons for worshiping together that go far beyond the level of obligation. Focus on the privilege of coming together in Christ as a community of faith to praise and thank God.

Reading	Message
1st reading from	
_____	_____
2nd reading from	
_____	_____
Gospel from	
_____	_____

12 | The Church Remembers
(Liturgical Year)

OUR LIFE

A wise teacher in the Old Testament once reflected:

There is a season for everything, a time for everything under heaven:
a time for being born,
a time for dying,
a time for planting,
a time for harvesting,
a time for tears,
a time for laughter,
a time for grieving,
a time for dancing.

Based on Ecclesiastes 3:1–4

These words tell us that there is a season, a time, for everything. Talk about your favorite time of the year.

How is each time different and special?

How does each season prepare us, and the world, for the next season?

SHARING LIFE

Are there "seasons," times of change, in our human lives?

Discuss why we have times for planting and harvesting, for tears and for laughter, for grieving and for rejoicing.

At what time is God with us? How?

Work in small groups to make a mural or a poster on the theme "Seasons of God's Grace in Our Lives." Choose photographs or make drawings that show special times of God's blessing.

Share your work with the whole group. Explain why you chose these times and what they mean to you. You might want to combine what you have made into a single mural or poster and display it in your classroom or in the school.

Form two groups. Read the words from the Book of Ecclesiastes in the Bible.

All: There is an apointed time for everything, and a time for every affair under the heavens:

Group 1: a time to be born,

Group 2: a time to die;

Group 1: a time to plant,

Group 2: a time to uproot the plant;

Group 1: a time to weep,

Group 2: a time to laugh;

Group 2: a time to mourn,

Group 2: a time to dance.

Ecclesiastes 3:1–4

This week we will explore the seasons of the Church year.

We Will Learn

- The liturgical year of the Church has different seasons to remember the life, death, and resurrection of Jesus.
- During the Church year we also honor and pray to Mary and the saints.
- The Church year reminds us that we always live in the presence of God.

117

ADVENT CHRISTMAS ORDINARY

O God, all times and seasons obey your laws.

What seasons of the year do you enjoy the most? How do you notice God's presence in that season?

The Liturgical Year

Every twelve months people live through the seasons of spring, summer, fall, and winter. The Church also has seasons that make up our liturgical year to remind us of Jesus' life, death, and resurrection. These seasons help us to remember that all time is a holy time to be lived in the presence of God.

Advent Season

The liturgical year begins with the four weeks of the Advent season, immediately before Christmas. During this time, we remember that the Jewish people waited and hoped for a Messiah. We wait and hope for the coming of Jesus at Christmas and at the end of time.

Christmas Season

The Christmas season celebrates the birth of Jesus and the announcement to the world that he is the Messiah promised by God. The best way to thank God for the gift of Jesus is to try to give ourselves to others by living the Law of Love.

Lenten Season

The season of Lent is a time of preparation for Easter and for the renewal of our Baptism.

Lent begins on Ash Wednesday and lasts for forty days. It is a time to remember the words of Jesus, "The kingdom of God is at hand. Repent, and believe in the gospel" (Mark 1:15).

Catholics for centuries have prepared for Easter in special ways during Lent. Adults *fast*, or eat less and do without snacks between meals on Ash Wednesday and Good Friday.

ORDINARY

a crazy ordinary lala eats
advent x-mas time lent easter
easter bunnys Tridu um

Those fourteen or older *abstain,* or do not eat meat on Ash Wednesday and the Fridays of Lent. We do without things so that we can have more to *share* with the poor.

We *pray* each day and try to keep God first in our lives. These practices help us to live Jesus' new commandment to love others as he loves us.

Passion, or Palm, Sunday is the last Sunday of Lent and the first day of Holy Week.

Easter Triduum

3) Holy Thurs. evening *Easter Sunday*

The Easter Triduum, or "three days," is the most important time of the entire Church year. It begins with the Mass of the Lord's Supper on Holy Thursday evening and continues through Good Friday and the Easter Vigil on Holy Saturday. It concludes with Evening Prayer on Easter Sunday. During these three days we remember the Last Supper and Jesus' gift of himself in the Eucharist. We recall his passion and death on the cross. We celebrate his resurrection.

Easter Season

On Easter Sunday, the greatest feast of the liturgical year, we celebrate Jesus' resurrection and our new life with God. The Easter season continues for fifty days until Pentecost Sunday.

On Pentecost we remember the day the Holy Spirit came to Jesus' first disciples. We recall that without the Holy Spirit we could not live as God's people.

The gifts of the holy spirit
speak all languages

Ordinary Time

The weeks of the year that are not part of the seasons of Advent, Christmas, Lent, the Triduum, or Easter are known as Ordinary Time. The Church reminds us that God is always with us and present in our lives, no matter what the time.

- Why are there different seasons in the Church, or liturgical, year?
- What will you do to remember God's presence in your life?

OUR CATHOLIC FAITH

- All holy men and women, pray for us.
- Think of someone special who tries to live as a disciple of Jesus. Tell about that person.

Celebrating Mary and the Saints

The Church has named certain people as saints. They are women and men, young people and grown-ups who tried very hard to follow Jesus in their ordinary lives. The Church asks us to admire and to imitate the way they lived the Law of Love.

The ceremony in which the Church names a person a saint is called *canonization*.

Mary, the Mother of God, is the greatest of the Church's saints. Because Mary was the Mother of God's own Son and did what God wanted during her whole life, God blessed her in many ways. Jesus gave us Mary to be our mother, too.

Mary's Song of Praise

After Mary learned from God that she would be the mother of the Messiah, she was filled with joy and hurried to her cousin Elizabeth. Elizabeth, filled with the Holy Spirit, said to Mary, "Most blessed are you among women, and blessed is the fruit of your womb" (Luke 1:42).

Mary responded to Elizabeth by praising God for the blessings she received. Mary's beautiful prayer is called the Magnificat.

Annunciazione, Domenico Ghirlandaio, (15th century)

what mary said to Elizabeth

Mary's Song of Praise

"My soul proclaims the greatness of the Lord;
  my spirit rejoices in God my savior.
For he has looked upon his handmaid's
    lowliness;
    behold, from now on will all ages call me
     blessed.
The Mighty One has done great things for me,
  and holy is his name.
His mercy is from age to age
    to those who fear him.
He has shown might with his arm,
  dispersed the arrogant of mind and heart.
He has thrown down the rulers from their
    thrones.
    but lifted up the lowly.
The hungry he has filled with good things;
  the rich he has sent away empty.
He has helped Israel his servant,
  remembering his mercy,
according to his promise to our fathers,
    to Abraham and to his descendants
     forever."

Based on Luke 1:39–56

Feast Days

Many feast days are celebrated during the
liturgical year. The chart shows some of
the feast days on which we remember the
lives of Jesus, Mary, and the saints.

Advent Season
Immaculate Conception,
  December 8
Our Lady of Guadalupe,
  December 12

Christmas Season
Christmas, December 25
Mary, Mother of God, January 1
Epiphany

Ordinary Time
Presentation of the Lord, February 2

Lenten Season
Ash Wednesday
Joseph, Husband of Mary, March 19
Annunciation, March 25
Passion, or Palm, Sunday

Easter Triduum
Passion, death, and resurrection
  of the Lord

Easter Season
Easter
Ascension
Pentecost

Ordinary Time
Assumption, August 15
Birth of Mary, September 8
All Saints, November 1
All Souls, November 2
Christ the King

OUR CATHOLIC FAITH

Holy Mary, Mother of God, pray for us. What is the name and feast day of your favorite saint? Why is this your favorite saint?

Living the Church's Year

Each year, the liturgical seasons and feasts come and go. We are shown the story of our faith over and over again. Jesus' life, death, and resurrection—the paschal mystery—is the heart of the story. The stories of Mary and the other saints give us many examples of ways to live each day like Jesus.

If the saints of the past were living today, there probably would be no newspaper or television stories about their lives. They did not wake up each day thinking about doing some great, heroic deed for Jesus that would put them in the headlines.

In fact, many of the saints like Saint Francis of Assisi, Saint Thérèse of Lisieux, Blessed Kateri, and Saint Martin de Porres never considered themselves as special. Each day they tried to live for the reign of God by doing God's will.

Each of us can be a saint, too. Each of us has already begun our journey to sainthood. We are initiated into the Church, the body of Christ, in the three sacraments of initiation.

In the sacraments of Baptism and Confirmation, we receive God's new life and the Holy Spirit to help us to live the Law of Love. In the sacrament of the Eucharist, Jesus gives us himself as our Bread of Life to strengthen us in following his way.

But living and growing in our faith is a lifelong journey. The liturgical year helps us to remember that we live our daily, ordinary lives in the presence of God.

When we do this, we can grow to become saints who will live after death in the eternal presence of God in heaven.

Liturgical Colors

The Catholic Church has many ways to help us pray during the different seasons of the liturgical year. We have different music and different prayers. But we also use different colors to help us enter into each season.

Advent: The colors violet or purple help us to remember that we are preparing for the coming of Christ.

Christmas: To celebrate the joy of Christ's birth, we use the colors white or gold.

Ordinary Time: During the longest season of the year, we use the color green, which reminds us of our hope in God.

Lent: This season of penance and renewal also uses the colors violet or purple.

Easter Triduum: Holy Thursday evening is white; Good Friday is red for Christ's passion; the Easter Vigil and Easter Sunday are white in celebration of the resurrection.

Easter: This season, too, is white or gold as we celebrate our new life in Christ.

Liturgical Year/ Liturgical Day

Our liturgical year does not begin on January 1, as the calendar year does. It begins with the first Sunday of Advent and ends with the feast of Christ the King, the last Sunday in Ordinary Time.

A liturgical day is different, too. Our liturgical day of 24 hours begins in the early evening and continues until the evening of the next day. This is a very ancient way of telling time from the Bible, reminding us of God's presence with us from sunset to sunset. Share with a partner which season is your favorite, and why.

THE YEAR OF GRACE

Learn by heart Faith Summary

- The liturgical seasons of the Church year are Advent, Christmas, Lent, the Easter Triduum, Easter, and Ordinary Time.
- During the liturgical year we also honor and pray to Mary and the other saints.
- The liturgical year reminds us that we always live in the presence of God.

COMING TO FAITH

How would you explain the liturgical year to a fourth grader?

With a team, make up a key word for each season. Share your key words with the whole group.

PRACTICING FAITH

†Gather in a prayer circle.

Reader 1: Loving God, we thank you for the gift of time.

All: (Response) Thank you for your presence with us always.

Reader 2: For Advent, when we take time to prepare for the coming again of your divine Son. (Response)

Reader 3: For Christmas, when we celebrate the birth of our Savior. (Response)

Reader 4: For Lent, when we do penance and grow as disciples of Jesus. (Response)

Reader 5: For the Easter Triduum, when we celebrate the death and resurrection of Jesus. (Response)

Reader 6: For the Easter season, when we rejoice in the new life of the risen Christ. (Response)

Reader 7: For Ordinary Time, which reminds us that you are with us in the everyday events of our lives. (Response)

Now pray the Glory to the Father prayer. Then take turns and pray:
Loving God, in this season of _____, help us to live as disciples of Jesus by

_____.

Talk with your teacher about ways you and your family might use the "Faith Alive" section. You might especially want to pray the Family Prayer together.

REVIEW · TEST

Match the seasons of the Church year with the descriptions.

Seasons	Descriptions
1. Ordinary Time	_4_ preparation for Easter
2. Easter Season	_3_ Holy Thursday, Good Friday, Holy Saturday
3. Lenten Season	_1_ the weeks of the year not in the other seasons
4. Easter Triduum	_5_ the birth of Jesus Christ
5. Christmas Season	___ Jesus ascends to his Father
	_2_ the resurrection of Jesus Christ

6. Choose one liturgical season and tell how you will celebrate it so as to grow in your faith.

_____

_____

FAITH ALIVE AT HOME AND IN THE PARISH

The paschal mystery, Jesus' life, death, and resurrection, is the heart of the liturgical year of the Church. In addition, the stories of Mary and the other saints give us many examples of the way to live each day as disciples of Jesus Christ. The liturgical year reminds us that all time is sacred because it is permeated with the presence of God and the guidance of the Holy Spirit.

Our identity as Catholics is strongly influenced by the rituals we celebrate in our parish and home during Advent, Christmas, Lent, the Easter Triduum, Easter, and Ordinary Time.

We have a wealth of feast days in which we celebrate the life of Christ and the lives of Mary and the other saints.

†Family Prayer

Leader: Let us praise the Lord of days and seasons and years, saying: Glory to God in the highest!

Family: And peace to God's people on earth!

Our lives are made of days and nights, of seasons and years, for we are a part of our universe. We mark ends, and we make beginnings, and we praise God for the grace and mercy that fills our days. Amen.

13 Celebrating Advent

Hail Mary, full
of grace, the
Lord is with
you.

Our Life

Here is an old legend that
might have something
true to say to us today.

Once long ago three
children were playing in
their garden. A messenger came along the
road. "The king will pass this way today," he
announced. The children were so excited.
"Perhaps the king will stop by our garden!
Let's make it beautiful!" So the children
worked to make their garden beautiful,
and they made sure they had fruit and bread
and cool drinks. Then they waited...
and waited...and waited.
It was almost sunset when an old man
stopped at their garden wall. "What a
beautiful garden," he said. "It looks so shady
and cool. May I come in and rest awhile?"

The children did not know what to do. They
were waiting for the king! But then—the
poor man looked so tired and hungry.
"Come in," they said and they had him sit in
the shade and they brought him food and
drink. Then they told him that they had
worked to make everything ready for the
king. But the king hadn't come. They were
so disappointed.

Suddenly a lovely light shone around the
man. He wasn't old or shabby anymore. He
was handsome. He smiled at the children.
"Your king *did* pass today," he said, "and you
welcomed him."

Share what you learned from this story for
your own life.

Sharing Life

Discuss together: what are the ways that
Jesus comes into our lives today?

How can we recognize him?

Talk about ways we might get ready for
his coming.

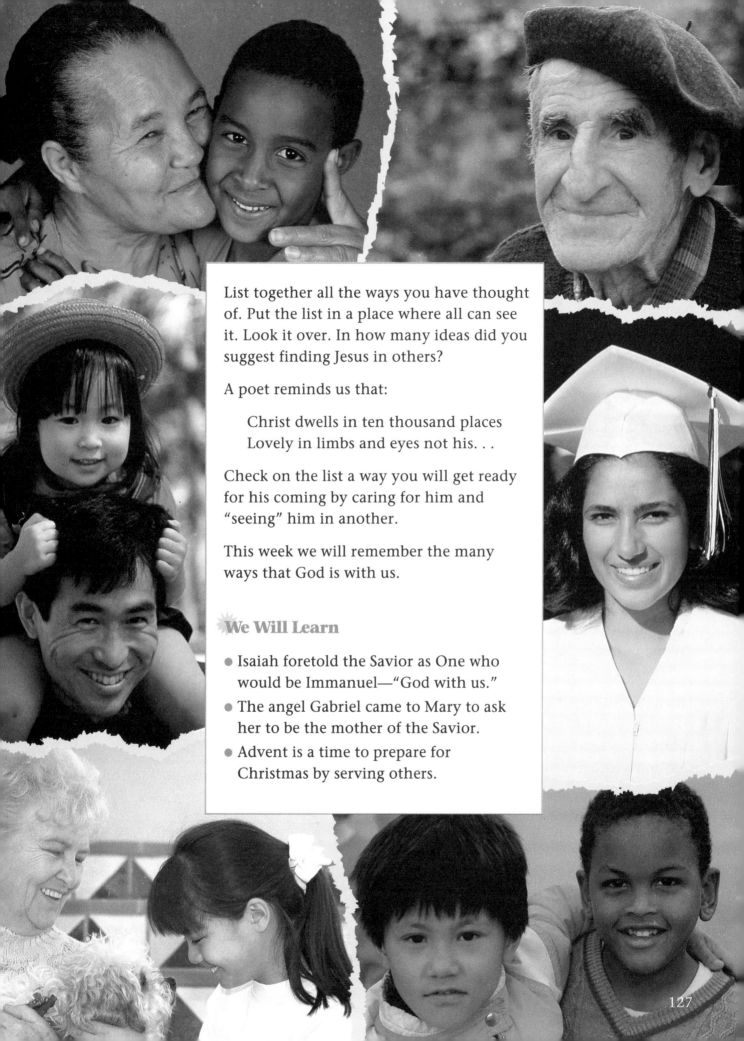

List together all the ways you have thought
of. Put the list in a place where all can see
it. Look it over. In how many ideas did you
suggest finding Jesus in others?

A poet reminds us that:

Christ dwells in ten thousand places
Lovely in limbs and eyes not his. . .

Check on the list a way you will get ready
for his coming by caring for him and
"seeing" him in another.

This week we will remember the many
ways that God is with us.

We Will Learn

- Isaiah foretold the Savior as One who
  would be Immanuel—"God with us."
- The angel Gabriel came to Mary to ask
  her to be the mother of the Savior.
- Advent is a time to prepare for
  Christmas by serving others.

127

Waiting for a Savior

Hundreds of years before Jesus was born, a prophet named Isaiah told the Israelites many things about the promised Savior, or Messiah, for whom they were waiting. Isaiah told the people that the Savior would be born of a young woman who would name him Immanuel. *Immanuel* means "God with us."

Isaiah said that the Savior would rule the people of Israel wisely. Isaiah wrote,
"The spirit of the LORD shall rest upon him:
    a spirit of wisdom and of understanding,
A spirit of counsel and of strength." (Isaiah 11:2).

Isaiah also described the Savior as a descendant of David, who was Israel's best loved king. The Messiah would be the great champion of justice. Isaiah told the Israelites,
"His dominion is vast and forever peaceful,
From David's throne, and over his kingdom,
    which he confirms and sustains
By judgment and justice,
    both now and forever." (Isaiah 9:6)

Isaiah also said that the child born to be their Savior would be called
"Wonder– Counselor, God-Hero, Father
-   Forever, Prince of Peace" (Isaiah 9:5).

Like Isaiah, the other writers of the Bible often compared sin to darkness. At the time of Isaiah, many Israelites had turned away from God and were living in the darkness of sin. Isaiah compared the coming of the Savior to the breaking forth of light in darkness. The prophet said,
"The people who walked in darkness
    have seen a great light;
Upon those who dwelt in the land of gloom
    a light has shone." (Isaiah 9:1).

Isaiah also told the Israelites that they could recognize the Savior by his works. The

Savior would help the poor, heal the sick, and free the oppressed.

The Coming of the Savior

Israel waited in hope for the coming of the promised Savior.

Many years after Isaiah, the angel Gabriel was sent to the Virgin Mary in the town of Nazareth in Galilee. The angel told her, "Behold, you will conceive in your womb and bear a son…. He will be great and will be called the Son of the Most High, and the Lord God will give him the throne of David his father."

Based on Luke 1:26–33

During Advent we remember the words of Isaiah and think about what they mean for us today. We prepare for the feast of Christmas and for Jesus' coming again. We believe that Jesus Christ is Immanuel, "God with us," and the Light of the World. As disciples of Jesus, we must bring his light to the world.

During Advent we prepare ourselves to bring the good news of Jesus to the poor. We try even harder to help care for the sick. We try to do what we can to stop injustice, discrimination, and oppression of any kind. We remember to be peacemakers.

COMING TO FAITH

Tell what you think Isaiah meant when he said our Savior would be:

- Immanuel
- a wise and just ruler
- a light shining in darkness
- one sent to bring good news

Maybe your group would like to bring in gifts of canned food or games for the children of your parish who are in need. Plan what you will do and make it a part of your Advent celebration.

PRACTICING FAITH

An Advent Celebration

All sing:

O come, O come, Emmanuel,
And ransom captive Israel
That mourns in lonely exile here
Until the Son of God appear.
Rejoice! Rejoice, O Israel,
To you shall come Emmanuel!

Reading: (See Isaiah 61:1, 3)

I am filled with the Lord's spirit.
God has chosen me and sent me
To bring good news to the poor,
To heal the broken-hearted,
To announce release to captives
And freedom to those in prison
To give those who mourn
Joy and gladness instead of grief.

Leader: Let's pause now and think about these words of Isaiah. How can we bring Jesus' good news to the poor? healing to the broken-hearted? How can we bring freedom to those held captive by sin? How can we bring God's joy to others? (Silent reflection)

Leader: Jesus, we believe that you are Immanuel, God with us, our promised Savior.

All: Help us to live as your disciples in the world today.

Leader: Jesus, you are the Light of the World.

All: Help us to live as your disciples in the world today.

Leader: Jesus, you are the one sent by God to announce the good news.

All: Help us to live as your disciples in the world today.

Leader: Jesus, you are the Son of God.

All: Help us to live as your disciples in the world today.

Leader: Jesus, you are the Savior, who has come to free us. Help us to bring good news to the poor, to heal the broken-hearted, and to bring freedom to all.

Presentation of Gifts

Walking in procession, all carry gifts for needy children and place them on a prayer table or near an Advent wreath.

All stand and sing:

O come now Wisdom from on high
Who orders all things mightily,
To us the path of knowledge show
And teach us in your ways to go.
Rejoice! Rejoice! O Israel
To you shall come Emmanuel!

Talk with your teacher about ways you and your family might use the "Faith Alive" section. You might make the Angelus your family prayer for Advent. See page 290.

REVIEW ■ TEST

Answer each question.

1. What did the prophet Isaiah foretell about the coming of the Savior?

He told he world be Immanuel ing

2. What does the name Immanuel mean?

"God with us"

3. What message did the angel Gabriel bring to Mary?

to be the mother of a savior

4. Write an Advent prayer that you will say each day until Christmas.

_____

_____

FAITH ALIVE AT HOME AND IN THE PARISH

This Advent lesson introduced some of the Old Testament prophecies that promised the Savior, the Messiah—the one who would be a wise and just ruler, a light shining in the darkness, the bringer of good news, Immanuel (which means "God with us"). We believe that these prophecies are fulfilled in Jesus.

Advent is a season to prepare again for the coming of God's Son into the world and into our lives and his future coming in glory. It is a time to reflect on our Savior, who gives hope to the poor, heals the sick, and liberates the oppressed.

Learn by heart **Faith Summary**

- The prophet Isaiah foretold the coming of the Savior as One who would be Immanuel—"God with us."

- Years later the angel Gabriel was sent to Mary to ask her to be the mother of the Savior.

- During Advent we prepare for Christmas by trying to serve the needs of others.

14 Celebrating Christmas

O come let us adore him, Christ the Lord!

Our Life

In some Latin American countries the people celebrate a lovely Christmas custom called *Las Posadas* ("the dwellings"). Two children take the parts of Mary and Joseph as they look for a place to stay in Bethlehem. All the other children escort them as they go from house to house in the neighborhood. At each door all sing a carol. Then Mary and Joseph ask for a room. They are turned away until they come to the last house. Here they are welcomed in, and all join in singing a joyful carol. A party usually follows!

Does your family have any special Christmas customs? Tell about them.

Share what Christmas means to you.

Sharing Life

Share what you know about Christmas customs in other countries. Why do you think people celebrate Christmas in different ways?

Discuss: what is the most important thing to remember in our Christmas celebrations?

See whether you can learn a Christmas
carol in a language other than your own.
Try learning "Silent Night" in Spanish (see
page 136). If you speak a second language,
teach the words to a small group. Then
share the results together as your closing
prayer.

We Will Learn

- The name *Jesus* means "God saves."
- Jesus is the Light of the World.
- Jesus came to bring us everlasting life.

133

Our Catholic Faith

Newborn Savior of All People

On Christmas Day, we celebrate the birth of Jesus. We remember that the Son of God became one of us and was named Jesus, because he is our Savior. Jesus brings God's life and love to all people.

Here is what we read in the gospel about Jesus receiving his name.

Before Jesus was born, an angel appeared to Joseph in a dream to tell him that Mary would have a son. The angel told Joseph, "You are to name him Jesus, because he will save his people from their sins."

Based on Matthew 1:18–22

The name Jesus means "God saves."

A week after Jesus' birth, Joseph, his foster father, followed the Jewish custom and named the newborn Savior Jesus.

Later the Holy Family went to the Temple in Jerusalem to present Jesus to God. A man named Simeon, who had been praying for the Promised Savior, took Jesus in his arms. Praising God, Simeon said, "Now, Master, . . . my eyes have seen your salvation . . . a light for revelation to the Gentiles."

Based on Luke 2:21–32

People of many different languages, customs, and races celebrate the birth of Jesus because he is the Savior of all people. When we celebrate Christmas, we remember that Jesus Christ has united us to God and to people all over the world.

134

Celebrating the Birth of Jesus

During the first years of Christianity, pagans in Rome celebrated a feast of the sun on December 25. Our Church may have chosen that same day on which to celebrate Jesus' birth because we believe that Jesus is the true Light of the World.

Today Christians around the world celebrate Christmas in many different ways. All our Christmas preparations, customs, and decorations should help us to remember the meaning of Christmas.

The lights on our Christmas trees and in our windows remind us of Christ, the Light of the World. The Christmas tree, which is usually an evergreen tree, reminds us that Jesus brought us life that lasts forever. The Christmas cards and gifts that we give remind us that God shared his own life and love with us.

During the Christmas season, we celebrate that God loved us so much that his only Son became one of us. We celebrate Christmas best by sharing God's love with others.

COMING TO FAITH

Tell the story of Jesus' name.

Then have a *Las Posadas* procession. Choose someone to be Mary and someone to be Joseph. Go from group to group in your parish center asking for a room and singing carols like "O Come All Ye Faithful" and "Away in a Manger." Let the last "house" be the place where your group meets. Some of you can be the "hosts" who welcome Mary and Joseph. When all are gathered, share the prayer service.

135

Practicing Faith

Mary and Joseph kneel beside an empty crib. All the rest gather around them and sing:

O little town of Bethlehem
How still we see thee lie.
Above thy deep and dreamless sleep
The silent stars go by.
Yet in thy dark streets shineth
The everlasting light—
The hopes and fears of all the years
Are met in thee tonight!

Reader 1: While Mary and Joseph were in Bethlehem, the time came for Mary to have her baby. She gave birth to a son, wrapped him in cloths and laid him in a manger because there was no room for them in the inn.

(Someone places a wrapped doll or an image of the baby in the manger.)

Reader 2: There were shepherds in the area, living in the fields and keeping watch over their flock. An angel of the Lord appeared to them and the glory of the Lord shone around them, and they were very much afraid. The angel said to them:

Angel: You have nothing to fear. I come to proclaim good news to you to be shared by all the people. This day a Savior has been born to you. Let this be a sign to you: in a manger you will find an infant wrapped in swaddling clothes.

Angels: Glory to God in high heaven, peace on earth to those on whom God's favor rests!

Shepherds: Let us go over to Bethlehem and see this event that has come to pass, which the Lord has made known to us!

Reader 3: The shepherds went with haste and found Mary and Joseph—and the baby lying in the manger.

Based on Luke 2:6–16

All sing "Silent Night"
(in Spanish, if possible):

Noche de paz, noche de amor.
Todo duerme en derredor.
Entre los astros que esparcen su luz,
Bella anunciando al niñito Jesús
brilla la estrella de paz,
brilla la estrella de paz.

Talk with your teacher about ways you and your family might use the "Faith Alive" section. Think of ways the family can join in the parish celebration of Christmas.

REVIEW ▪ TEST

Complete the sentences.

1. The name Jesus means _"God saves"_.

2. On Christmas day we celebrate _the birth of Jesus_
_____.

3. Jesus came to bring us _eternal life,_.

4. What personal gift will you give Jesus this Christmas?
I will give Jesus my radio.
_____

FAITH ALIVE ▪ AT HOME AND IN THE PARISH

In this liturgical lesson your fifth grader was reminded that the name Jesus means "God saves." Jesus came to be our Savior and Liberator, and his saving grace is for all people. All Christians celebrate Christmas and, though customs differ in different parts of the world, we all rejoice in the truth that God loved us so much that God's Son came to dwell among us and to be like us in all things, except sin. If you have special Christmas customs from your own childhood, be sure to share them with your children. Explore parish customs as well, and plan to join in them as a family.

Learn by heart **Faith Summary**

- The name *Jesus* means "God saves."
- Jesus is the Light of the World.
- Jesus came to bring us everlasting life.

15 | Jesus Christ Forgives Us
(Reconciliation)

Jesus, forgive us
our trespasses
as we forgive
those who
trespass
against us.

Our Life

John Newton was a Scottish sea captain in the middle of the 19th century. He became very prosperous because of the cargo he carried—human cargo. Newton was a slave trader. He took people from Africa and sold them to slave traders in the new world. He did this for some years.
Then something happened to change him. Later he called it "grace."

Newton took a close look at his life and saw clearly the evil he was doing. He left the sea and the slave trade and spent his days in prayer asking God's mercy. As time went by he experienced great peace; he knew that he was forgiven. Newton tried to express in words the amazing grace of God's forgiving love. What he wrote has become one of the most loved Christian hymns in the world.

> Amazing grace, how sweet the sound
> That saved a wretch like me.
> I once was lost, but now am found;
> Was blind, but now I see.

What two "amazing" things did God's grace do for Newton?
Tell how you feel when you are forgiven.

Sharing Life

Discuss with one another what it means to be truly forgiven. Begin by saying, "True forgiveness means . . . ."

What part do you think forgiveness should play in the life of a Christian? in a family? in a parish?

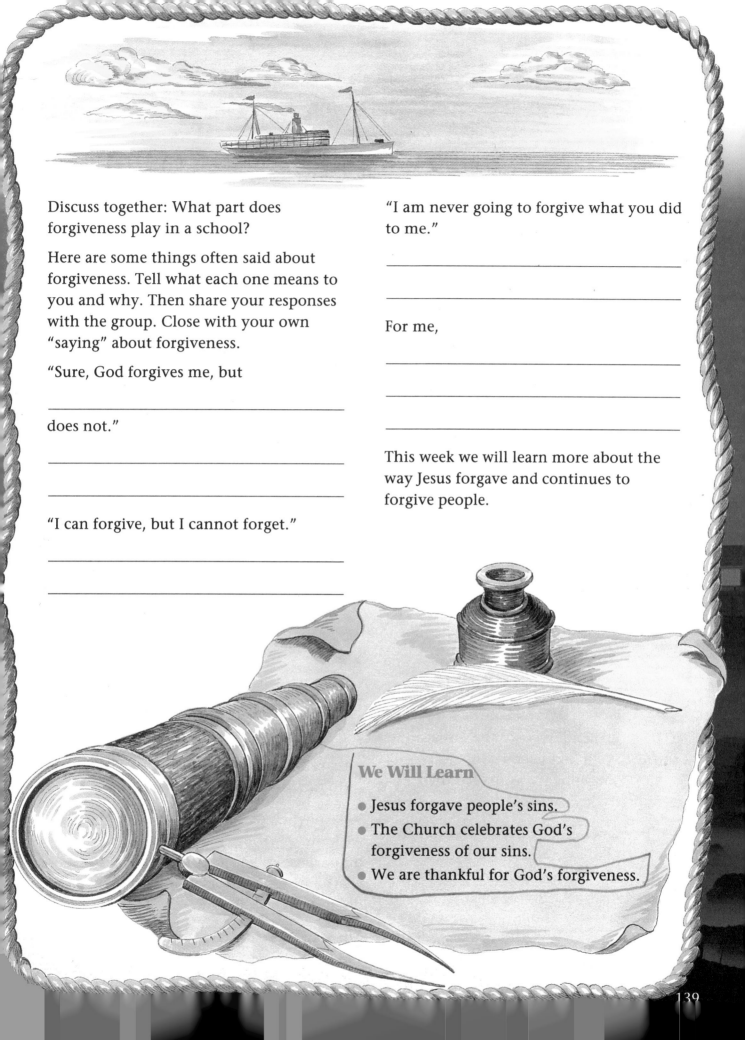

Discuss together: What part does forgiveness play in a school?

Here are some things often said about forgiveness. Tell what each one means to you and why. Then share your responses with the group. Close with your own "saying" about forgiveness.

"Sure, God forgives me, but

_____

does not."

_____

_____

"I can forgive, but I cannot forget."

_____

_____

"I am never going to forgive what you did to me."

_____

_____

For me,

_____

_____

_____

This week we will learn more about the way Jesus forgave and continues to forgive people.

We Will Learn

- Jesus forgave people's sins.
- The Church celebrates God's forgiveness of our sins.
- We are thankful for God's forgiveness.

■ Jesus, heal us from our sins.

■ When do you most need God's forgiveness? How do you ask for it?

Jesus Christ Forgives Sins

Jesus announced the good news that God always forgives our sins when we are sorry for them. Throughout the gospels we read how Jesus revealed God's great and compassionate love for us by forgiving people their sins.

One day some Jewish leaders brought to Jesus a woman who had committed a serious sin. Wanting to punish her, they said to Jesus, "In the law, Moses commanded us to stone such women."

Stooping down, Jesus wrote in the dirt. Then he said, "Let the one among you who is without sin be the first to throw a stone at her."

Jesus bent over and wrote in the dirt again. As the leaders thought about what Jesus had said, one by one they dropped their stones and walked away.

When Jesus was left alone with the woman, he said, "Has no one condemned you?" The woman looked around and replied, "No one, sir." Jesus spoke again, "Neither do I condemn you. Go, [and] from now on do not sin any more."

Based on John 8:1–11

Jesus forgives us when we sin just as he forgave the woman in the story. Jesus calls us to turn away from sin, too.

We sin when we freely choose to do what we know is wrong. We disobey God's law on purpose. When we sin, we fail to live as we should as members of the Church and disciples of Jesus.

The Catholic Church teaches us that we can sin in thought, in word, or in action.

FAITH WORD

Sin is freely choosing to do what we know is wrong. When we sin, we disobey God's law on purpose.

Other sins are less serious. These are called venial sins. By them we do not turn away completely from God's love. But they still cause hurt to other people, ourselves, and the Church. Repeated venial sins can also weaken us and lead to more serious sins.

All sins are personal sins. But whole groups of people can sin, too. We call this social sin. Social sin happens when groups of people choose not to do God's loving will. For example, members of a group commit social sin when they treat unfairly people who are poor or different from them.

Sin is never just between God and one person. Our sins always hurt someone else. We must try to heal the hurt we cause by our sin. We must do and say things that show we are truly sorry. We must try not to sin again.

We also have the responsibility to make up for the harm that our sins may have caused to others, for example, returning stolen goods. We call this making reparation.

Some sins are so serious that by doing them we turn completely away from God's love. We call them mortal sins.

A sin is mortal when:

● what we do is very seriously wrong;
● we know that it is wrong and that God forbids it;
● we freely choose to do it.

■ Why is sin never just between God and one person? Explain.

■ Imagine Jesus is sitting beside you. What will you tell him about the way you are trying to avoid sin?

141

OUR CATHOLIC FAITH

Holy Spirit, help me to make a good confession.

When you know that God or someone has forgiven you, do you ever feel like celebrating? Why or why not?

A Sacrament of Healing

Reconciliation, or Penance, is one of the two sacraments of healing. This sacrament is a powerful and effective sign through which Jesus shares with us God's mercy and forgiveness of our sins. We know we are united again, or reconciled, to God and to our Church community.

When we celebrate Reconciliation, we praise and worship God. In this sacrament we receive God's help to do his loving will, to avoid all forms of sin, and to live as his people. For this reason, we celebrate Reconciliation even when we are not guilty of serious sin.

We can celebrate Reconciliation individually or communally. These ways, or rites, of celebrating Reconciliation are given on page 143. In both rites, we meet with a priest privately. By the power of the Holy Spirit, the priest acts in the name of Christ and the Church to forgive sins in God's name.

We thank God for Reconciliation in our everyday lives. We try to bring God's peace to our families, our school, and our parish community.

The following describes some very important things to know about Reconciliation:

Examination of Conscience: We ask the Holy Spirit to help us think about how well we are doing God's loving will.

Contrition: We say an Act of Contrition to tell God that we are sorry for our sins. We promise to avoid sin and to make up to others for hurting them.

Confession: We confess our sins to God by telling them to the priest in private. We make sure that we confess all mortal sins to the priest. He advises us how to live each day for the reign of God as Jesus wants. The priest will never tell anyone what he heard in confession.

Penance: Our penance can be a prayer or a good deed that helps make up for the hurt caused by our sins. We do the penance the priest gives us to show God that we are sorry and want to change. Doing our penance helps us to avoid sin and grow closer to God.

Absolution: By the power of the Holy Spirit, the Father of mercies forgives sins through his Son; the priest acts in the person of Christ for the Church, and gives us absolution. He makes the sign of the cross over us and says in part, "Through the ministry of the Church may God give you pardon and peace, and I absolve you from your sins in the name of the Father, and of the Son,✝ and of the Holy Spirit." We respond, "Amen."

These words and actions show that God is with us, forgiving our sins. Jesus wants us to celebrate the gift of God's forgiveness by forgiving others.

Individual Rite of Reconciliation

● Before entering the Reconciliation room, we examine our conscience.

● The priest welcomes us in the name of Jesus Christ and the Church. We make the sign of the cross together.

● We listen to a reading from the Bible.

● We confess our sins to God by telling them to the priest. The priest talks to us about our sins. He gives us a penance.

● We pray an Act of Contrition like the one on page 290.

● In the name of God and the Church, the priest says the words of absolution and makes the sign of the cross. We know that God has forgiven us. We answer, "Amen."

● The priest then tells us to go in peace.

● We make sure to do the penance the priest gave us.

Communal Rite of Reconciliation

● We gather as a community and sing a song. The priest greets us and we pray together for God's mercy.

● We listen to readings from the Bible. The priest or deacon gives a homily, reminding us of God's mercy and our need for forgiveness.

● We examine our conscience by thinking about our sins. We pray an Act of Contrition together. We may pray a litany or sing a song. We tell God that we are sorry and ask for forgiveness.

● We pray the Our Father.

● We confess our sins to the priest individually. We receive our penance from the priest, and he gives us absolution from our sins.

● We gather together after our individual confessions. We show our thanks to God by singing or praying.

● The priest blesses us and we leave in God's peace to do our penance and try to sin no more.

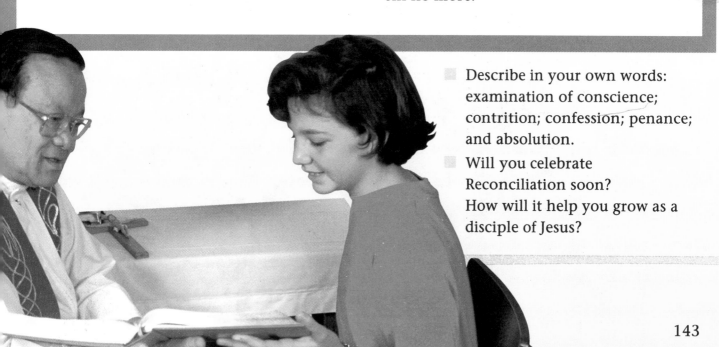

Describe in your own words: examination of conscience; contrition; confession; penance; and absolution.

Will you celebrate Reconciliation soon? How will it help you grow as a disciple of Jesus?

OUR CATHOLIC FAITH

Lord Jesus Christ, may your peace take root in our hearts.

Do you think Jesus wants you to be a forgiving person? Why?

Being Thankful for Forgiveness

We give thanks for God's great compassion and forgiveness that we experience in the sacrament of Reconciliation. We try to bring God's peace to our families, our school, and our parish community.

We show our thanks to God for forgiving us by asking for forgiveness from people whom we hurt.

We can also go to the people who hurt us and forgive them because God has forgiven us. We can be friends to those who are treated unjustly by others. We can offer them the gift of our support and friendship.

When we do these things, we carry on Jesus' ministry of reconciliation. The Holy Spirit helps us to share God's peace and forgiveness with others.

God's forgiveness also comes to us each time we celebrate the Eucharist. During the Mass we tell God we are sorry for our sins. We ask him to help us avoid sin. We grow closer to God and one another.

Celebrating the Eucharist is our greatest form of giving thanks to God for forgiving us and sending us to be peacemakers in our world.

The Seal of Confession

One of the wonderful things for Catholics about the sacrament of Reconciliation is that the confession of our sins is completely private and secret. No one will ever know what we tell the priest during the celebration of this sacrament.

Every priest is bound by a very serious obligation that we call the *seal of confession.* This means that the priest is absolutely forbidden to repeat or discuss what he hears in confession—no matter what!

The reason for this complete secrecy is that the priest, in hearing a confession, acts in the name of God, not in his own name. In fact, the priest's obligation is so total that he may not even talk to us later on about our own confessions unless we give him our permission to do so.

In addition, any person who discovers or overhears in any way what is told in the sacrament of Reconciliation is also bound to complete secrecy. We never need to be afraid to tell anything to the priest in our confession of sins.

A Story About the Seal of Confession

In 1393 Saint John Nepomucen was a priest in the royal court of Bohemia. When the king of Bohemia interfered with the running of the Church, Saint John disagreed and tried to stop him. But the king had Saint John tortured and killed.

The people considered Saint John a martyr. According to a popular story, it was said that Saint John Nepomucen had been killed because he refused to tell the king what the queen had said in confession. For this reason, Saint John Nepomucen became known as the patron saint of the seal of confession.

Faith Summary

- Reconciliation is the sacrament in which we are forgiven by God and the Church for our sins.
- Examination of conscience, contrition, confession, penance, and absolution are important steps in the celebration of Reconciliation.
- In Reconciliation we receive God's help to do his loving will, to avoid sin, and to live as God's people.

145

COMING TO FAITH

Challenge one another's knowledge of the key ideas of Reconciliation. Choose a card. Ask a group member to explain the term on the card. Check the answer by reading the definition on the back of the card. Key words are: conscience, contrition, Reconciliation, absolution, penance, confession.

PRACTICING FAITH

Gather in a circle. Sing "Amazing Grace."

Reader: God said,
"I have brushed away your
offenses like a cloud,
your sins like a mist;
return to me, for I have
redeemed you."

Isaiah 44:22

Reflection: Be very still. Talk to Jesus about forgiveness you need to receive, or forgiveness you need to give. Ask Jesus to help you do what you need to do.

Leader: To show our thanks for the amazing grace of God's mercy and forgiveness, let us offer one another a sign of God's peace. (Turn to those on your right and left and give a handshake of peace.)

Closing: All sing (or say) another verse of "Amazing Grace."
Through many dangers, toils, and snares
We have already come;
'Tis grace has brought us here thus far
And grace will lead us home.

Talk with your teacher about ways you and your family might use the "Faith Alive" section. Invite a family member to celebrate Reconciliation with you.

REVIEW ▪ TEST

Match the terms with the descriptions.

Terms	Descriptions
1. Confession	_____ thoughts about how we are living God's will
2. Absolution	__4__ sorrow for our sins and willingness to avoid sin
3. Penance	__1__ tell our sins to the priest
4. Contrition	__2__ sacramental sign of God's forgiveness
	__3__ a prayer or good work that helps make up for our sins

5. When do you find it hard to forgive? What do you do about it?

When some one kicks me then I kick them I find it hard to forgive. I say I am sorry then sometimes they would say sorry too.

FAITH ALIVE ▪ AT HOME AND IN THE PARISH

In this chapter your fifth grader explored the meaning of sin, forgiveness, and reconciliation. Fifth graders are at an age when they are beginning to recognize that they, like all of us, are in need of forgiveness in the sacrament of Reconciliation.

Throughout his ministry, Jesus challenged people to recognize their sinfulness and to seek forgiveness from God. He offered compassion and mercy to all sinners. The Church continues his ministry and reminds us of our need for sacramental forgiveness. This need exists whether we are seriously alienated from God, or simply need to confront periodically the sinful attitudes and habits that develop when our Christian life goes unexamined. This healing sacrament restores us to God's grace, reconciles us with the Church, and reminds us of our lifelong call to conversion and penance as disciples of Jesus.

†Family Prayer

God and Father of us all,
you have forgiven our sins
and sent us your peace.
Help us to forgive each other
and to work together to establish peace
   in the world.
We ask this through Christ our Lord.
Amen.

You, O God, are our strength and our hope.

OUR LIFE

Ten-year-old Danny Cardo was dying. Leukemia was destroying his blood cells and without a bone marrow transplant his life would end in a matter of weeks. No one in his family was a close enough match to his bone marrow for a transplant—not even his twin sister. His family turned to God in prayer. His school friends and his whole parish joined in.

In California, far away from Danny's home in Vermont, a young woman named Clare had recently become a bone marrow donor. The computer linked her blood type with Danny's as a real match. The surgery was done "just in time," the doctor said.

Today Danny is a healthy, active eleven-year-old. He would like to meet Clare someday. "I thank God for my life," Danny says. "I would like to thank her, too."

Why do you think Danny's family and parish turned to God in prayer?

How do you think Danny felt to know so many people were praying for him?

What or who helps you when you are sick?

SHARING LIFE

Imagine you were Danny. How would it make you feel to be facing death?

What would you want your family and friends to do?

Discuss together the best way to handle serious illness.

Now take a few moments to become very still. Close your eyes and listen to the words and music being played. Then listen to it a second time. Let the words "sink in."

Share what the song said to you about our Christian hope in God's loving care for us, no matter what burden we might have to carry.

Pray the Our Father and Hail Mary together for all young people who are sick or suffering. You might want to do this often this week as we learn more about a great sacrament of healing.

We Will Learn

- Jesus cared for the sick and dying.
- The sacrament of Anointing of the Sick is for the sick, the elderly, and the dying.
- We respect our bodies by caring for them. We can help the Church bring God's healing power to all the world.

OUR CATHOLIC FAITH

The last rites

- O God, we turn to you in our need.
- Why do you think Jesus helped the sick?

Jesus' Care for the Sick and Dying

In many stories, Jesus tells us that each of us is like a traveler or a pilgrim on a journey to God in heaven. We are born. We journey through life. Many of us will suffer illnesses. Then each of us must die to complete our journey into God's presence. God created us—body and soul—to be with God forever. The soul is immortal and is what gives life to the body. It makes us able to think, choose, and love. *St. Paul*

Jesus always cares very much for us and helps us on our journey, especially when we are suffering in mind or in body. In his public ministry, Jesus showed great care and compassion for people who were sick. His most frequent miracles were those of healing. Jesus told his disciples to carry on this ministry of healing.

Healing of a Man Born Blind

One day Jesus and his disciples met a man who had been blind since birth. The disciples thought the man's blindness was his own fault because he was a sinner.

But Jesus said, "Neither he nor his parents sinned; it is so that the works of God might be made visible through him."

Jesus spit into the dirt and made some mud. Rubbing the mud on the man's eyes, Jesus told him, "Go wash in the Pool of Siloam."

The man went to a nearby pool of water. After he washed the mud out of his eyes, he could see for the first time in his life!

Based on John 9:1–6

Jesus healed the blind man to show how much God loved him. The man, who could now see, became a sign to the people that sickness is not a punishment for sin.

Jesus showed us that God always loves and cares for the sick. God wants us all to be healthy and happy in mind and body.

Jesus will help us, too, whenever we are sick or suffering. Jesus may not cure us miraculously as he did the blind man. But if we pray, Jesus will help us to be patient and brave. His love will help us to bear the burden of being ill.

Jesus, who suffered and died on the cross for us, knows the meaning of sickness and pain. He will fill us with hope that God loves us. He will unite our suffering and pain with his own and offer it to God.

God will certainly bless and give strength to all who journey through life with faith. How we face troubles and sickness shows the way in which we are trying to journey as followers of Jesus.

List ways you can be helpful and a sign of God's love to a sick person.

_____

_____

_____

_____

_____

- How do you think Jesus helps a person today who is blind, or lame, or deaf to journey through life?
- How will you ask Jesus to help you when you are sick?

OUR CATHOLIC FAITH

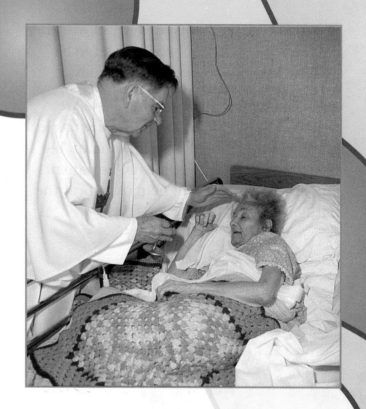

- Lord Jesus, you healed the sick. Lord, have mercy.
- Name a time you helped a sick, or elderly person. Why did you help?

Anointing of the Sick, A Sacrament of Healing

If someone in our family gets sick, our home just does not seem right. In the same way, if someone in the Catholic community suffers illness, every one of us is affected by it. We are all part of the body of Christ. *St. Paul*

Jesus gave his Church the work of bringing God's healing power to the sick, the elderly, and the dying. By the power of the Holy Spirit, the Church carries on this mission of healing in the sacrament of the Anointing of the Sick.

Anointing of the Sick is one of the two sacraments of healing. This sacrament is a powerful and effective sign of Jesus' presence that brings strength and healing to the elderly, the sick, and the dying.

The celebration of this sacrament sometimes helps sick people to get well again. When that does not happen, the sacrament helps the sick face their illness with faith and trust. It also helps dying people to continue their journey to God in heaven.

Saint James writes in his New Testament letter that in this sacrament our sick bodies can be healed and our sins forgiven. He wrote that if anyone was sick the church elders would come and pray for and rub oil on the sick person in the name of the Lord. James said, "The prayer of faith will save the sick person... If he has committed any sins, he will be forgiven."

Based on James 5:14–15

Celebrating the Sacrament

The sacrament of Anointing of the Sick often takes place during a Mass after the Liturgy of the Word. Family, friends, and other members of the parish come together with the sick and elderly to pray for and support them.

Anointing of the Sick is also given at home and in the hospital to those who are very ill or dying. Wherever the sacrament is celebrated, it also comforts the family and friends and helps them to pray for the elderly, sick, or dying person.

The two most important signs of the sacrament are the laying on of hands and anointing with oil.

The priest first lays his hands on the head of each sick or elderly person. This is a sign of God's blessing.

He then anoints the person's forehead with oil, saying,

"Through this holy anointing
may the Lord in his love
and mercy help you
with the grace of the Holy Spirit."

He then anoints the person's hands, saying, "May the Lord who frees you from sin save you and raise you up."

Every Catholic should understand how this sacrament is celebrated. When a Catholic is seriously ill, a priest should be notified. In this way we help our friends and relatives who are sick.

The sacrament of **Anointing of the Sick** brings God's special blessings to those who are sick, elderly, or dying.

Viaticum
When Holy Communion is given to a dying person, it is called *Viaticum*. Viaticum means "food for the journey." Viaticum is often received along with Anointing of the Sick.

▪ What two signs does the priest use in the Anointing of the Sick?

▪ How will you help those in your parish who are sick or elderly?

153

OUR CATHOLIC FAITH

■ Holy Spirit, grant us courage to carry on Jesus' mission.

■ Share some simple ways that you can take better care of your body to prevent sickness.

Respecting Our Bodies

God wants us to respect our bodies by taking care of them. Some sickness or disease cannot be avoided. Other illnesses can be avoided if we eat healthful foods, get enough sleep, and exercise properly.

Most importantly, we must not abuse and harm our bodies. Drinking alcohol to excess and smoking tobacco are bad for our health.

No matter what our friends do or ask us to do, God will give us the courage to say no to illegal drugs. God will also help us to try again if we fail.

The Catholic Church has shelters to care for the hungry and the homeless, and places to treat those suffering from alcohol and drug addiction. The Church has nursing homes and hospitals to care for people who are elderly, injured, or dying.

The Church encourages the study of ways to prevent disease. The Church, as Jesus' peacemaker, also preaches against the evil of war, which needlessly kills and injures so many people.

We can continue Jesus' mission of bringing God's healing power to all the world. We can respect our bodies. We can support our Church's efforts to eliminate disease, suffering, hunger, homelessness, and war in our world.

Preparing for a Sick Call

When someone in the family is very sick or elderly, and not able to go out, we ask the parish priest to visit that person. Catholics often call this visit of the priest a *sick call*. The priest comes to pray with the sick person, to bring Holy Communion, and sometimes to celebrate the sacrament of Anointing of the Sick. The whole family can join in the celebration.

This is the way a family can prepare for a sick call.

If possible, a small table covered with a white cloth should be placed near the person who is sick. In this way, the priest can place the holy oil on the table and the *pyx*, or small round container for the Blessed Sacrament. A small crucifix and two blessed candles are often placed on the table, too.

The priest may use holy water to sprinkle and bless the sick person. Then, after the anointing, the priest may wish to remove the holy oil from his fingers. It would be helpful to have cotton, a small piece of lemon, and a small towel on the table for this purpose.

When you ask the priest to visit a sick or elderly person in your family, ask him what preparations he would like you to make for his visit. Sometimes families have special *sick call sets* that have been handed down from generation to generation. How can you help now to prepare for a sick call?

Faith Summary

Learn by heart

- The sacrament of Anointing of the Sick brings God's special blessings to those who are sick, elderly, or dying.
- Anointing of the Sick is one of the two sacraments of healing.
- We must respect our bodies by caring for them. We must work to eliminate sickness and evil from the world.

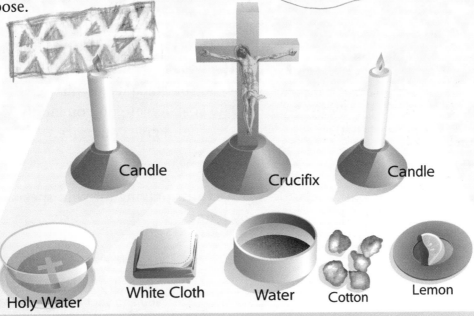

Candle

Crucifix

Candle

Holy Water

White Cloth

Water

Cotton

Lemon

COMING TO FAITH

Act out a celebration of the sacrament of Anointing of the Sick.

Tell how we can live this sacrament in our daily lives.

PRACTICING FAITH

Ask your catechist about some people in your parish who are in need of your loving care.

Decide together some things that you, your friends, or your family will do to help these people.

†Praying for the Sick

Place in a bowl on a prayer table the names of people who are sick. Pray this blessing from the Bible for all these people.

Leader: In the name of the Father, and of the Son, and of the Holy Spirit. Amen.

All: The LORD bless you and keep you!
The LORD let his face shine upon you, and
    be gracious to you!
The LORD look upon you kindly
    and give you peace.

Numbers 6:24–26

Take turns praying for your special person by name.

Talk with your teacher about ways you and your family might use the "Faith Alive" section. Ask a family member to visit a sick or elderly person with you.

REVIEW ▪ TEST

Match.

1. Viaticum   _____2_____ a sacrament of healing

2. oil and laying on of hands   _____1_____ "food for the journey"

     _____3_____ the signs of the sacrament

3. hope

     _____3_____ an effect of the sacrament

4. soul

     _____4_____ gives life to the body

5. What can you do to take care of your own health?

I can stick to healthy foods and say no to drugs

FAITH ALIVE AT HOME AND IN THE PARISH

In this chapter your fifth grader has learned more about the sacrament of Anointing of the Sick. The sacrament used to be called Extreme Unction. The Catholic Church has returned to the early Christian understanding of this sacrament as one of healing, and not simply a sacrament limited to the dying. This is why the sacrament is now called Anointing of the Sick.

Faithful to the healing mission of Jesus, the Church invites the sick and dying to come to him, seeking physical and spiritual health. The anointing with holy oil is a powerful sign of Jesus' loving presence to the one who is suffering.

Caring for the Sick

Visit someone who is sick or who is elderly and perhaps has few visitors. You might take the person a small gift (a few flowers, a large-print prayer booklet). Be prepared to listen to the person with patience. Let the person know by your interest, gentleness, and compassion that you really care for him or her.

Loving God, help us to grow as people who understand and keep our promises.

OUR LIFE

Most fairy tales end with the prince and princess "living happily ever after." It is an ending we expect. Real life, however, can be very different. People who get married plan to live happily ever after, too.

The couples promise to stay together "until death us do part." But real life is full of good times and bad times, joys and sorrows, sickness and health.

How do couples make marriage work? Here are some responses from real people.

● "We try to love each other. That's what is most important."
(Jennifer and Steven, newlyweds)

● "We keep trying to grow and change together—we're partners in everything."
(Gilberto and Maria, married 10 years)

● "When we have problems, we work them out. Marriage takes *work*!"
(Roy and Linda, married 21 years)

● "We are best friends. We always will be."
(Jim and Tiana, married 46 years)

What do you think about what these couples are saying about marriage?

Then ask yourself: How well do I keep promises?

SHARING LIFE

Discuss together:

● things that make it difficult for couples to keep their promises

● things couples might do to help them keep their promises

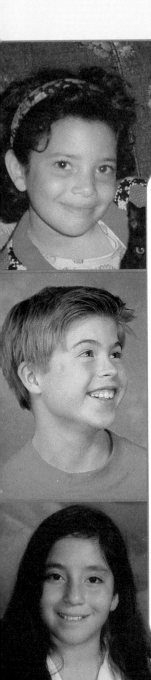

Here is a description of love Saint Paul once wrote. After each description, explain why this kind of love is important in a marriage or a friendship.

Love is patient.   _____
                          _____

Love is kind.   _____
                          _____

Love is not jealous.   _____
                          _____

Love is not selfish.   _____
                          _____

Love is not angry   _____
or irritable.   _____
                          _____

Love forgives all.   _____
                          _____

See 1 Corinthians 13:4–5

Share your thoughts with the group. This week we will explore how one prepares for and lives the sacrament of Matrimony.

We Will Learn

- Jesus Christ blessed the marriage covenant.
- Our Church celebrates the sacrament of Matrimony.
- We need to practice being faithful to our friends.

- O God, fill us with your love.
- Make a list of ways that the family and friends of married people can help them live their marriage vows.

Matrimony, A Sacrament of Service

Jesus calls all his disciples to love God, love others, and love themselves. The Church celebrates that call to love in a special way in the sacrament of Matrimony, or marriage. We see Jesus' compassionate care for newlyweds in the story of the wedding feast at Cana.

One day Jesus went with Mary, his mother, and his disciples to a wedding in the village of Cana. Everyone was having a great time. But suddenly the wine began to run out.

Mary knew how embarrassed the bride and groom would be over this, so she whispered to Jesus, "They have no wine."

Jesus asked that six huge stone jars holding over twenty gallons each be filled to the top with water. He then instructed the servants, "Draw some out now and take it to the headwaiter."

The new wine was so good that the headwaiter said to the couple, "You have kept the good wine until now."

Based on John 2:1–11

Jesus wants to help every couple live out their marriage covenant. A *covenant* is a special agreement that joins two parties together forever.

The marriage covenant is like the covenant the Church lives with Jesus. Jesus promises to love us forever. We promise to try always to follow the Law of Love and to live for the reign of God.

In the sacrament of Matrimony, a bride and groom promise to love and honor each other as equal partners forever. Such a love demands that each partner love the other unconditionally, no matter what happens. This means they do not promise "I will love you if ...," but rather "I will love you always."

Matrimony is one of the two sacraments of service. Married couples promise to serve each other with love and to serve the whole Church. They enter into a lifelong covenant of love. This is their vocation.

They serve the Church by their love and share in God's creation in a very special way when they give birth to children. Every married couple must be ready to welcome and raise lovingly the children God wishes them to have. In Matrimony God gives a man and woman the special grace and blessings to build a truly Christian family together.

You can try to help your family do this. You can return their love by caring for them and by helping out at home.

You can always pray for your whole family, too.

You can share your family's love with others who do not experience love in their own family. By doing these things you help support the marriage promises parents make.

■ Explain in your own words how the marriage covenant is like Jesus' love for the Church.

■ How will you help your parents live their marriage covenant?

161

OUR CATHOLIC FAITH

- Lord Jesus, bless all married couples.
- Why do you think a man and woman decide to marry?

The Church Celebrates Matrimony

In the sacrament of marriage, the Church brings God's love and blessing to the newly married couple. Their love is a sign of God's love in the world. Jesus himself becomes a special partner in their relationship. Jesus wants to help every couple live out their marriage covenant. The Holy Spirit gives the couple the grace to live this sacrament faithfully and well.

Celebrating the Sacrament

Catholics celebrate marriage as a sacrament. It is usually celebrated in the parish of the bride or groom. Families and friends take part in the celebration. They promise to try to support the couple during their married life.

In the Catholic understanding of marriage, the couple themselves are the ministers of the sacrament. After the Liturgy of the Word, the bride and groom stand before the priest or deacon, who witnesses the couple's promises for Christ's community, the Church.

Individually they vow to each other, "I, (*Name*), take you, (*Name*), to be my wife [or husband]. I promise to be true to you in good times and in bad, in sickness and in health. I will love you and honor you all the days of my life." These are called the marriage vows, or promises.

Holding hands and saying these words are signs in the sacrament that the bride and groom have made a lifelong covenant with one another.

Jesus Christ comes to the couple and unites them in love as Christ loves his Church. The Holy Spirit strengthens and blesses their love. Their married love becomes a sign of God's love for the world.

After they exchange their vows, the bride and groom usually give each other wedding rings as a sign of their new union.

Name some ways couples can remind themselves of their marriage covenant of love and service.

_____

_____

_____

_____

_____

After the Our Father, the priest or deacon gives the nuptial blessing. In this prayer, the Church asks God to help the couple love each other as Jesus loves us, share their love with their children, and raise them to be Jesus' disciples.

As another sign of their union, the bride and groom, if both are Catholics, may receive Holy Communion together. They ask Jesus to help them live their marriage promises with love all their lives.

Sometimes husbands and wives struggle in their marriages. But children are not to blame when their parents separate or divorce. Separation or divorce does not mean people are bad. This is a very difficult time for the whole family. No matter what happens, God continues to love each person and always offers the help that is needed.

God's covenant with us never fails. God always loves us.

Name three signs used in the sacrament of Matrimony. Which one is the most important? Why?

Do you think you would like to marry some day? What will you do now to prepare yourself to live the sacrament of Matrimony well?

OUR CATHOLIC FAITH

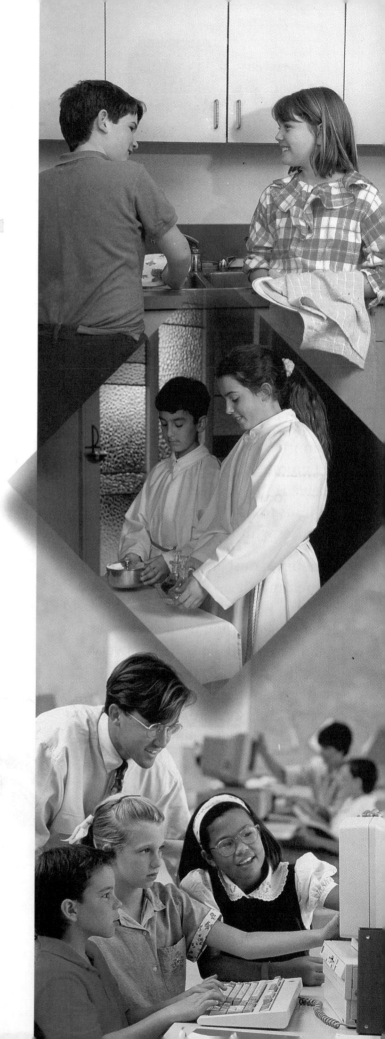

■ God the Holy Spirit, grant us the gift of faithfulness.

■ What can you do to show someone today that you are a good friend?

Practicing Being Good Friends

Marriage is a long way off for us. We can prepare now for this sacrament by learning to love, respect and care for our family and friends in the same way that God always loves us.

We can learn to love others unconditionally. This means that we do not stop loving others because they do something that bothers us. We can also ask others for their forgiveness if we hurt them.

We can prepare for marriage by being faithful to our friends. We can ask God to help us stand by them even when it is not easy to do so.

God created men and women to be equal. Marriage is a covenant between equal partners who treat each other with love and respect. Boys and girls can learn now how to work together as equal partners.

We should learn to practice unselfish love. Parents often place their children's needs before their own. We can practice this kind of unselfish love now by doing things generously for our parents, for our brothers and sisters, and for our friends.

The Ministers of Marriage

Tell what you think is wrong with the following statement: "That young couple was married by Father Smith."

Sometimes Catholics are surprised to learn that the bride and groom themselves are the ministers of the sacrament of Matrimony, not the priest. The priest is the official witness of the Church. He offers the prayers, celebrates the nuptial Mass, and blesses the couple. He receives the couple's consent in the name of the Church. He joins with the entire assembly at a wedding in witnessing to a couple's marriage vows.

When Catholics are married, they are required to celebrate their exchange of vows before a priest and two witnesses. This is because marriage is a sacrament. A sacrament belongs to the whole Church, not just to the couple.

Exchanging Rings

Wedding rings are a sign of the love and faithfulness that a married couple pledge to each other. The Church has no rules or regulations concerning the style of a wedding ring. Very often rings are just simple bands.

A long time ago, it was customary for some Catholics to inscribe the inside of the wedding ring, or band, with a prayer or phrase. One favorite prayer was: *In Christ and thee my love shall be.* What words would you put on the inside of a wedding ring to help a young couple remember the meaning of the sacrament of marriage?

Learn by heart Faith Summary

- The sacrament of Matrimony is a powerful and effective sign of Christ's presence that joins a man and woman together for life.
- Married couples promise to serve each other and the whole Church. Matrimony is a sacrament of service.
- We can prepare now for Matrimony by trying to love others as God loves us.

Coming To Faith

Reread the marriage vows on page 162. These are the promises the man and woman make to each other on their wedding day and forever. Describe in your own words what they are promising.

Why do you think the Church considers Matrimony a sacrament of service?

Practicing Faith

† **Praying for Married Couples**

Praying for married couples is one of the most important ministries, or services, young people can offer.

Offer the following prayer together.

Leader 1: Jesus, you shared the joy and laughter of wedding celebrations.

All: Share your joy with all married couples—especially those who are closest to us.

Leader 2: Jesus, you treated women and men equally.

All: Help wives and husbands to live together as equal partners and loving friends.

Leader 3: Jesus, you want marriage to last forever, like God's love for us.

All: Guide those whose marriages are in trouble. Help divorced or separated couples.

Leader 4: Jesus, help all your disciples to follow your command to love and to be faithful friends.

All: Amen.

Talk with your teacher about ways you and your family might use the "Faith Alive" section. Pray the Family Prayer together before doing the activity.

REVIEW ■ TEST

Circle the letter beside the correct answer.

1. At the wedding in Cana, Jesus
   a. changed water into wine.
   b. ignored the problem.
   c. did not work a miracle.

2. The ministers of the sacrament of Matrimony are
   a. the priest and witnesses.
   b. Jesus and the Church.
   c. the bride and groom.

3. The most important sign of Matrimony is
   a. the marriage vows.
   b. the wedding rings.
   c. the nuptial blessing.

4. Married love is a sign of
   a. the Trinity.
   b. Christ and the Church.
   c. God's love for us.

5. Can you be a sign of God's love in your family? How?
   Yes. By being helpful, respectful
   and generous.

FAITH ALIVE AT HOME AND IN THE PARISH

Your fifth grader has learned more about the sacrament of Matrimony. Invite her or him to tell you what the sacrament means and what young people can do now to learn to prepare for marriage.

Read the Bible story in John 2:1–11 about the marriage feast at Cana. Talk about God's love for married couples and families. Also talk about the fact that God does not abandon families separated by death or divorce.

Saying Thank You

Design an original card or write a thoughtful letter of thanks to your parents or grandparents. Do something special for their next wedding anniversary (bake a cake, write a poem or a song, participate in a Mass together as family on their anniversary day).

†Family Prayer

May the Lord Jesus, who was a guest at the
   wedding in Cana,
bless my family and friends. Amen.

18 Jesus Christ Calls Us to Serve
(Holy Orders)

Loving God, fill your Church with the spirit of courage, love, and service.

OUR LIFE

In each of these pictures a priest is ministering, or offering some service, to his parish. Tell:
● how each priest is serving.
● what difference the priest may be making in the lives of the people served.

Name other ways by which priests minister to, or serve, their people.

SHARING LIFE

If you were a priest, what would you want to do for those you serve? Circle one of the priestly ministries listed below.

baptizer	confessor	teacher
preacher	leader	friend
Mass Celebrant and presider		spiritual guide

Think of a priest who has served you or your family in this ministry. How did he help?

Discuss as a group what qualities are needed to be a good priest. Why?

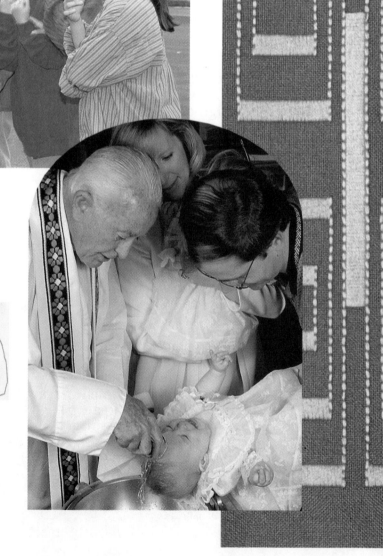

168

Here are two candidates for a top leadership position. Which one would you pick? Why?

Description #1

This person is …

intelligent, shrewd

good business skills

ambitious, wants to "get ahead" wants to do great things but doesn't care who gets hurt on the way

likes to get things done

ADUJS Judas

Description #2

This person is …

intelligent but stubborn

honest, tough

proud, boastful

often takes on more than he can handle

short tempered, but has a kind heart and can say "I'm sorry."

EETRP Peter

My choice is _____

because _____

Now unscramble the names on each resume to find which apostle is being described. This week we will learn more about the vocation to the ordained ministry.

We Will Learn

- Jesus Christ gives us leaders in the Church.
- Our Church celebrates Jesus' priesthood.
- We experience the sacrament of Holy Orders through the ministry of bishops, priests, and deacons.

OUR CATHOLIC FAITH

- O God, we give you thanks for the gift of Holy Orders.
- Do you think priests need our help? Why or why not?

Jesus Christ Gives Us Leaders

When Jesus began his public mission, he invited all his disciples to help him. From among the disciples, he chose twelve special helpers, called apostles, to be the first leaders of his Church.

After choosing his apostles, Jesus often taught them what it meant to be a leader. What Jesus said about being a leader was very surprising to the apostles. He showed them that being a leader meant being a servant, not one who is served.

Jesus told them, "Whoever wishes to be great among you, will be your servant.... For the Son of Man did not come to be served but to serve and to give his life as a ransom for many."

Based on Mark 10:35–45

By his words and actions Jesus showed his apostles that they were not to seek power and glory over others. He called them instead to be compassionate servants who would serve as he served.

After Jesus Christ ascended into heaven and after the coming of the Holy Spirit, the apostles led the early Church in two special ways:

- They went everywhere teaching the good news of Jesus to all.
- They led the community in carrying on the mission of Jesus to the world.

The Church grew so rapidly that soon more helpers were needed. The apostles, with the help of the Christian community, chose others to continue their work of teaching and leading the Church in worship and service. The apostles laid their hands on them and prayed that they would be strengthened by the Holy Spirit.

In time these successors of the apostles were called bishops. The bishops ordained still others as priests to help them. Deacons also were chosen to make sure that the needs of the poor, the lonely, the widowed, and the orphaned were met.

Tell why you think our pope is called "the Servant of the Servants of God."

_____

_____

_____

How did Jesus explain what it meant to be a leader in his Church?

How will you help the leaders of our Church today?

The leader of the apostles was Saint Peter. As bishop of Rome, the pope carries on the ministry of Saint Peter. The pope leads the other bishops just as Peter led the apostles.

Today our bishops, priests, and deacons continue the mission of the apostles. Our pope is the leader of the whole Catholic Church. Bishops lead and serve our dioceses.

In our parish, priests help us to be a Christian community caring for one another. They lead us in celebrating the sacraments and teach us how to live Jesus' good news. They serve the whole community and encourage us to use our gifts in service, too. Deacons have a special concern and ministry for the poor and those in need.

Together with our bishops, priests and deacons, we must all work together to bring about the reign of God.

OUR CATHOLIC FAITH

■ Lord Jesus, you call all your disciples to a life of service.

■ What do you imagine it would be like to be ordained a priest?

Holy Orders, A Sacrament of Service

Holy Orders is the sacrament through which the ordained ministry of bishops, priests, and deacons is conferred by the laying on of hands followed by the prayer of consecration.

Our ordained ministers serve the Catholic community in four ways:

● They preach and teach the good news of Jesus Christ.

● They lead us in celebrating the sacraments.

● They lead us in working together to build up the Christian community.

● They help us to serve the poor and all those in need.

Celebrating Holy Orders

Bishops, priests, and deacons are ordained in the sacrament of Holy Orders. The sacrament of Holy Orders is celebrated during a Mass. The celebrant is always a bishop. Only a bishop can ordain another bishop, priest, or deacon.

The bishop asks the whole community whether they find the men acceptable for ordination. Then he asks the candidates whether they will serve the Church.

The bishop then instructs them about their duties. The candidates promise to respect and obey their bishop, to celebrate the sacraments faithfully, to preach and explain Catholic teachings, and to give their lives in service to God. They are to act in the person of Christ as they lead and serve his Church.

In ordaining priests, the bishop lays his hands on the head of each candidate and prays silently. This is the most important sign of the sacrament of Holy Orders. Then the bishop prays a prayer of consecration, or the prayer that "makes holy."

Each candidate for the priesthood is also anointed with holy oil. This is a sign of his special sharing in Christ's own priesthood through the ordained ministry.

Each receives a paten and chalice. With these the priest leads the community in celebrating the Eucharist.

Bishops and deacons are also ordained using a similar ritual. When bishops are ordained, they receive a mitre (headpiece), ring, and crozier (shepherd's staff). These symbols remind us that the bishops are the successors of the apostles. They are to teach, govern, and sanctify the Church.

When deacons are ordained, they receive the gospel book. They proclaim the good news to us and can lead us in celebrating some of the sacraments. Deacons have a special ministry to serve the poor and those in need.

FAITH WORD

Holy Orders is the sacrament that confers the ordained ministry of bishops, priests, and deacons.

Bishops, priests, and deacons are our ordained ministers. Today our Church is much in need of loving and caring priests. We need to ask the Holy Spirit to give those called to the ordained priesthood the strength to accept and live this vocation.

By Baptism each of us is given a share in the priesthood of Jesus Christ. We are not ordained ministers. But we, too, are called to share the good news of Jesus Christ and carry on his mission. We too, must serve the poor and all in need. By doing this we help bring about the reign of God in our families, our parish, and our world.

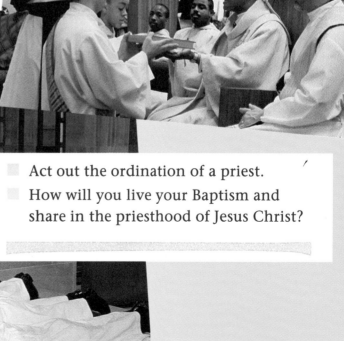

- Act out the ordination of a priest.
- How will you live your Baptism and share in the priesthood of Jesus Christ?

OUR CATHOLIC FAITH

▪ Holy Spirit, guide the ordained ministers of the Church.

▪ Name ways that you can help a priest make a difference in people's lives.

Holy Orders and Our Lives

Each one of us experiences the sacrament of Holy Orders through the ministry of the priests and deacons in our parish. Here are some ways we can support the ordained ministers in our parish:

● Pray for them, especially at Mass. At Mass we pray for our pope, our bishop, and for all who teach the Catholic faith that comes to us from the apostles.

● Help them when they celebrate the sacraments. For example,

— babysit for the parents of a new baby so they can attend baptismal instructions to prepare for their baby's Baptism.

— be an altar server.

— prepare the altar, the gifts, the readings, and the music for a Mass with a group of classmates.

— spend time examining our consciences so we can talk over with the priest in Reconciliation about who or what makes it hard for us to follow Jesus.

● Help them in one of your parish programs. For example,

— tell the priest about people in the parish who are new, in need, or ill.

— collect food and clothing for the hungry and poor.

— help with the religious education program in the parish.

The Ministry of Deacons

The Church has always held the holy order of deacons in high honor. Men who are ordained priests are first ordained deacons. But many men remain deacons for the rest of their lives. They are called *permanent deacons.* This is their special call, or vocation, in the Catholic Church.

Permanent deacons receive the sacrament of Holy Orders and spend a long time in preparation for it. They may be married, but the marriage must take place before they are ordained. A deacon may not remarry when his wife dies. Once men are ordained by the bishop as permanent deacons, they may never go on to the priesthood. Their ministry is a permanent and special ministry of service to the whole parish community.

BISHOP HEALY

A Daring Priest

When young James Healy decided to become a priest, he knew he was asking for trouble. He was ordained in 1854. Racism and anti-Catholic prejudice were common.

As the son of an African-American mother and an Irish-American father, James Healy was often the target of racial insults. Even some of his own parishioners in Boston treated him with cruelty. But he loved the priesthood and he would not give it up.

James Healy went on to become the first black bishop of an American diocese in 1875. The people of his diocese in Portland, Maine soon learned to love and honor him as a good shepherd.

We can honor Bishop Healy by following his example of courage and faithfulness to our own vocation.

Learn by heart **Faith Summary**

- Jesus chose the twelve apostles to lead our Church in teaching and worship.

- Bishops, priests, and deacons are ordained in the sacrament of Holy Orders.

- Our ordained ministers lead us in building up the Christian community.

COMING TO FAITH 12

Work together and imagine a day in the life of a priest. Make a list of all the ways he serves the community.

_____

_____

_____

_____

_____

PRACTICING FAITH

Think about some people in your parish who may not have been touched by the ministry of a priest. Will you tell your priest about these people?

Name one way you will help the priest in your parish serve the people who are:

hungry _____

_____

elderly _____

_____

ignorant of their faith _____

_____

Circle the one you will do this week.

✝Now gather together. Each one extend hands in prayer and say: "Lord Jesus, you ask us to serve and not be served. We pray for our ordained ministers. May those called to the priesthood respond with generous hearts. Amen."

Talk with your teacher about ways you and your family might use the "Faith Alive" section. Pray the vocation prayer with your family.

REVIEW ■ TEST

Match each ordained minister with his primary role.

Ministers	Roles
1. priest	_____ proclaims the gospel; celebrates some of the sacraments
2. bishop	_____ always leads the community in song
3. pope	_____ leader of the whole Catholic Church
4. deacon	_____ leads the celebration of the Eucharist
	_____ successor of the apostles

5. Jesus said, "Whoever wishes to be great among you will be your servant." (Mark 11:43)
What do these words mean to you?

_____

_____

FAITH ALIVE AT HOME AND IN THE PARISH

What a great responsibility parents have in helping their children grow in faith. It is something that they do all their lives. The same is true in helping children to make their vocational choice in life.

The Church reminds us that vocations to the priesthood and to the religious life are gifts from God that first need to be supported and cared for by parents. Parents must encourage their children to consider that God may be calling them to the priesthood or to the religious life.

Take time to find out more about the different vocations in the Church and the best way to prepare for a vocation. Discuss ideas as a family and the need for vocations to the ordained ministry in the Church today.

Then take time to share this vocation prayer.

†Prayer for My Vocation

Dear God,
You have a great and loving plan
for our world and for me.
As a disciple of Jesus,
I wish to share in that plan fully,
faithfully, and joyfully.
Help me to understand what it is
you wish me to do with my life.
Help me to be attentive to the signs
that you give me about preparing for the future.
And once I have heard and understood
your call, give me the strength
and the grace to follow it
with generosity and love. Amen.

Holy Spirit, help us to carry on the mission and ministry of Jesus.

Our Life

The parish council of St. Rose's Parish was upset to learn that so many young people between the ages of 18 and 30 and adults aged 30 to 45 seemed not to be active in the Church.

The council decided to invite these people back to the Church with a very special "Come Home for Easter!" celebration. Then they began to talk about who had the responsibility to organize the drive. This is what different members of the parish council said:

1. "Father Thomas is the priest and pastor. So he's the only one who can bring Catholics back to the Church. Of course, Sister Teresa and Mrs. Brown, the pastoral ministers, could help him."

2. "We're the people of the parish. Let's all work together with our ministers to build up our parish."

What answers do you think each of the following would give and why?

Your parish council	You
Your parents	Jesus

Sharing Life

Why do you think the Church needs priests, religious brothers and sisters, and lay pastoral ministers?

Discuss how Baptism calls all Christians to share in the ministry of Jesus.

What are some of the gifts that you can share with your parish community?

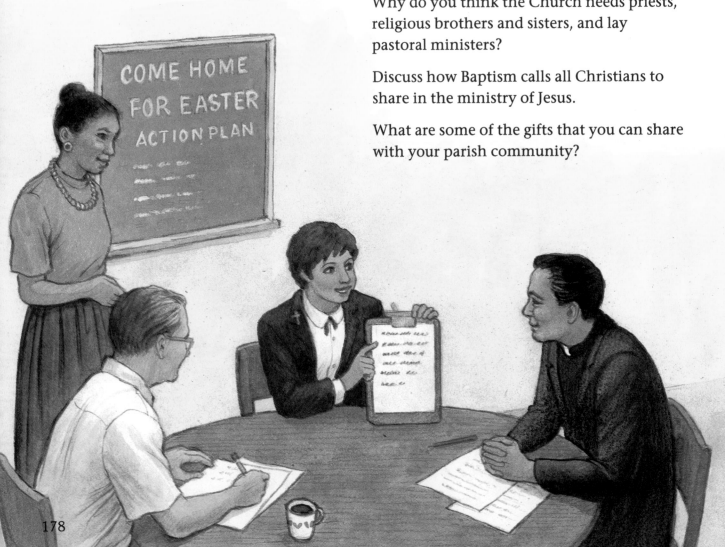

I CAN SHARE MY GIFTS BY:

I CAN SHARE MY GIFTS WITH...

- a lonely person by...
- a "left-out" classmate by...
- a youth group by...
- a sick person by...
- my parish by...
- my family by...

Play this association game with a small group.

Complete each sentence by saying the first thing that comes to mind. Have someone write the associations that are suggested.

After each one has had a chance to respond, share some of the associations your group has suggested. Talk about what you learned from this activity. It can prepare you to understand better the meaning of vocation, which we will explore this week.

We Will Learn

- Jesus Christ calls each one of us to a specific vocation to carry on his priestly mission.
- There are many vocations—married, ordained, religious, and single.
- We can prepare for our vocations now.

- O God, help us to share the good news of Jesus everywhere.
- In what ways do you serve your school, parish, or community?

Sharing Christ's Priestly Mission

Before Jesus ascended into heaven, he said to his disciples, "Go, therefore, and make disciples of all nations, baptizing them in the name of the Father, and of the Son, and of the holy Spirit, teaching them to observe all that I have commanded you. And behold, I am with you always, until the end of the age."

Matthew 28:19–20

Jesus wants his work to be carried on by all who are baptized. By Baptism all of us share in the great mission of Jesus to bring about the reign of God. This means that each of us has been called to live a holy life of service in our Church and our world.

This call is named our *Christian vocation.* Our Christian vocation begins at Baptism, the first sacrament of initiation. At Baptism we receive God's life and are called to bring this life to others.

In Confirmation we are sealed with the Gift of the Holy Spirit and strengthened to live our Christian faith with courage.

In the Eucharist we are given the daily help we need to carry out our vocation as Christians.

Through Baptism every Christian shares in Jesus' priestly mission. We call this the *priesthood of the faithful.* This means that every baptized person has a vocation to live as Jesus lived. As disciples, we share in the priesthood of Jesus Christ.

The priesthood of the faithful is not the same as the ordained priesthood. Those in Holy Orders share Christ's priesthood in a special way. Through the priesthood of the faithful, each one of us helps to carry on Jesus' mission in the world.

Evangelization means spreading the good news of Jesus Christ and sharing our faith by our words and actions.

Our pope and bishops have written special letters to all Catholics, reminding us of our responsibility to share the good news of Jesus. This responsibility is called evangelization. Every Catholic has many opportunities to share his or her faith with others.

By using our everyday opportunities for evangelization, it is hoped that:

● all Catholics—lay, ordained, and religious—will try harder to live as disciples of Jesus;

● Catholic people who do not take part in parish life will begin again to worship and serve;

● more people who have not been baptized will hear the good news and receive Jesus' new life in Baptism.

Find out what your own parish is doing about evangelization.

Saint René Goupil

René Goupil was a young Frenchman who had studied medicine. He wanted to help in the work of evangelization among Native Americans in the New World.

In 1638 he went to Quebec, where he worked for four years. During this time, Goupil became a Jesuit brother. Then, while on a journey with a Jesuit priest, Saint Isaac Jogues, he was captured by the Iroquois, and killed near Albany, New York. René Goupil was the first of the North American Martyrs.

What does it mean when we say all baptized Catholics share in the priesthood of the faithful?

In what ways will you live the priesthood of the faithful at home? in school?

181

OUR CATHOLIC FAITH

■ Lord Jesus Christ, to whom shall we go? you have the words of eternal life.

■ Name some of the many different ways people serve in our Church.

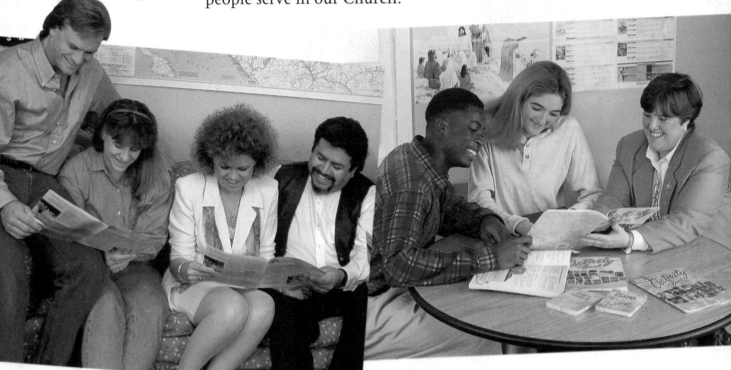

Carrying on Jesus' Mission

Sometimes people ask us, "What do you want to be when you grow up?" We cannot know for sure right now what we will do.

But as baptized Catholics, Jesus calls us to work for the reign of God in whatever vocation we choose. These are some of the vocations to which Jesus calls his people.

Married People: Jesus calls many women and men to the vocation of marriage and being parents.

Single People: Some people have a vocation to serve the Church as single, or non-married, men and women. By their daily words and actions, single people can show the world what it means to follow Jesus.

Ordained Ministers: Those who receive the sacrament of Holy Orders are called by Jesus to serve his Church as bishops, priests, and deacons.

Laity: These are the single or married people in our Church. They serve our Church in many ways. Some dedicate years in serving as lay missionaries or as volunteers with religious communities in our country and around the world.

Pastoral Ministers: Pastoral ministers are religious brothers or sisters and lay people who have received special training to serve the needs of our Church. Some dedicate their entire lives to the tasks of parish leadership and education. Others serve by working with the poor and the homeless and for justice and peace.

6. *Religious:* For many hundreds of years, men and women have joined religious communities as religious sisters, brothers, or priests. Religious serve our Church in parishes, hospitals, schools, and anywhere the good news needs to be preached. They make promises, or vows, of poverty, chastity, and obedience.

These vows are serious promises made to God and to the Church.

- The vow of poverty calls a person to live a life of detachment from material things. It does not mean that a person goes without the necessities of life. However, it does mean that a person vows to live a simple life as Jesus did in his ministry and without owning anything.

- The vow of chastity calls a person to dedicate his or her life totally to unselfish love through the religious community. It also means that men and women in vowed religious communities must live a celibate life. This means they do not marry but dedicate their lives to the wider community of the Church.

- The vow of obedience means that religious will listen to and obey in a special way their superiors, who may call them to serve the Church in ministries or in places they may not expect.

Each of us has been called by Jesus to continue his mission of building up the reign of God on earth. All of us have a vocation to do something that only we can do.

† Pray
"Holy Spirit, help me to know and follow my vocation."

▪ Explain some of the vocations by which we can serve our Church.

▪ Right now, which vocation interests you the most? How will you learn more about it?

183

OUR CATHOLIC FAITH

■ Holy Spirit, grant us the courage to be Christ's faithful witnesses.

■ What can you do now to prepare for your vocation?

Preparing for Your Ministry

It is important that every young person prepare for a life of service to others. What can you do now to live the new life you received in Baptism and to be a disciple of Jesus?

You can take part in the sacraments, especially Eucharist and Reconciliation, and share in God's own life of grace. This will enable you to live each day as a disciple of Jesus.

You can pray each day that the Holy Spirit will guide you and give you courage to accept the vocation God has for you.

You can learn about and grow in living your faith by:

● reading the Bible frequently;

● spending time trying to understand what is in this religion book so that you can explain it to others;

● listening carefully to the homilies at Mass and the faith stories told by your family;

● reading the lives of your favorite saints.

You can select one way to serve your parish now. You can be a compassionate person to others and also work for justice and peace. But you must serve faithfully, and not just when you feel like it.

Most of all, use your wonderful smile to brighten up everyone's day. Let everyone say, "See the smile of those Christians. See the joy that following Jesus brings them."

Young Missionaries

The work of evangelization goes on in many ways in the Catholic Church. Recent popes have challenged us to make this ministry our own in new and exciting ways.

Many young people have accepted this challenge of ministry and have volunteered for mission work. Joining with their own diocese or with one of several religious communities, they have given weeks, months, or even one or two years of their lives to help build up the reign of God, especially in poorer parts of the world.

The Society of Jesus (the Jesuits), the Order of Friars Minor (the Franciscans), Maryknoll, the Glenmary Home Missioners, and some dioceses, for example, each have special programs through which high school and college-age young people or Catholic families may volunteer for missionary work. The volunteer work can be done in the United States or sometimes in other countries of the world.

When volunteers go to a particular area to serve others, they live with the people and share in every part of their lives. By studying the language and customs of people different from themselves, these volunteers come to serve with respect and love. In this way, they not only help their brothers and sisters in Christ but come to understand better the causes of poverty and injustice in the world.

Do you have dreams of serving the needs of others? Tell about some of your dreams.

Learn by heart Faith Summary

- Jesus calls each of us to a specific vocation to carry on his priestly mission.
- Evangelization means spreading the good news of Jesus Christ and sharing our faith by our words and deeds.
- There are many vocations—married, ordained, religious, and single life. We are all called to carry on Jesus' mission.

COMING TO FAITH

Tell what a vocation is.
What is the Christian vocation of a
baptized person?

List the talents and abilities God has given
you. How can you use them to help others?

_____

_____

_____

_____

PRACTICING FAITH

Work together in your group to choose one
of the following ways you will serve others
this week.

● Offer to visit the sick with a eucharistic
minister.

● Offer to help your catechist.

● Volunteer to work in a community project
for the poor or the homeless.

● Volunteer as a tutor for younger or
handicapped children.

● Other: _____

Write the plan for your project.
What will you do?
How and when will your group do it?
Who will lead the project?

† Loving God, help us to live our Christian
vocation in following Jesus.

Talk with your teacher about ways
you and your family might use the
"Faith Alive" section. Encourage family
members to support you in what you
and your group plan to do.

REVIEW ▪ TEST

Define.

1. Evangelization: _Spreading the good news of Jesus._

2. Vocation: _Is our call to live Holy lives of service in our church._

3. Laity: _Single married people who belong to the church._

4. Pastoral minister: _minister who are religous brother and sisters_

5. How can you prepare now for your future vocation? What do you think that vocation might be?

_____

_____

_____

_____

FAITH ALIVE ▪ AT HOME AND IN THE PARISH

In this lesson your fifth grader has deepened his or her understanding that each of us has a particular vocation to build up the reign of God on earth. Ask your fifth grader to describe the different vocations presented in the lesson. It is not too early for fifth graders to consider what their special vocation might be. Encourage your fifth grader to pray and read about this vocation and to talk to those who follow it. Then discuss how she or he can prepare now for a life of Christian service to others. Parents would do well to be informed of the beauty of religious vocations and the Church's great tradition in this regard.

A Family of Service

Look around at your neighborhood, your school, your parish, your community. Consider who needs the kind of help your family can offer. Recognize that whatever you do out of love for God is part of your family vocation.

† Praying to the Holy Spirit

Take a few moments to ask the Holy Spirit to help your family know the talents or abilities you have been given. Use these talents to help others and be an even greater sign of God's love.

Jesus, help us to follow you this Lent so that we may live in Easter joy.

Our Life

A report tells us that during one year the average person in the United States eats about:

- 144 pounds of meat
- 81 pounds of vegetables
- 63 pounds of sugar
- 22 pounds of cheese
- 18 pounds of ice cream

It is also reported that during an average year people spend about:

- 26 billion dollars on television products
- 8.6 trillion dollars on clothes
- 20 billion quarters on video games

What do you think about this report?

Which of your possessions is the last you would give away? Why?

Sharing Life

Discuss with your group whether there are people who have:

- not enough food and things?
- just enough food and things?
- more than enough food and things?

Why are things the way they are, and what can be done about them?

Do you believe that Jesus wants us to share with others, especially the poor? Why or why not?

Work with a partner to suggest what Jesus might say to each of these comments.

	JESUS SAYS...
I am too young to do anything about hungry people.	You are never too young to do something about poor people
Our family is too poor to share with others.	You can never be too poor to share
It's not my problem that people are homeless.	It is our job to help those in need.

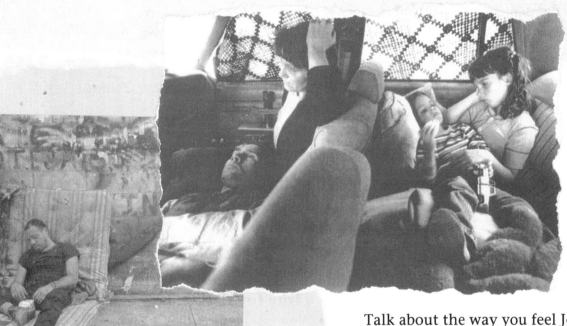

Talk about the way you feel Jesus would respond and why. Then think about what we will learn this week.

We Will Learn

- We learn how Jesus prepared himself to preach the good news.
- We prepare to live the new life we receive in Baptism.
- Lent prepares us to enter more fully into the passion, death, and resurrection of Jesus.

Jesus in the Desert

Before Jesus began to preach the good news of God's love to the people, he went into the desert to prepare himself. After many days Jesus was very hungry, and the devil tempted him, saying, "If you are the Son of God, command that these stones become loaves of bread."

Jesus must have looked at the rocks around him. Some of them may even have been shaped like loaves of bread. How easy it would have been to hold a rock in his hands and turn it into a hot, good-smelling loaf of bread.

But Jesus answered, "It is written:
One does not live by bread alone,
    but by every word that comes forth
        from the mouth of God."

The devil next took Jesus to Jerusalem. Setting him on the highest point of the Temple, the devil said, "If you are the Son of God, throw yourself down. For it is written: 'He will command his angels . . .
    [and] they will support you.'"

Jesus answered, "Again it is written, 'You shall not put the Lord, your God, to the test.'"

The devil finally took Jesus to a very high mountain, and showing him all the kingdoms of the world, said, "All these I shall give to you, if you will prostrate yourself and worship me."

Jesus answered, "Get away Satan! It is written:
    'The Lord, your God, shall you worship
        and him alone shall you serve.'"

Then the devil left Jesus.

Based on Matthew 4:1–11

After this, Jesus went out and began to preach the good news to all the people.

A Time for Preparing

During the season of Lent we prepare for Easter. Lent helps us to understand the meaning of the death and resurrection of Jesus. We remember that in our Baptism we die to sin and rise to new life in Jesus. During Lent we try to prepare ourselves to live better the new life we received in Baptism. We also pray for those who are about to be baptized.

Sometimes we spend too much time eating, shopping, and playing games. We become so busy with our possessions that we can forget about God and others.

During Lent many Catholics give up snacks or eat less at meals. We help poor and hungry people. We spend more time with God by praying and reading from the Bible. These Lenten practices help us put God and people before our possessions.

During Lent we try more than ever to love God and others, as Jesus showed us, without expecting something in return.

We must prepare ourselves to carry on the mission of Jesus. We try to do this during Lent.

COMING TO FAITH

Here are some things we can do during the season of Lent.
Check off the thing that you will do to share in Jesus' mission.

_____ Spend more time reading the Bible
_____ Give away some toys or games
_____ Take part in Mass more often
_____ Forgive someone who has hurt me
_____ Be kind to someone who is ignored by others
_____ Give up one of my favorite foods
_____ Pray the stations of the cross
_____ Visit someone who is lonely
_____ Pray for the leaders of our Church

_____ Celebrate Reconciliation
_____ Pray with my family or friends
_____ Care for the environment
_____ Pray for those preparing for Baptism
_____ Bring food to the parish to give to a hungry family
_____ Work with people who are trying to make peace
_____ Reach out to someone who is being treated unfairly

Other things I can do:

_____   _____

PRACTICING FAITH

A Prayer Service for Lent

† Gather in a circle.

Opening Hymn

"Come Back to Me" (Hosea)
or "Earthen Vessels"

Prayer

Leader: Jesus, we come together
to begin our preparation for Easter.
During the season of Lent, we
want to renew our desire to live
the way you taught us.

Gospel

Leader: A reading from the
holy gospel according to Mark.

(Read Mark 1:12–15)

Time for Reflection

Think about the Gospel reading. Read over
the list of Lenten practices you checked on
page 191. Now discuss together quietly what
your group might do together to join in
Jesus' mission this Lent.

Then pray the following prayer
together.

Jesus, during these forty days of Lent,
help us to follow you. Help us to live
more fully the new life we received in
Baptism. As your disciples, we have
decided to do the following acts:

We will pray more by _____

_____

_____

We will act as peacemakers by _____

_____

_____

We will serve the poor and hungry by

_____

Closing Hymn

"Let There Be Peace on Earth"
or "Prayer of Saint Francis"

Talk with your teacher about ways
you and your family might use the
"Faith Alive" section. Share with
family members ways your family
can pray, fast, and give to the poor.

REVIEW ▪ TEST

Give Jesus' answers to each of the devil's temptations.

1. "If you are the Son of God, command that these stones become loves of bread."
Jesus:

_____

_____

2. "If you are the Son of God, throw yourself down" (from the mountain).
Jesus:

_____

_____

3. "All these I shall give to you, if you will worship me."
Jesus:

_____

_____

4. How will you follow Jesus this Lent?

_____

_____

FAITH ALIVE AT HOME AND IN THE PARISH

In this chapter your fifth grader has learned that Lent is a time to strengthen our hearts and wills against temptation as Jesus did when he prayed and fasted in the desert. Prayer, fasting, and almsgiving are traditional Lenten practices to help us renew the gift of faith that we first received in Baptism. Besides fasting on Ash Wednesday and Good Friday, Catholics also abstain from meat on these days and the other Fridays of Lent.

Your child has also learned that during Lent we join in prayer with catechumens preparing for Baptism. We give our support to those preparing for membership in our Church.

Learn by heart **Faith Summary**

● Lent prepares us to enter more fully into the passion, death, and resurrection of Jesus.

● During Lent we try to love God and others without expecting something in return.

Alleluia! Jesus is risen and is still with us. Alleluia, alleluia!

Our Life

It was a forgotten patch of earth almost lost among the dingy apartments. Full of weeds, garbage, and abandoned junk, it was just another piece of ugliness in this very tough part of the city. But not to Mr. Catelli. He had a dream. This plot of earth could live again. So one day Mr. Catelli went out and began to work.

Some neighbors saw what he was doing and offered to help. Soon the garbage was packed into bags and left for the sanitation trucks. Young people in the neighborhood started to drop by to help with the weeding. Soon

Mr. Catelli was laboriously turning the soil and adding loam. By now the whole neighborhood was involved, and Mr. Catelli had gifts of seeds, plants, and even trees. The planting began. "Now what?" the children asked. "Now we wait and water and let God work," Mr. Catelli answered.

Spring came and the lot was now a park full of flowers and grass and young trees. "Our park is beautiful!" everyone said. Mr. Catelli smiled. What was dead had come back to life.

What do you learn from this story of Mr. Catelli?

Name some things that give you new life.

Sharing Life

Have you ever helped something that seemed dead have new life? Tell about it.

Why are these experiences so full of surprise and joy?

Sometimes there are things that we do or say that can bring a feeling of "new life" to another person. Can you think of or imagine ways this might happen?

Share your ideas and list all of them below. Maybe they will suggest ways you can be a "life-giver," especially during the season of Easter.

NEW LIFE IDEAS

_____

_____

_____

_____

_____

_____

_____

We Will Learn

- We remember Jesus' entry into Jerusalem.
- We remember the paschal mystery of Jesus Christ.
- We celebrate the Easter Vigil.

OUR CATHOLIC FAITH

Honoring Christ, Our Savior

The Sunday before Easter Sunday is called Passion, or Palm, Sunday. Passion Sunday is the first day of Holy Week. It prepares us for the Easter Triduum, the three days that begin on Holy Thursday evening and end with Evening Prayer on Easter Sunday.

On Passion Sunday we remember that Jesus and his friends went to the city of Jerusalem shortly before his arrest and crucifixion. The Gospel of Mark tells us the story as follows:

Jesus, riding on a donkey, came into the city of Jerusalem. As Jesus rode by, people spread their cloaks before him on the road. Others cut branches off the trees and laid these on the road in front of Jesus. Others followed Jesus, shouting, "Hosanna!
  Blessed is he who comes in the name of the Lord!…
  Hosanna in the highest!"

Based on Mark 11:1–11

Jesus came into the city of Jerusalem in triumph. He was honored and welcomed by the crowds. But within a few days, he would suffer, be crucified, and die.

On Passion Sunday, palm branches are blessed and given to us. We walk in procession into the church, singing and waving palm branches to honor Jesus.

The Easter Triduum

During the Easter Triduum we celebrate the paschal mystery. The word *paschal* means "passing over" or "passover." The paschal mystery is a remembering and celebrating of the events of Jesus' "passing" through suffering and death to new life in his resurrection.

On Holy Thursday evening we celebrate the Mass of the Lord's Supper. We remember that Jesus gave us the gift of himself in the Eucharist.

On Good Friday in the Celebration of the Lord's Passion, we remember that Jesus was crowned with thorns, suffered, and died on the cross for our sins.

On Holy Saturday night we celebrate the Easter Vigil. We await the resurrection of Jesus and remember that we are baptized into his death and resurrection. On this night we welcome new members into the Church through the sacraments of initiation.

On Easter Sunday we celebrate the resurrection of Jesus and our new life in Christ. The Easter Triduum concludes with Evening Prayer on this day. Then all during the Easter season, we remember how Jesus Christ brought us the fullness of God's life and love.

COMING TO FAITH

Below is a list of some important celebrations of the Easter Triduum. Tell what we remember and celebrate during each. Write how you can take part in each celebration.

Evening Mass of the Lord's Supper

We celebrate ——————————
————————————————
————————————————

I can ——————————————
————————————————
————————————————

Celebration of the Lord's Passion
We celebrate ——————————
————————————————
————————————————

I can ——————————————
————————————————
————————————————

Easter Vigil
We celebrate ——————————
————————————————
————————————————

I can ——————————————
————————————————

PRACTICING FAITH
An Easter Celebration

Opening Prayer

Leader: Jesus, we have prepared ourselves to share in the joy of your resurrection. Open our hearts to receive your new life.

An Easter Story

Group 1: Are you the only visitor in Jerusalem who does not know what things happened there to Jesus of Nazareth?

Group 2: What things?

Group 1: We had hoped that Jesus was the one who would set Israel free. But he was crucified. After his death, some women in our group went to the tomb and told us, "He is alive!"

Group 2: How slow to believe you are! Wasn't it necessary for the Messiah to suffer these things?

Narrator: Jesus explained many other things to them. As they came near the village toward which they were going, Jesus acted as if he were going on.

Group 1: Stay with us. It is getting dark.

Narrator: Jesus sat down to eat with them, took the bread, and said the blessing; then he broke the bread and gave it to them. Their eyes were opened and they recognized Jesus. Jesus then disappeared from their sight.

Renewal of Baptismal Promises

Leader: Do you reject Satan?

All: I do.

Leader: And all his works?

All: I do.

Leader: And all his empty promises?

All: I do.

Leader: Do you believe in God, the Father Almighty, creator of heaven and earth?

All: I do.

Leader: Do you believe in Jesus Christ, God's only Son, our Lord, who was born of the Virgin Mary, was crucified, died and was buried, rose from the dead, and is now seated at the right hand of the Father?

All: I do.

Leader: Do you believe in the Holy Spirit, the holy Catholic Church, the communion of saints, the forgiveness of sins, the resurrection of the body, and life everlasting?

All: I do.

Blessing with Holy Water

All come to a prayer table on which a small bowl containing holy water has been placed. All bless themselves with the holy water by making the sign of the cross to remember the gift of new life given in Baptism.

REVIEW ■ TEST

Tell what we remember and celebrate on these days.

1. Holy Thursday: _____

_____

_____

2. Good Friday: _____

_____

_____

3. Easter Vigil: _____

_____

_____

4. Easter Sunday: _____

_____

_____

FAITH ALIVE AT HOME AND IN THE PARISH

This lesson is a preparation for the Easter experience of moving with Jesus through death to new life. Your child followed the events of Palm Sunday and the Easter Triduum—which begins with the Evening Mass of the Lord's Supper on Holy Thursday and ends Easter Sunday with Evening Prayer. Easter is the greatest celebration of the Church year. The resurrection of Jesus is the ultimate foundation of Christian faith.

Learn by heart **Faith Summary**

- The paschal mystery celebrates the events of Jesus' "passing" through suffering and death to new life.

- On Holy Thursday we celebrate the gift of the Eucharist. On Good Friday we remember Jesus' suffering and death. On Easter we celebrate Jesus' resurrection.

Loving God, bless the Church. Help us to live as your people.

OUR LIFE

Groups such as youth organizations and sports teams have marks, or qualities, that clearly show what kind of a group each one is or would like to be. Choose one of the following situations and work with a partner to draw up your expectations, qualities, or "marks" for each one.

- You are putting together a "dream team" in any sport you wish.

- You are a musician and are assembling a band or an orchestra.

- You are organizing a youth service group.

What qualifications would you expect from individual members? from the group as a whole?

SHARING LIFE

We are members of the Church. Discuss together: What marks, or qualities, do you think the Church should have? Make a list.

Do you show that our Church has these qualities? How?

Now imagine for a moment that the leaders of the Church have asked you to represent all Christians in the United States. You will be part of a computer link with Christians your age throughout the whole world. Your task will be to describe the Church to young people from other lands and cultures. What ideas will be part of your description? Write them here.

Priest, Pope, and Bishop are what make up the church.

What do you think the young men and women will tell you about the Church in their parts of the world—Japan, China, Brazil, Honduras, France, Nigeria, South Africa? Imagine yourself listening to their descriptions. How is their experience of the Church similar to yours? How is it different? Let everyone in the class share his or her ideas. You might want to role-play a meeting of young people from around the world talking about what the Church means to them.

This week we will learn more about the qualities or marks of the Church and what it means to live them.

We Will Learn

- The Church of Jesus Christ is one and holy. We are to be united in faith in leading holy lives.
- The Church of Jesus Christ is catholic and apostolic.
- We are to live the marks of the Church.

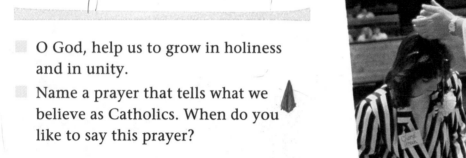

OUR CATHOLIC FAITH

- O God, help us to grow in holiness and in unity.
- Name a prayer that tells what we believe as Catholics. When do you like to say this prayer?

The Marks of the Church

The Church has four great identifying "marks," or qualities, that let people know the kind of community Jesus began. We say that the Church is one, holy, catholic, and apostolic.

Every Sunday or Saturday evening at Mass, we stand to profess our faith together. We say the Nicene Creed. When we say "We believe in one, holy, catholic, and apostolic Church," we profess that the Church has these four marks. We believe that the Church is to show these four qualities, or marks, to the whole world. In this way the Church may be recognized as the Church of Christ.

The Church Is One

Jesus wants all his disciples everywhere to be one with him and with one another in the Holy Spirit.

On the night before he died, Jesus prayed to his Father, "I pray not only for them, but also for those who will believe in me through their word, so that they may all be one, as you, Father, are in me and I in you, that they also may be in us, that the world may believe that you sent me."

John 17: 20–21

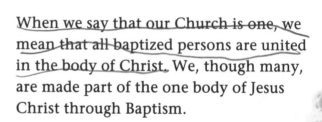

When we say that our Church is one, we mean that all baptized persons are united in the body of Christ. We, though many, are made part of the one body of Jesus Christ through Baptism.

Our Church has many members who have different roles and responsibilities. Our leaders help us to be one and work together. We are to be united in our faith and in our love of Jesus Christ and of one another.

As Catholics we are united by the leadership of the pope and bishops. We celebrate our unity with Jesus and with one another in the Eucharist.

But not all Christians share the same beliefs and practices. Over the centuries, some Christians became separated from the Catholic Church.

Today all Christians are called to pray and work for the full unity of the Church. Saint Paul once described the unity we should have: "One Lord, one faith, one baptism; one God and Father of all, who is over all and through all and in all."
Ephesians 4:5–6

The Church Is Holy

God alone is perfectly holy. The Church is holy because it is the body of Christ and because the Holy Spirit is present in the Church.

Jesus called his disciples to live holy lives, as he did. The holy lives of the apostles, the saints, and of all disciples of Jesus show the holiness of the Church.

God says to us, "Be holy, for I, the LORD, your God, am holy" (Leviticus 19:2).

We begin to share in God's holy life when we are baptized. The Church helps us to grow in holiness, especially through the sacraments.

We can show that the Church is holy by leading holy lives and by working for the reign of God in the world. We try to put God first in all we say and do. We try to live the Law of Love and work for justice and peace.

What do we mean when we say that in the Church we are to be united and to lead holy lives?

How will you try to grow in holiness today?

OUR CATHOLIC FAITH

Consegna delle Chiavi, **Perugino, Sistine Chapel, Vatican**

■ Lord Jesus, thank you for inviting us to be members of your Church.

■ What does the word *catholic* mean to you?

The Church Is Catholic

The word *catholic* means "universal" or "worldwide." The Church is to be a community in which all people of every race, color, nationality, and background are welcome. All are to hear the good news of Jesus Christ.

Jesus invited everyone to belong to his community and to follow him. He commanded his disciples to be just as welcoming and to include everyone in carrying on his mission.

Before his ascension into heaven, Jesus told his disciples, "Go into the whole world and proclaim the gospel to every creature" (Mark 16:15). The disciples carried out Jesus' command.

Today the Church continues to show it is catholic. Missionaries carry the good news to every country on earth. The Church works for the salvation of all people everywhere. We try to share our faith and welcome everyone to Jesus' community of disciples.

We welcome all people to become part of our parish community. We are to treat everyone with love and compassion.

The Church Is Apostolic

When Saint Paul wrote to the early Christians, he reminded them that they were "built upon the foundation of the apostles and prophets, with Christ Jesus himself as the capstone" (Ephesians 2:20). The Church is apostolic, because it was founded on the apostles and tries to be faithful to the mission and beliefs Jesus gave them. The Church can trace itself back to the apostles.

Saint Peter led the first apostles as they carried on Jesus' mission. In the Catholic Church, Peter's successors are the popes. Today our Holy Father, the pope, carries on the work of Saint Peter. The other bishops carry on the work of the first apostles.

The Church shows it is apostolic because it proclaims and teaches the good news of Jesus Christ that comes to us from the apostles. All Christians are to carry on the mission of Jesus in the world today.

Our pope and bishops lead us as the apostles led the first Christian communities. All of us work together to make the Church truly apostolic and faithful to Jesus.

We can show that our Church is apostolic by learning all we can about our Catholic faith. We can pray for and help our missionaries. We can do our part in carrying out the mission Jesus gave to the first apostles.

The **pope** is the bishop of Rome. He is the successor of Saint Peter and the leader of the whole Catholic Church.

Each time we pray the Nicene Creed at Mass, we say that we believe in the one, holy, catholic, and apostolic Church. Jesus asks each one of us to develop these marks, or qualities, in our own lives. In this way we show others that we are true disciples of Jesus Christ.

Find out and write the name of the bishop of your diocese. Tell how he serves you.

Name of our diocese: _____

_____

Name of our bishop: _____

_____

How our bishop serves us:

_____

_____

_____

■ After studying this lesson, what does the word *catholic* mean to you?

■ How will you help to show that our Church is apostolic?

205

Holy Spirit, help us to grow as one, holy, catholic, and apostolic Church.

Tell what you think about this statement, "We are the Church."

Living the Marks of the Church

As disciples of Jesus Christ, we believe in the one, holy, catholic, and apostolic Church. Here are some things we can do to show we are trying to live these four marks of the Church.

● We can show that we are *one* with others in our parish by celebrating the Eucharist with them, especially every weekend. We try to better understand the Creed we publicly say together. We pray for the unity of all Christians. We forgive others and ask for their forgiveness.

● We can show that we are *holy* by living the Law of Love and working for the reign of God. We help the Church grow in holiness by loving God, by praying frequently, and by celebrating the sacraments.

We grow in holiness by treating all people justly and by living in peace with them. We love ourselves when we respect and take good care of our bodies.

● We can show that we are *catholic* by reaching out to new people in our school, parish, or neighborhood. We welcome everyone and treat them as important because they are loved by God.

● We can show that we are *apostolic* by learning how to live and share our Catholic faith as we work for the reign of God.

We pray that the Holy Spirit will guide our pope and bishops. We ask the Holy Spirit to help us to carry on the mission of Jesus Christ.

Youth On Pilgrimage

A pilgrimage is a journey made with other believers to a sacred place in order to pray and renew one's faith. Pilgrimages have been a Catholic custom since the first century. In modern times, millions of young people have made pilgrimages to celebrate World Youth Day in many parts of the world.

In 1993 World Youth Day was held in Denver, Colorado. Pope John Paul II celebrated the liturgy and preached the gospel to huge crowds of young people. Many had walked for miles, slept on the ground, and stood in line for hours in order to participate.

Like true pilgrims, the young people were eager to pray together and share their Catholic identity. Many said they experienced the Church as a family in a way they had never known before.

Find out what you can about World Youth Day for young Catholics. Where will it be held next? When?

A Time to Be One and Holy

The 90,000 young people who gathered for World Youth Day in Denver in 1993 demonstrated to the world what it means to be one and holy. They came from many countries. But they accepted one another as sisters and brothers in Christ. They shared their food and belongings. They welcomed strangers like old friends.

Many spent all night praying before the Blessed Sacrament. Some prayed the rosary. Others spent time in silent prayer. They celebrated Reconciliation. And they sang hymns at the top of their lungs!

Find out whether a special religious event for young people is being held in your area. How can you participate? Are there places that you can visit that will help you express your faith?

Learn by heart **Faith Summary**

- The marks of the Church are one, holy, catholic, and apostolic.
- The Church of Jesus Christ shows it is one and holy when we are united in faith and live holy lives.
- The Church of Jesus Christ shows it is catholic and apostolic by welcoming all and being faithful to the mission and beliefs Jesus gave to the apostles.

Coming to Faith

Tell the name of:
your diocese, bishop, parish, pastor.

Now imagine that your bishop has asked your group to make a short TV spot showing how your diocese or parish tries to live the marks of the Church today. Plan your ideas together. Use the marks of the Church as an outline. You may draw sketches, write a script, or act it out.

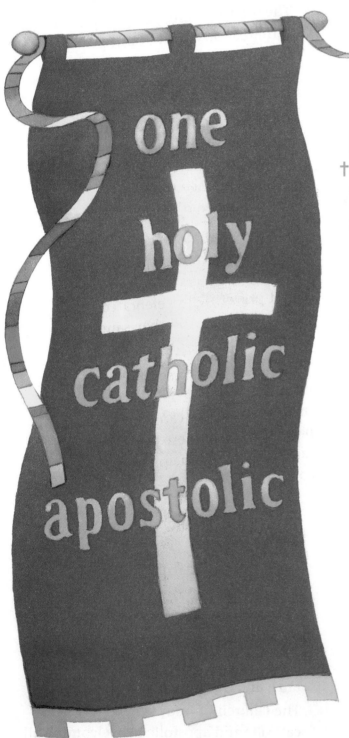

Practicing Faith

† Gather in a prayer circle. Be very still and let the Holy Spirit guide us.

Side 1: May the Holy Spirit help us to live in unity with Jesus and one another.

(*Action idea*: Decide to help someone who is sick or lonely or poor this week.)

Side 2: May the Holy Spirit guide us to be like Jesus in all things.

(*Action idea*: Decide to set aside time for prayer this week.)

Side 1: May the Holy Spirit help us to be open and welcoming to all people.

(*Action idea*: Invite a friend, who does not usually go to Mass, to come with you this week.)

Side 2: May the Holy Spirit give us courage to proclaim the good news of Jesus.

(*Action idea*: Read a gospel story with a friend or family member. Talk about what it means.)

All: We believe in the one, holy, catholic, and apostolic Church. Amen.

Talk with your teacher about ways you and your family might use the "Faith Alive" section. Ask a family member to do the activity with you.

REVIEW ▪ TEST

Match the marks of the Church with the correct descriptions.

Marks	**Descriptions**

1. apostolic

2. holy

3. catholic

4. one

_____ all believers are united in the body of Christ

_____ signs of Jesus Christ's community

_____ a community where all are welcome

_____ the good news of Jesus comes to us from the first leaders of the Church

_____ sharers in God's holiness

5. What does it mean to you to be a Catholic?
What kind of Catholic do you want to be?

_____

_____

_____

_____

_____

_____

 **FAITH ALIVE** AT HOME AND IN THE PARISH

In this chapter your fifth grader has learned more about the four marks of the Church. The Church is one, holy, catholic, and apostolic. Beyond a confession of faith, these four marks are challenges that the whole Church and every member is called to live faithfully. Ask your son or daughter to name and describe each mark. Discuss with the family how each of you as a member of the Church can live these marks today. Then, the next time you join with others at Mass and profess your faith, let the words you speak (one, holy, catholic, and apostolic) remind you of the challenge to live your faith each day.

Being Catholic

Discuss with your family what you will do together to welcome people into your parish. You might invite a family (or a person) who does not attend church regularly to come to Mass with you. You might invite someone who does not belong to a church community to come with you to some parish event.

23 | All People Are God's People

Prejudice — comes from ignorance & fear

Dear Jesus, help us to love one another as you love us.

OUR LIFE

It was almost the last day of the summer Olympics. Some athletes who had just completed the track and field competition were being interviewed for TV.

"Let me ask you," the interviewer said looking at the group that included young people from many different countries. "What is the highlight of this experience for you?"

What do you think was the answer?

The athletes did not talk about competition, or gold medals, or national honor. To a person they said their deepest memory would be of meeting people from different cultures, different backgrounds, different races, different languages, and discovering how very much they all shared in common.

"The Olympic circles are the color of the races of the world," one athlete remarked, "but they are all linked together as one."

What do you think this story says about prejudice?

How do you try to live this "Olympic" dream?

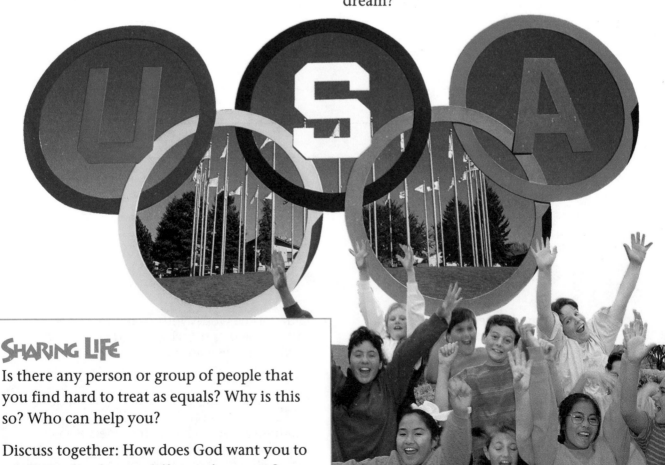

SHARING LIFE

Is there any person or group of people that you find hard to treat as equals? Why is this so? Who can help you?

Discuss together: How does God want you to treat people who are different from you? Explain.

210

Where do you think prejudice comes from? Share your ideas. Then work with a partner to draw up an explanation of what is wrong in each of these cases. Share your explanations with the whole group.

Case

Prejudice

Case	Prejudice
Don Miller was not given the job he deserved and for which he was qualified because the boss wanted someone younger in the office.	He was older.
Some of your classmates refuse to accept two new Vietnamese students into the group. They make fun of the new students' efforts to speak English.	He couldn't speak good English, he could speak Vietnamese. They were different
On Saturday night some vandals spray painted swastikas on the local synagogue.	they hated jews
Carol Redding and Mark Lest have similar jobs in the same company. They have the same amount of work and responsibilities. Mark makes $10,000 more a year than Carol.	Carol makes less money than mark in a year because they like men working better than women

This week we will be exploring the root and the evil of prejudice and how we can work to overcome it.

We Will Learn

- We are created in God's own image and likeness.
- We respect the ways other people worship God.
- We can fight against prejudice in our life by coming to know and appreciate people who are different from us.

OUR CATHOLIC FAITH

God said, "Let us make man in our image, after our likeness." So God created human beings in his image and likeness. God created them male and female. Then he blessed them. God looked at all creation and was very pleased.

Based on Genesis 1:26–31

O God, you have created us out of love and filled the whole world with your greatness.

Do you think all people are made in God's image and likeness? Why or why not?

Created in God's Image

We meet many different people who differ from us in color, religion, age, language, or wealth. Although people are different, all are created in God's image and likeness. We must treat everyone with respect.

In the Book of Genesis, the first book of the Bible, we read that God the Father created women and men in his own image and likeness.

Jesus knew how good God's creation was and how important each person was in God's eyes. Jesus never mistreated anyone, even if others did not like a person.

Jesus welcomed women as well as men as equal members of his community of disciples. He brought God's love to the poor and sick as well as to the rich and healthy. He brought the good news to the young as well as to the elderly, to Gentiles as well as to Jews. Jesus himself gave us the perfect example of living the Law of Love.

In our world, and even in our own lives, prejudice exists. *Prejudice* is a dislike for or hatred of people because they are different

from us in race, sex, religion, age, or any other way. The Catholic Church condemns all prejudice as a sin.

We can be prejudiced ourselves, or we can practice prejudice as a group. We can exclude people from our love and treat them unjustly in our own lives.

Groups can deny other people jobs, food, housing, and education because they are different. When groups do this, it is a type of social sin.

Prejudice can also show in the way we speak about people. We may make remarks or tell jokes at their expense. We may speak unkindly about people because they seem different from us. We may also be victims of prejudice ourselves.

We must follow Jesus' example and try to reject all prejudice because it is a sin against the Law of Love. The Law of Love demands that we treat everyone equally and with justice.

Two forms of prejudice that seem to come up in every age are racism and sexism. As Catholics, we must be ready to fight against racism and sexism wherever we find them—in the Church community and in society at large. God expects nothing less from us.

Can we be prejudiced and follow the Law of Love? Why or why not?

What will you do today to show that all people are God's children?

213

OUR CATHOLIC FAITH

■ We adore you, O Christ, and we praise you because by your holy cross you have redeemed the whole world.

■ Do you know anyone who is not a Catholic or a Christian? Tell how that person worships God.

Respecting Other Religions

The word *prejudice* often makes us think about racial prejudice. People can also practice religious prejudice. This is a dislike for people who worship God differently from the way we do or do not worship God at all.

God calls us to reject prejudice of any kind. There are many religions in the world other than Christianity. Jesus wants us to respect all people, even those who do not believe in him. As Catholics, we respect all people. We seek unity with those Christians who are not members of the Catholic Church.

We have a special relationship with the Jewish people. Jesus himself was a Jew and grew up practicing the Jewish religion. Mary, his mother, Saint Joseph, and the apostles were all devoted Jews. Christians must have a great respect for the Jewish people.

Christians and Jews share these beliefs:

● Both religions believe in the one true God, who is our creator.

● Both religions read, study, and believe the Jewish Scriptures, which Christians call the Old Testament.

● Both religions follow the Ten Commandments.

Christianity itself is made up of all the baptized disciples of Jesus. Originally, there was only one Church. However, over the centuries, divisions took place among Christians.

Eddie Maracich   April 12, 2000
Religion

1. Prejudice - a dislike for or
hatred of people because the are
different from us in race, sex, religion, age, or any
other way.

2. We must follow Jesus' example and
try to reject all prejudice.

3. No. You can not because prejudice
is a sin.

4. racism - a sin of prejudice

5. They both believe in one truer
God. Both religions read, study, and
believe Jewish Scriptures. Both
religions follow the ten commandments.

6. worship the one true god father, son,
and holy spirit.
believe in Jesus Christ, and Bible
is inspired word of God.

7. Ecumenism - the search for reunion of the Christian Churches,

These divisions were the result of disputes over certain beliefs and practices of the Church. Our popes and bishops have pointed out that all sides share in the blame for these divisions.

Among the Christian Churches that became separated from the Catholic Church are the Eastern Orthodox Churches and the Protestant Churches (for example, the Lutheran and Episcopal). Some other Protestant Churches found in America today include the Baptist, Congregationalist, Methodist, and Presbyterian.

By Baptism all Christians are united as brothers and sisters in Christ. We share many important beliefs in common. Here are some beliefs Christians share.

know these

- We believe in and worship the one true God: Father, Son, and Holy Spirit.
- We believe in Jesus Christ, who is both divine and human. Jesus died out of love for us and to save us from our sins. He rose from the dead to bring us new life.
- We believe that the Bible is the inspired word of God.
- We believe in one Baptism for the forgiveness of sins.

- We believe that we are to live the Ten Commandments and the Law of Love, and to carry on Jesus' mission in the world.
- We believe in the resurrection of the dead on the last day and in everlasting life.

Even though Christians are divided, we join together in working for the reign of God.

What beliefs do Christian and Jewish people share?

What will you do to help someone who is not Catholic to better understand your Catholic beliefs?

OUR CATHOLIC FAITH

▪ Holy Spirit, keep us ever faithful and alert to the virtue of justice.

▪ What can you do to help end prejudice in our world today?

Working Against Prejudice

Prejudice of any kind prevents us from living the way Jesus taught. To avoid being guilty of prejudice, we can learn about people whom we consider "different." We can be friendly with the children in our neighborhood or parish or school who are of another color or religion.

As we get older, we can study more about other Christian traditions and about other religions. Learning what others believe and how they worship God can enrich our own faith.

Ecumenism is the search for the reunion of the Christian Churches. The Catholic Church is very involved in this ecumenical work all over the world in which the leaders of various Christian groups meet to discuss their differences in a spirit of love and reconciliation.

We can talk about our faith to our friends who are not Catholic. We can pray each day for the success of the ecumenical movement. We can pray that some day all Christians will be united in one Church.

Profile of a Witness—
Sister Thea Bowman

Know for
Bonus

For thousands of Americans, she was a remarkable singer and storyteller who used songs to express her deep faith and love of God. She was Sister Thea Bowman, a Franciscan sister who followed the way of Saint Francis of Assisi.

Sister Thea's own story started in the small community of Canton, Mississippi. The granddaughter of a slave, she knew from the age of twelve that she wanted to serve as a religious sister. Her gift of music and song started in her childhood. She had heard those around her use music as a way of sharing their stories of faith and their struggle for justice and freedom. Later, as a singer and music director, she helped others, especially Catholics in the African American community, to realize how important it is to express our cultural heritage and our roots in the Church.

Sister Thea's remarkable faith became even more evident when she became terminally ill with cancer. She continued to speak and sing of God's love and mercy in spite of her illness. She said that it was a gift God had given her to share with all God's people. She shared her gift to the very end. Sister Thea died in 1990.

You, too, have a gift to share with all God's people. Have you discovered it yet? Think about how you can develop your gift, then share it. It's not too soon to begin.

Learn by heart Faith Summary

- As Catholics we must fight against prejudice in our lives.
- We respect those who worship God in other religions.
- We have a special bond with the Jewish people. We seek unity with all Christians.

217

COMING TO FAITH

Discuss: Why does our Catholic faith teach that all prejudice is a sin?

What can we do to avoid prejudice?

Challenge one another to name the beliefs all Christians have in common.

PRACTICING FAITH

Form five groups, each representing a group that faces prejudice. Cut five large circles out of different-colored paper.

Group 1: Our circle stands for the physically and mentally challenged. Things are sometimes harder for us. But we are just like everyone else.

Group 2: Our circle stands for those who face prejudice because of their skin color. Jesus' followers must be "color blind." (Group 2 makes a slit in its circle and joins it with Group 1's.)

Group 3: Our circle stands for those who face prejudice because of their religious beliefs. We know that God loves all people. (Group 3 joins circles with Group 2.)

Group 4: Our circle stands for those who meet prejudice because of gender. Men and women, girls and boys are equal in God's eyes. (Group 4 joins circles with Group 3.)

Group 5: Our circle stands for poor and homeless people. We have very few material things, but Jesus calls us his very own people. (Group 5 joins with Group 4 and Group 1, linking all circles together.)

All: In Christ, there is no east or west,
In him no north or south,
One great family bound by love
Throughout the whole wide earth!

Talk with your teacher about ways you and your family might use the "Faith Alive" section. Talk with family members about ways to fight prejudice.

218

REVIEW ■ TEST

Circle the letter beside the correct answer.

1. All people are created
   a. unequal.
   b. in God's image.
   c. exactly the same.

2. We fight against prejudice when we
   a. treat all people with dignity and respect.
   b. look down on those who are different.
   c. put down the religious beliefs of others.

3. Christians and Jews share the same belief
   a. in Jesus, the Messiah.
   b. in the Ten Commandments.
   c. in the Eucharist.

4. All Christians share belief
   a. in the seven sacraments.
   b. that the Pope is Peter's successor.
   c. in Jesus' Law of Love.

5. Think for a moment. Have you ever treated anyone with prejudice? What will you do to change your attitude?

Yes, I will show sorrow for what I did.

FAITH ALIVE AT HOME AND IN THE PARISH

Children are not born prejudiced or bigoted. Others teach them this sin. Any kind of prejudice is evil. Our world and our society constantly face the sin of prejudice—racial, religious, gender prejudice, and prejudice against those who are physically or mentally challenged, against the elderly, against the ill, or against the poor. Prejudice is usually the result of ignorance and fear, both of which can be overcome by God's grace and our good will. God created all people in his image. This fundamental belief of our Christian faith should help to root out any semblance of prejudice in our lives. In addition, we must work to ensure that we ourselves, our parish, and our school are free of all prejudice.

Family Discussion Time

Talk together about people you know who have been victims of prejudice and discrimination, including victims of religious or gender prejudice. Then talk about ways your family can heal the hurt caused by the evil of prejudice and about ways you can try to work against this sin. Share ideas with other neighbors and friends.

24 The Gift of Faith

Lord Jesus, we believe that you have the words of eternal life.

Our Life

Jesus said to the people, "I am the living bread that came down from heaven; whoever eats this bread will live forever." Many of his followers could not understand this teaching.

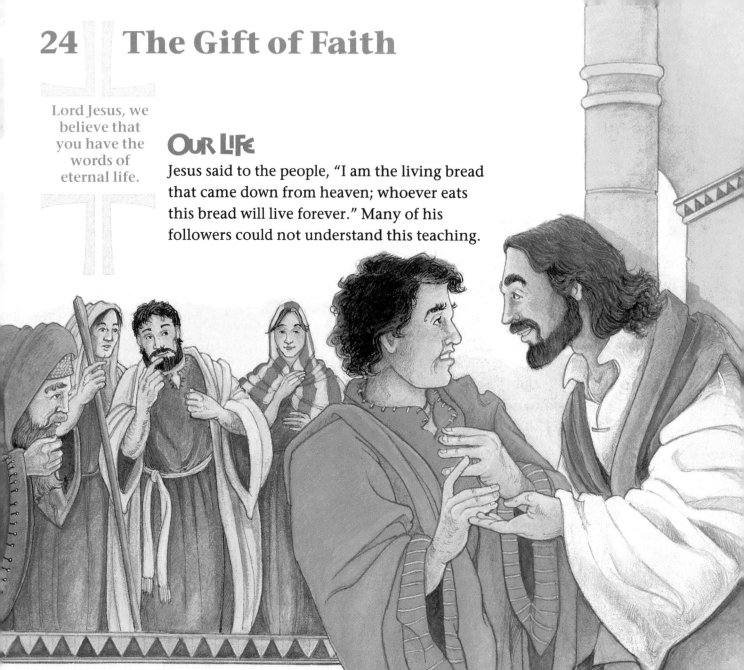

They turned away from him. So Jesus asked the twelve disciples, "Do you also want to leave?"

Simon Peter answered for all of them. "Master," he said, "to whom shall we go? You have the words of eternal life. We have come to believe and are convinced that you are the Holy One of God."

Based on John 6:51, 60, 66–69

What do you learn from this Scripture story?

Suppose Jesus asked you, "Would you also like to leave?" What would be your answer?

Sharing Life

Talk together about these ideas.

- What is it about a person that makes us believe in him or her?
- What is the hardest thing about believing in someone?
- Share the reasons why you believe in God.

Work together and make a poster that lists your reasons for believing in God. Label your poster "We believe in God because...." Display your poster in the school hall if possible, as a way of sharing your faith.

This week we will discover more about what faith means to us as Catholics and the ways we can grow in living our faith.

We Will Learn

- Faith is the virtue that enables us to trust and believe in God.
- In creeds we find summaries of what we believe.
- Living our Christian faith changes our lives for the better.

OUR CATHOLIC FAITH

- O God, increase our faith in you each day.
- When do you find it easy to place your trust in God? When is it hard? Why?

The Virtue of Faith

A *virtue* is the habit of doing something good. We find virtues such as courage, honesty, and justice in many people.

In our relationship with God we are asked to practice the special virtues of faith, hope, and love every day. Each of these virtues is a gift from God.

Here is a story about Jesus teaching his disciples to trust in God. It is about having faith in Jesus, God's own Son, at all times and in all situations.

Peter Walks on Water

One day after preaching by a lake, Jesus sent the crowds away. Before going up into the hills to pray, he told his disciples to get in their boat and cross the lake without him.

When morning came, the boat was still out in the middle of the lake battling strong winds. Jesus came down from the hills and began walking on the water toward the disciples. Seeing someone walking on the water, the disciples became terrified.

Then Jesus spoke to them across the waves, "Take courage, it is I; do not be afraid."

Then Peter called out, "Lord, if it is you, command me to come to you on the water. " Jesus answered, "Come."

Peter got out of the boat and started walking on the water. But then Peter, afraid of the wind and the waves, doubted Jesus. He began to sink into the water and cried out to Jesus, "Lord, save me!"

Peter Walking on Water, H.V. Kulmbach, circa 1500

Faith is a virtue that enables us to trust and believe in God, to accept what he has revealed, and to live according to his loving will.

water, wine, land, pulled peter out water, fish & bread, boat, dove

So it is with us. We must always place our trust in God to help and save us. We must live our faith every day as disciples of Jesus. We must believe that God will help us and will always be with us.

Once we have done the best we can, we must leave the rest to God. That is how we practice the virtue of faith.

In the Church the cross is a symbol of faith. Make your own symbol of what faith means to you. Maybe the Scripture story will give you an idea.

The Great Virtues

Faith, hope, and love are called theological virtues because they strengthen our relationship with God. *Theological* means "having to do with God." Each of these virtues is a gift from God.

Jesus immediately grabbed Peter, and said to him, "O you of little faith, why did you doubt?"
Based on Matthew 14:22–33

Peter was lost once he forgot to believe in the power of God. He began to rely only on himself instead of trusting in Jesus' love and care for him.

- What do you learn for your life from the story of Jesus and Peter?
- Tell how you will try to practice the virtue of faith today. Ask the Holy Spirit to help you.

223

OUR CATHOLIC FAITH

- Lord Jesus, you are the Word made flesh.
- Tell about some of the things that you believe as a Catholic. Why are they important to you?

Our Church as Teacher

Our Catholic faith is a gift from God. Jesus taught us that faith is necessary for us to gain eternal life. Faith comes to us only because God gives us this gift. We do not earn the gift of faith.

In response to God's love, we live our faith as disciples of Jesus Christ and as God's own people. Jesus is the greatest teacher of our faith. Jesus also gave us the Church to help us learn about and live our faith together.

Sometimes it is difficult to understand everything about God and our faith. Many things about God are called mysteries of faith, such as the Blessed Trinity. No one can fully understand these mysteries. We believe them because God has revealed, or made them known, to us. The Church teaches them to us, and they are part of our faith.

Our Church has several prayers called creeds that summarize what we believe. We pray the Nicene Creed at Mass.

On this page is another creed. It is called the Apostles' Creed because it developed from the very early teachings of the Church. The Apostles' Creed describes the most important truth of our Catholic faith: There is one God but three divine Persons in the one God. We call this truth the mystery of the Blessed Trinity.

The Apostles' Creed

I believe in God, the Father almighty, creator of heaven and earth.

I believe in Jesus Christ
his only Son, our Lord.
He was conceived by the power
of the Holy Spirit
and born of the Virgin Mary.
He suffered under Pontius Pilate,
was crucified, died, and was buried.
He descended to the dead.
On the third day he rose again.
He ascended into heaven,
and is seated at the right hand of the Father.
He will come again to judge
the living and the dead.

I believe in the Holy Spirit,
the holy, catholic Church,
the communion of saints,
the forgiveness of sins,
the resurrection of the body,
and the life everlasting.
Amen.

The Apostles' Creed tells the story of God's love for us. It is divided into three parts. The first part of the Apostles' Creed tells us about God the Father, who gives us life.

The second part speaks of God the Son, who became our Savior and the Savior of all people. God the Son became one of us to save us from sin. Jesus died on the cross and rose from the dead to bring us new life. He redeemed us and freed us from the power of sin. He is the perfect sign of God's love for us.

The third part of the Apostles' Creed talks first of God the Holy Spirit, who is our sanctifier, the One who makes us holy.

Then the Creed reminds us that we are to believe that the Church was founded by Jesus. We are in union with all baptized persons, living and dead.

We believe that our sins will be forgiven if we are truly sorry for them, and that we will rise again to live with God forever in heaven.

Which truths in the creed are easier for you to understand? more difficult?

How will faith make a difference in your life today?

OUR CATHOLIC FAITH

- Glory to the Father, and to the Son, and to the Holy Spirit.
- How do you think we put our faith into action?

Faith in Our Life

We believe in God the Father, our creator; God the Son, our redeemer; and God the Holy Spirit, our sanctifier. But we are called to do more than just believe. In order for our faith to change our lives, we must practice it as well.

One of the first Christians, Saint James, wrote about practicing faith. He said, "What good is it . . . if someone says he has faith but does not have works? . . . faith of itself, if it does not have works, is dead."

James 2:14–17

Saint James was saying that we should respond to God's gift of faith by living it.

Our faith requires that we practice what we believe and put our faith into action. Here are some ways we can do this:

- We should learn as much as we can about our faith.

- We should celebrate the sacraments often, especially Eucharist and Reconciliation, to receive strength and guidance. Celebrating these sacraments helps us live our faith courageously.

- We should make decisions each day that show we are living the Law of Love and building up the reign of God.

- We should avoid all forms of prejudice.

- We should try to be peacemakers in our lives and pray for peace in the world.

The gift of faith is a gift God wants us to care for our whole lives. It is also a gift we live out in the community of the Church. Pray that you will always be strong in faith.

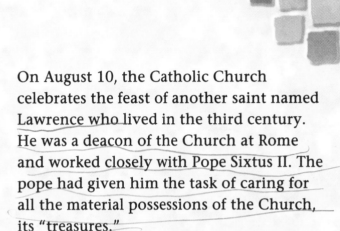

Saints New and Old

The saints whom we honor in the Catholic Church are women and men of all times, races, and cultures. They stand as models of faith in action for us today. Here are several saints who may be new to you.

Between 1839 and 1867, one hundred and three Koreans were martyred for their faith. They were young and old, priests and lay people. Among them was Saint Andrew Kim of Taegu. He was the first native priest of Korea. We celebrate his feast on September 20. On the same day we celebrate another Korean martyr, Saint Paul Chong. Paul was a catechist, a teacher of religion. He, too, gave his life for his faith.

Another saint, Lawrence Ruiz, lived two hundred years before the Korean martyrs. Lawrence was a married man and a Filipino missionary who was martyred in Japan. He was canonized in 1987 and is honored today as the first canonized Filipino saint. His feast day is September 28.

On August 10, the Catholic Church celebrates the feast of another saint named Lawrence who lived in the third century. He was a deacon of the Church at Rome and worked closely with Pope Sixtus II. The pope had given him the task of caring for all the material possessions of the Church, its "treasures."

It was a time of suffering and persecution for the Church. After the pope had been arrested and killed, Lawrence sold what had been entrusted to him so that he could help the poor and needy. Soon after this, he was arrested and ordered to bring all the Church's treasures to the authorities. Standing before a judge, he gathered the poor and lowly around him and said, "These are the treasures of the Church." The angry judge ordered Lawrence to be killed.

These saints were people of faith. How can you imitate their example today?

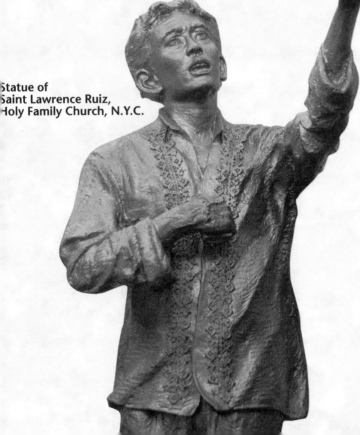

Statue of
Saint Lawrence Ruiz,
Holy Family Church, N.Y.C.

Learn by heart **Faith Summary**

- The virtues of faith, hope, and love are gifts from God.
- Faith is a virtue that enables us to trust and believe in God, to accept what he has revealed, and to live according to his will.
- The creeds of the Church summarize what we believe.

227

Coming To Faith

Take turns sharing what your Catholic faith means to you.

Then help one another remember what the Apostles' Creed teaches us about:

- God the Father.
- God the Son.
- God the Holy Spirit.

Practicing Faith

Do your best to memorize the Apostles' Creed. Try learning two or three lines each day until you have memorized it.

Think about what it means to have faith, to believe in God the Father our loving creator, in Jesus our redeemer, and the Holy Spirit our sanctifier. Then express your faith by drawing a symbol or by writing a poem, or by just writing key words that say what your faith means to you.

Take turns sharing what you have made. Listen carefully as your friends speak. We can help one another strengthen our faith.

† Close by praying together the words of the Apostles' Creed.

Talk with your catechist about ways you and your family might use the "Faith Alive" pages. Pray the prayer together.

REVIEW ■ TEST

Match.

1. virtue

2. Apostles' Creed

3. a theological virtue

4. faith

___4___ enables us to trust and believe in God

___3___ love

_____ the habit of doing good

___2___ a profession of our faith

___1___ is a statement about sainthood

5. How will you share the gift of faith at home?

_____

_____

_____

FAITH ALIVE AT HOME AND IN THE PARISH

In this chapter your fifth grader has learned more about the virtue of faith and its necessity for our salvation. This is the first of the three great virtues that are at the core of our Catholic identity. They are sometimes called the theological virtues because they pertain to our relationship with God.

Read together the Bible story of Jesus walking on the water (Matthew 14:22–33). Think about the hard times that each family member has faced in trying to practice faith. Then talk about the kind of faith that Jesus wants us to have in him. Faith is a gift from God. But we are to nurture this gift in the community of the Church throughout our lives. The family, too, is essential in nurturing faith. Ask God to help the members of your family to give one another the example of a lived Christian faith.

† An Act of Faith

Here is a short prayer called an Act of Faith. You can learn it and pray it whenever you feel anxious or doubtful. Pray it with your family during the week.

O God, we believe in all that Jesus has taught us about you. We place all our trust in you because of your great love for us. Amen.

25 | God Fills Us with Hope

Jesus, we place all our hope in You.

OUR LIFE

Pope John Paul II loves young people. He enjoys being with them and hearing what they have to say about their lives and about their faith. He always brings them a message of hope.

After meeting with the Holy Father, here is what a group of young people had to say:

"I think the pope is great! He makes me feel that things are better than I thought."

"Wow! He told us how much the Church needs us and how important we are. That's cool!"

"He told us that we are the future of the Church. He made me feel that young people like us can make a difference."

Do you know anyone who is filled with hope? Tell about him or her.

What do you think it means to be a person of hope?

What does hope mean in your life now?

SHARING LIFE

Have you ever been in a situation in which you felt hopeless? Tell about it. Explain what you did and why.

Talk together and share reasons why Christians should always have hope.

Sometimes we use the word *hope* when we mean "wish." *Wish* means something you would like to have happen. *Hope* means a trust that God will always love and care for you because that is what he promised.

In the chart below write, some of your *wishes* and some of your *hopes* to show you know the difference. Share your completed chart with the group.

My Wishes | My Hopes

My Wishes	My Hopes
get a dog	his love for us
To be a famous soccer player	his care for us
have a goat kart & moonwalk.	for my sins to always be forgiven always

This week we will discover more about the virtue of hope.

We Will Learn

- Hope is the virtue that enables us to trust that God will always help us.
- Mary, the Mother of the Church, is a sign of hope for us.
- We must live our Christian lives with hope, believing that we can make a difference.

231

Our Catholic Faith

- O God, how great are your promises to us and your truth.

- What do people your age hope for today? Why?

The Virtue of Hope

Often we use the word hope to mean "wish and expect." When we say, "I hope it will be nice this weekend," we are wishing for good weather. The virtue of hope means much more than this kind of wishing or expecting.

We practice the virtue of hope when we trust that God will help us in every situation, no matter what our problem is.

Hope, like faith, is a gift from God. We are able to have hope because God promises to love us always. Our confidence in God helps us to live as people with hope.

Jesus is our greatest source of hope. We trust in Jesus' promise that our actions will make a difference. When Christians hope that God's reign will really come, we are not just wishing. We do all that we can each day to make it happen. With the help of the Holy Spirit, we do our best to do God's loving will, knowing that our lives can make a difference.

Through the life, death, and resurrection of Jesus, we live as people of hope. We know that the risen Christ is truly with us. He is our Savior and has conquered sin and evil. This gives us the hope of new life in him. Now we live in hope because we know we can be happy with God forever.

The Easter Story

Early on Sunday morning, Mary Magdalene stood crying outside the tomb of Jesus. The tomb was empty and his body was gone. Turning around, she saw a man who she thought was the gardener standing there.

He asked her, "Why are you weeping? Whom are you looking for?"

Mary answered, "Sir, if you carried him away, tell me where you laid him." Jesus said to her, "Mary!" In hearing her name spoken, Mary realized that it was not a gardener but Jesus. She turned toward him and joyfully cried out, "Teacher!"

Jesus then told Mary, "Go to my brothers and tell them, 'I am going to my Father and your Father, to my God and your God.'" Mary Magdalene immediately went to find the disciples and share with them the wonderful news that she had seen the risen Lord.

Based on John 20:1–18

Because of Jesus' resurrection, the Holy Spirit has come upon us so that we may live in the hope of eternal life.

Some people look around at all the poor and hungry people. They look at all the unfairness in our world and say, "God has forgotten us." They find it difficult to hope that Jesus can help us. Other people may even lose hope that our life and this world can ever be better.

We must not be like these hopeless people. We must always hope and trust God. We must be confident that, with God's help, we can make a difference in our world. We can make our world a better place.

As Christians we have the hope of eternal life as well. This hope encourages us to pray for the souls in purgatory. At Mass we pray for those who have died in the hope of rising again. We also hope to enjoy forever the vision of God's glory in heaven.

How can hope make a difference in your life?

How will you make a difference in your family? school? parish?

OUR CATHOLIC FAITH

■ Lord Jesus, help us to live as people of hope.

■ What are some things that make it difficult for us to have hope?

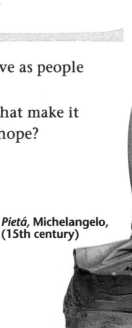

Pietá, **Michelangelo, (15th century)**

A Message of Hope

Everyday we read about sadness and suffering. We are tempted to wonder if God has forgotten us. To hope does not mean to wait for God to solve all our problems. We must work together for the reign of God.

God gives us the gift of hope so that each of us will do what we can to change the world. Guided by the Holy Spirit we are partners with God in bringing about a better world.

Two thousand years ago, Saint Paul also lived in a world filled with problems. Christians were being persecuted and killed for their faith in Jesus Christ. It looked as if the Church, which had just begun, would not last.

Even the early Christians were forgetting Jesus' promise that his Church would last forever. Here is what Saint Paul wrote in a letter to the Christians in Rome to encourage them to have hope.

"For I am convinced that neither death, nor life, nor angels, nor principalities, nor present things, nor future things, nor powers, nor height, nor depth, nor any other creature will be able to separate us from the love of God in Christ Jesus our Lord" (Romans 8:38-39).

Mary, A Sign of Hope

Mary is a special sign of hope for us. The Blessed Virgin Mary was Jesus' first and greatest disciple. Mary is the Mother of the Church.

Mary loved Jesus and followed him. She shared in the joy of his resurrection on Easter Sunday. Mary was a person of great faith, hope, and love.

The Church teaches that at the end of her life, Jesus brought Mary, body and soul, to be with him forever in heaven. We call this Mary's assumption. We celebrate this event on August 15. Mary's assumption strengthens our hope that we, too, will live forever in heaven.

We can ask Mary to help us hope that we can make things better in the world. Then one day our hope will be fulfilled. We, too, like Mary, will enjoy life with God forever in heaven.

The Church today continues to bring a message of hope to the whole world. Each time we pray and celebrate the sacraments with our parish community, we show that we have hope that God's reign will come.

Create a design for a banner or poster honoring Mary, a woman of hope.

- What does it mean for you to practice the virtue of hope?
- How will you imitate Mary as a person of hope?

OUR CATHOLIC FAITH

- O Holy Spirit, guide the Church to be a community of hope.
- When is it hard to have hope in your family? your school? your neighborhood? Why?

People of Hope

All Christians are called to be people of hope. With God's help, we believe that our lives can make a difference.

Some people give up helping other people because they doubt it does any good. Some people try to escape from their problems through addiction to alcohol or drugs. Others commit the most hopeless act of all, suicide. We must speak with an adult if we have, or one of our friends has, given up hope and is thinking of using drugs or alcohol or committing suicide.

We must pray for people who are tempted by these hopeless actions and ask God to give them hope.

As Christians, we try never to give up. That is what hope means for our lives. There will always be times when we can help another person by welcoming, forgiving, healing, or serving as Jesus showed us.

We can always do something to overcome prejudices and to make peace. No matter how small our help may seem, we offer it. With God's help, it can make a difference. We are confident that God works through us in small as well as big ways.

We get the help we need to be hopeful people by praying, especially to the Holy Spirit, and by receiving Holy Communion.

We also pray to Mary and the saints. They lived through very difficult times, too. But they trusted in God and now experience their reward in heaven.

Christ Our Light

One symbol of hope that is often used in the Catholic Church is the Easter candle. It is also called the paschal candle, since it reminds us of Christ and the paschal mystery—Jesus' life, death, and resurrection.

The Easter candle is blessed on Holy Saturday night during the Service of Light, the first part of the Easter Vigil. In the darkness, the priest blesses a new fire and then prepares the candle.

Very often the priest traces a cross, the numbers of the current year, and the first and last letters of the Greek alphabet on the candle. He says as he does this:

Christ yesterday and today
the beginning and the end
Alpha
and Omega
all time belongs to him
and all the ages
to him be glory and power
through every age for ever. Amen.

Sometimes the priest may insert 5 grains of incense in the candle in the form of a cross. He may say:

By his holy
and glorious wounds
may Christ our Lord
guard us
and keep us. Amen.

Whenever you see the Easter Candle lit in church—at a Baptism or a funeral and all during the Easter season—remember that it is a symbol for Christ our Light. Our hope is in him, who has risen from the dead.

Alpha and Omega

The first and last letters of the Greek alphabet—alpha and omega—are used as a symbol of Christ. According to the Book of Revelation in the Bible, Jesus said of himself, "I am the Alpha and the Omega, the first and the last, the beginning and the end" (Revelation 22:13).

Faith Summary

Learn by heart

- Hope is the virtue that enables us to trust that God will be with us in every situation.
- Jesus is our greatest source of hope.
- Mary, the Mother of the Church, is a sign of hope for us.

COMING TO FAITH

As Christians we can show hope in God in many ways. Discuss what you would do to live the virtue of hope in each of these situations. Why?

- Everything at home seems hopeless. No one seems to understand you. You feel like running away.
- People are being treated unfairly and with prejudice because of their race or religion.
- Violence seems to be a way of life; young people are losing their lives on our streets.

PRACTICING FAITH

Share with one another ways you can be signs of hope in your homes and neighborhood. Write on the candle one way you will do this. Then gather in a circle with your friends. Take turns holding up your candle and reading aloud your decision of hope. Pray together:

†**Leader:** Let us pray for hope for others and for ourselves.

All: We are people of hope.

Leader: God, our Creator, help those who have given up hope.

All: We are people of hope.

Leader: Jesus Christ, our Redeemer, help those who suffer from addiction. Free them from their hopeless actions.

All: We are people of hope.

Leader: Holy Spirit, our Sanctifier, help all people, especially those our age, who want to hurt themselves or even end their lives. Take away their hopelessness.

All: We are people of hope.

Leader: Loving God, help each one of us to be a person of hope.

All: Amen.

Talk with your teacher about ways you and your family might use the "Faith Alive" section.

REVIEW • TEST

Circle the letter beside the correct answer.

1. At the assumption, Mary
   a. heard the angel's message.
   b. was taken, body and soul, into heaven.
   c. gave birth to Jesus.

2. Hope means trusting that
   a. God will be with us in every situation.
   b. everything will be just the way we wish.
   c. we will never have any problems.

3. God gives us hope so that we
   a. will never suffer.
   b. will do what we can to change the world.
   c. will love others.

4. The Christian's greatest source of hope is
   a. the wonders of creation.
   b. the example of the saints.
   c. the life, death, and resurrection of Jesus.

5. How can you be a sign of hope to someone this week?

_____

_____

_____

FAITH ALIVE AT HOME AND IN THE PARISH

In this chapter your fifth grader has learned more about the virtue of hope. Help your family to understand that for Christians, the paschal mystery—the life, death, and resurrection of Jesus—is our greatest source of hope. Because of Easter, we know that the risen Christ is truly with us. He is there to bring us new life, to help us avoid sin, and to do God's loving will. We can live in hope because we know that we can always rely on God.

Talk about things your family can do to be a sign of hope to others. Ask the Holy Spirit to guide your family and the entire community of the Church in hope. Remember Jesus' words to us, "I am with you always, until the end of the age" (Matthew 28:20). Finally, look to Mary as an exemplar of true Christian hope.

†An Act of Hope

Pray this Act of Hope together this week.

O God, we never give up on your love. We have hope that your kingdom will come and that we will live with you forever in heaven. Amen.

OUR LIFE

Jesus, help us to love others as you love us.

The apostle John once wrote a long letter to the Christians of the early Church. He was concerned that some might be overcome by the pressures of the world and forget the most important teaching of Jesus' way of life.

What do you think is the most important teaching of Jesus about the way we should live?

Here is a part of John's letter. Listen to it as if he is writing it directly to you.

Dear friends,
Let us love one another, because love is of God. Whoever loves is a child of God and knows God. Whoever is without love does not know God, for God is love.... This is what love is: it is not that we have loved God, but that God has loved us, and sent the Son to forgive our sins.

Dear friends, if this is how God loved us, then we should love one another.

Based on 1 John 4:7–11

What did you hear from John's letter for your life?

John uses the word *love* ten times! What do you think John means by *love*?

SHARING LIFE

Discuss: how can we love those who are
- strangers to us?
- different from us?

What does Jesus, and John, expect of us when they say "love one another"?

WALK FOR HUNGER

Imagine that you have been asked to write a letter to the Christian community about love. What ideas would you want to share with the community?

Take a few moments and write some of your ideas below. Then share them with a partner. Then work together to write a letter that includes your ideas.

Find out where you can display all the letters of the class. Were there any ideas that your group had in common? Do you think it was easy to write a letter about love? Why or why not?

This week we will explore more about the virtue of love.

We Will Learn

- Love is a virtue that enables us to love God, our neighbor, and ourselves.
- Our Church teaches us that love is the greatest of the three theological virtues.
- We can practice the virtue of love through the Corporal and Spiritual Works of Mercy.

DEAR FRIENDS,

OUR CATHOLIC FAITH

O God, your love fills the whole universe.

Explain what real love means to you.

The Virtue of Love

The virtues of faith and hope, we have learned, are gifts from God that enable us to trust and believe in God and to live our Catholic faith. The virtue of love is also a gift from God. It is one of his greatest gifts to us.

We know God loves us because he created us and our wonderful world. But, most of all, God sent Jesus to be one of us. Jesus, in his life, death, and resurrection, revealed the truth that "God is love" (1 John 4:8).

Because we are created in God's image and likeness, we are made to love and be loved. Living the virtue of love is what makes us most like God.

We practice the virtue of love not just with words and feelings, but especially by what we do for others. We should not give to others or do for others only when it is convenient for us. To live the virtue of love we must often sacrifice, or give up something, to show our love for God and others.

Here is a story that Jesus told to show who really practices the virtue of love.

The Good Samaritan

One day a man who was going to Jerusalem was robbed and beaten and left by the side of the road. After a while, a priest came down the road and saw the man. But he did not help him.

A second man came by, went over to look at the wounded man, and continued on his way.

Then a Samaritan came by. He saw the beaten man and went to help him. He bandaged his wounds, put him on his donkey, and took him to an inn.

"Take care of him," the Samaritan said to the innkeeper. "If you spend more than what I have given you, I shall repay you on my way back."

Based on Luke 10:30–35

The priest, the second man, and the Samaritan all saw the wounded man lying on the road. Only the Samaritan delayed his trip to care for him. Only the Samaritan truly practiced the virtue of love.

Each day we, too, can see ways to practice the virtue of love. We must decide to do what we can for those who need us and not walk away. We must try to practice the virtue of love with compassion as Jesus did.

What does this statement mean to you? "Living the virtue of love often means that we go out of our way to help."

How will you practice the virtue of love in your family? your school? your parish?

243

OUR CATHOLIC FAITH

Thank you, Jesus, for the good news of God's love.

What are some ways your family practices the virtue of love? What do you do to help them?

Our Church Teaches Us Love

Jesus' whole life was an act of love. Jesus' mission was to show everyone how to live the Law of Love. Jesus once told his followers this powerful story to help them better understand how important the virtue of love is in living for God's reign.

Jesus said that at the end of time he will say, "Come, you who are blessed by my Father. Inherit the kingdom prepared for you from the foundation of the world."

"For I was hungry and you gave me food, I was thirsty, and you gave me drink, a stranger and you welcomed me, naked and you clothed me, ill and you cared for me, in prison and you visited me."

His followers will ask Jesus when they did all these things for him.

Jesus will reply, "I say to you, whatever you did for one of these least brothers of mine, you did for me."
Based on Matthew 25:31–40

Jesus was teaching his disciples that love demands action. The virtue of love demands that we reach out to others, especially to people in need. The true love that Jesus taught us demands that we treat others fairly and with justice.

One of the letters of Saint Paul to the people of Corinth is an especially beautiful description of what real love is like when it is lived as Jesus taught. Paul wrote:

"Love is patient, love is kind. It is not jealous, [love] is not pompous, it is not inflated, it is not rude, it does not seek its own interests, it is not quick-tempered, it does not brood over injury, it does not rejoice over wrongdoing, but rejoices with the truth. It bears all things, believes all things, hopes all things, endures all things."
1 Corinthians 13:4–7

Saint Paul was teaching what it means to practice true love as Jesus did. The love Saint Paul urges us to practice often demands that we willingly give up something we want in order to help others.

In living for God's reign, what we actually do is more important than what we say. But words and feelings help us keep our love growing.

Each day we should reach out to those we love, especially family, give them a hug and whisper, "I love you."

244

oral and Spiritual
to practice love.

d for one of these
s mine, you did

test of the
virtues.

Eddie Maraeich

1. Feed the Hungry,
shelter the homeless,
for the sick, help
the dead.

2. Share knowle
who need it, l
it, be patient w
who hurt you
those who nee

3. Love is a virtue
love God, our

4. St. Paul told us
believes all thing
endures all th
Jesus did.

5. The corporal w
to care fore th
our neighbors,
how to care for

When we practice the virtue of love we come to know why Saint Paul ends his description of love by saying that of the three virtues, faith, hope, and love, "the greatest of these is love" (1 Corinthians 13:13).

Make a Love Calendar. Write one way you will try to practice the virtue of love each day. Keep a record of how many times you practiced the love Saint Paul describes.

Love Is

Monday

Tuesday

Wednesday

Thursday

Friday

Saturday

Sunday

- In your own words tell about the love Jesus taught us. What does it ask of you?
- How will you show love to your family? your Church? someone who doesn't like you?

OUR CATHOLIC FAITH

Holy Spirit, guide the Church in love.

What do you think it takes to practice the virtue of love each day?

Practicing the Virtue of Love

In our Catholic tradition, we know some very specific ways to practice the virtue of love. These are called the Corporal and the Spiritual Works of Mercy.

The Corporal Works of Mercy show us how to care for the physical well-being of our neighbors.

The Spiritual Works of Mercy show us how to care for their spiritual well-being.

Corporal Works of Mercy

- Feed the hungry.
- Give drink to the thirsty.
- Shelter the homeless.
- Clothe the naked.
- Care for the sick.
- Help the imprisoned.
- Bury the dead.

Spiritual Works of Mercy

- Share knowledge.
- Give advice to those who need it.
- Comfort those who suffer.
- Be patient with others.
- Forgive those who hurt you.
- Give correction to those who need it.
- Pray for others.

Prison Ministry

Not long after his election as pope, John XXIII did something that surprised many people. He left the Vatican and went to visit the inmates of a local prison in the city of Rome. The prisoners rejoiced that the Holy Father had remembered them and showed his care and love for them.

It should not be surprising for Catholics today to realize that the Church has a special ministry to those who are in prison. To help the imprisoned is one of the Corporal Works of Mercy.

At certain times in history, prisons were places of harsh and inhuman treatment. The Church has worked constantly to speak against injustices committed against men and women in prison.

In our country, most prisons have Catholic chaplains. Chaplains may be priests, sisters, or other trained individuals. They work in this pastoral ministry by helping prisoners to celebrate the sacraments, to know and experience God's love for them, and to rehabilitate their lives. In this way, they help to bring about the reign of God.

Prison ministry is not easy work. But with the help of the Holy Spirit, prison ministers can do so much to help men and women return to freedom and once again live as free children of God. Is there some way that you could help with the Church's prison ministry?

Learn by heart Faith Summary

- Love is a virtue that enables us to love God, our neighbor, and ourselves.
- The Corporal and Spiritual Works of Mercy are some very specific ways to practice the virtue of love.
- Saint Paul tells us that love is the greatest Christian virtue.

Coming to Faith

Rewrite these Corporal and Spiritual Works of Mercy as action statements so that it is easier for you to practice them. For example, you could rewrite "Comfort those who suffer" as "I can invite someone who is suffering from prejudice to spend time with my group of friends."

MY ACTION PLAN

■ Share knowledge.

_____

_____

_____

■ Be patient with others.

_____

_____

_____

■ Feed the hungry.

_____

_____

_____

■ Shelter the homeless.

_____

_____

_____

■ Pray for others.

_____

_____

_____

Practicing Faith

Talk together about a work of mercy that you might take on as a group project this coming week. For example:

● Does your parish work for the poor and homeless? How can you help?

● Could a catechist use some help with younger children?

Plan what you can do. Then do it! End by listening again to the words from Saint John's letter on page 240.

Talk with your teacher about ways you and your family might use the "Faith Alive" section. Pray the Act of Love with your family.

REVIEW ■ TEST

Answer.

1. What does the virtue of love enable us to do?

_____

_____

2. How did the Samaritan in the story Jesus told practice the virtue of Love?

_____

_____

3. Name a Corporal Work of Mercy.

_____

4. Name a Spiritual Work of Mercy.

_____

5. Name one way you will practice the virtue of love this week.

_____

_____

FAITH ALIVE AT HOME AND IN THE PARISH

In this chapter your fifth grader has learned more about the greatest virtue of all, love. Ask her or him to tell you what Jesus and John and Paul mean by love. We can see the true meaning of love each and every time we look at a crucifix. It is a longstanding custom for Catholics to have a crucifix displayed in their homes. It reminds us of Jesus' words about his sacrifice—"Greater love than this no one has." The closer we are to Jesus in our lives, the more we will comprehend love's truest meaning.

In Catholic tradition love always demands justice; true love means much more than a sentimental feeling. Go over together Saint Paul's description of love and the examples of it that your fifth grader did on page 245. Then talk about other ways your family and parish can live the virtue of love. Remind your son or daughter that true love is achieved only by a lifetime of practice. Help him or her to rely on the guidance of the Holy Spirit and the help of the Church community to grow as a loving person throughout life's journey.

† An Act of Love

Pray this prayer as a family.

O God, we love you above all things. Help us to love one another with patience, kindness, and unselfishness. Amen.

Jesus help us to see signs of your love in our daily lives.

Our Life

Our country honors people in many ways. One special way is by placing statues of two people from each state in the National Statuary Hall located in the Capitol building in Washington, D.C. Among those selected for this honor are thirteen Catholics—so far.

Arizona: Father Eusebio Kino, Jesuit

California: Father Junipero Serra, Franciscan

Hawaii: Father Damian of Molokai, Sacred Heart Fathers

Illinois: General James Shields

Louisiana: Justice Edward D. White

Maryland: Charles Carroll

Nevada: Patrick A. McCarren

New Mexico: Dennis Chavez

North Dakota: John Burke

Oregon: Dr. John McLoughlin

Washington: Mother Mary Joseph Pariseau, Sister of Charity of Providence

West Virginia: John E. Kenna

Wisconsin: Father Jacques Marquette, Jesuit

Father Damian of Molokai

Do you know why any one of these Catholics is honored this way?

What things do you or your family have that remind you of someone?

Sharing Life

What things in your parish church help you to remember Jesus, or Mary, and the saints?

Why are these things a help?

Work with a partner. Ask each other: What object would help you remember me when I'm not with you? Why would this be a special way to remember me? In the space below draw the symbols that would best describe your partner and yourself. Then share with the group why each symbol would be an appropriate remembrance.

This week we will learn more about symbols in our Church that help us live our faith.

We Will Learn

- The Church uses sacramentals to help us remember Jesus, Mary, and the saints, and to live in the presence of God.
- The Church uses signs and blessings, actions and objects as sacramentals.
- Praying the rosary helps us to remember the life of Jesus and Mary.

Sacramentals

There are many things in our daily lives that remind us of God. Our Church uses blessings, actions, and objects to help us remember God, Jesus, Mary, and the saints. We call these *sacramentals*.

We bless ourselves with *holy water* as we enter the church. Holy water is a sacramental that reminds us that we have been baptized by water and the Holy Spirit and have become God's own children.

The *altar* in our church is also a sacramental. The altar is the symbol of Jesus Christ. It is sometimes called the Lord's table because it reminds us of the Last Supper.

We may wear a *cross* to help us remember the death and resurrection of Jesus. Or we may wear a *medal* to help us remember Mary or the saints. Looking at a *statue* of Jesus, Mary, or one of the saints while we are praying helps us to remember their love and care for us.

We also use sacramentals during the liturgical year. We light *Advent candles* to help us remember that Christ is the Light of the World. On Ash Wednesday we receive *ashes* on our foreheads. This reminds us to turn away from sin and to turn to the good news of Jesus. On Good Friday we kiss the *crucifix* as a sign of respect and love for Jesus crucified.

During the Easter season we light the *Paschal* or *Easter Candle* to remember the resurrection of Jesus.

The Rosary

The *rosary* is also a sacramental. Praying the rosary helps us to remember the lives of Jesus and Mary.

We begin praying the rosary with the sign of the cross. The rosary has a cross on which we then pray the Apostles' Creed and remember the beliefs of our faith. The cross is followed by one large bead and three smaller beads. We pray the Our Father on the large bead and one Hail Mary on each of the small beads.

Then there is a circle of five groups of beads, or "decades." Each decade has one large bead and ten smaller ones. We pray an Our Father on each of the large beads and one Hail Mary on each of the small beads. We end each decade by praying the Glory to the Father.

As we pray the rosary, we think about the joyful, sorrowful, and glorious events in the lives of Jesus and Mary. We call these the mysteries of the rosary. There are fifteen mysteries of the rosary. They are:

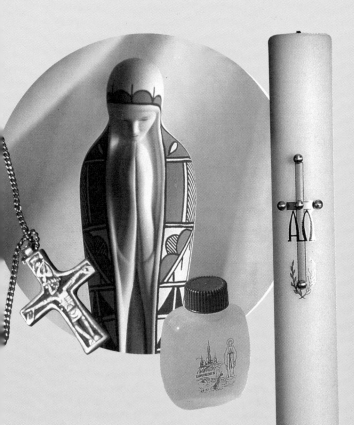

The Five Joyful Mysteries

1. The annunciation
2. The visitation
3. The birth of Jesus
4. The presentation of Jesus in the Temple
5. The finding of Jesus in the Temple

The Five Sorrowful Mysteries

1. The agony in the garden
2. The scourging at the pillar
3. The crowning with thorns
4. The carrying of the cross
5. The crucifixion and death

The Five Glorious Mysteries

1. The resurrection
2. The ascension
3. The descent of the Holy Spirit upon the apostles
4. The assumption of Mary into heaven
5. The coronation of Mary as Queen of heaven

Saint Frances Cabrini

COMING TO FAITH

How do sacramentals help you to remember God's presence in your life?

Name a sacramental that you have learned about. Tell what it helps you to remember.

_____

_____

Draw a picture or a symbol of your favorite sacramental. Then gather together and share your ideas.

PRACTICING FAITH

Statues and medals remind us of the saints who were faithful disciples of Jesus. Their lives can encourage us and remind us of how we can live our faith today.

Read about the saints below and then share together your ideas about ways you can be like them, faithful followers of Jesus Christ.

Saint Thomas More (1478–1535) was a devoted husband, parent, and a successful

lawyer. He rose to great power in the government of England when Henry VIII was king. But Henry VIII made himself the head of the Church in England and demanded that Thomas More take an oath against the pope. Thomas refused and was sentenced to death. Thomas More remained loyal both to the Church and to England. He said, "I am the king's good servant, but God's first."

What quality in Thomas More's life will help you to live as Jesus' disciple?

_____

_____

Saint Frances Cabrini (1850–1917) was an orphan who became a school teacher. Frances Cabrini founded the Missionary Sisters of the Sacred Heart to teach orphaned children in Italy. She and some of her Missionary Sisters came to America in 1889. In America Frances founded many schools, orphanages, and hospitals to help the immigrants.

What quality in Frances Cabrini's life will help you to live as Jesus' disciple?

_____

_____

Another saint I like is _____

The quality I admire and will try to imitate in this saint's life is

_____

_____

Talk with your teacher about ways you and your family might use the "Faith Alive" section. Pray the Our Father with your family this week.

REVIEW · TEST

Match the sacramentals with the descriptions.

Sacramentals	Descriptions
1. holy water	_____ reminds us of the death of Jesus
2. altar	_____ remind us to turn away from sin
3. cross	_____ reminds us of our Baptism
4. ashes	_____ reminds us that Christ is our Light
	_____ is a symbol of Christ; the Lord's table

5. What sacramental will you be especially mindful of this week?
What will you do?

_____

_____

_____

 FAITH ALIVE AT HOME AND IN THE PARISH

Sacramentals are blessings, actions, or objects that help us remember God, Jesus, Mary, the saints, and our call to discipleship. Sacramentals include blessings, medals, relics, shrines, blessed water, candles, palms and ashes, rosary beads and stations of the cross. They are material, visible realities that help us to be more aware of the invisible loving presence of God, Jesus, Mary, and the saints in our lives. Sacramentals enrich our Catholic life by directing our attention to God, who reaches out to us through all the gifts of his creation.

Learn by heart **Faith Summary**

- Sacramentals are blessings, actions, and objects that remind us of God, Jesus, Mary, and the saints.

- The rosary is a sacramental that helps us reflect on the lives of Jesus and Mary.

God, we remember and celebrate all the gifts of your love.

Mass
of the
Holy Spirit

Opening Hymn:
Write title here.

_____

First Reading

The Holy Spirit comes to the disciples as Jesus promised. (Read Acts 2:1–11.)

Responsorial Psalm

Choose an appropriate psalm from the Lectionary or Bible, for example—Psalm 23 or Psalm 145. Write your selection here.

_____

Response: Lord, send out your Spirit, and renew the face of the earth.

Gospel

A reading from the holy gospel according to John. (Read John 20:19–23.)

Prayer of the Faithful

Leader: Come, Holy Spirit. Renew the face of the earth.

All: Come, Holy Spirit. Renew the face of the earth. _(This response is said after each of the following)_

Reader: Come, Holy Spirit. Give us the gift of wisdom.

All: (Response)

Reader: Come, Holy Spirit. Give us the gift of understanding.

All: (Response)

Reader: Come, Holy Spirit. Give us the gift of right judgment.

All: (Response)

Reader: Come, Holy Spirit. Give us the gift of courage.

All: (Response)

Reader: Come, Holy Spirit. Give us the gift of true knowledge.

All: (Response)

Reader: Come, Holy Spirit. Give us the gift of reverence.

All: (Response)

Reader: Come, Holy Spirit. Give us the gift of wonder and awe in your presence.

All: (Response)

Reader: Come, Holy Spirit. Fill our hearts with your gifts, and come upon us as you came upon the disciples on the first Pentecost.

All: Amen.

Presentation of the Gifts

Write the names of those who will carry the bread and wine to the altar.

Gift	Presenter
_____	_____
_____	_____
_____	_____

Communion Hymn

Closing Hymn

WE HONOR OUR IMMACULATE MOTHER

Entrance Procession

You may carry flowers that you have bought, made, or grown. Put them on or next to the place that has been set up to honor Mary, our Immaculate Mother.

Opening Hymn

"Immaculate Mary"

Leader: Today, we honor the Blessed Virgin Mary as the woman God chose to be the Mother of God's own Son. We remember that the Immaculate Conception means that Mary was always sinless, even before she was born. We honor Mary as the patroness of our country on December 8, the feast of the Immaculate Conception.

In our litany prayer today, we pray to Mary, using some of the titles with which the Church honors her. These titles help us to remember Mary's role in God's plan of salvation.

Leader: Holy Mary,

All: O Mary, conceived without sin, pray for us who have recourse to you. *(This response is said after each of the following.)*

Leader: Holy Mother of God,
Mother of Christ,
Mother most pure,
Mother most lovable,

Mother of our Creator,
Mother of our Savior,
Virgin most faithful,
Cause of our joy,
Health of the sick,
Refuge of sinners,
Comfort of the afflicted,
Help of Christians,
Queen of angels,
Queen of apostles,
Queen of martyrs,
Queen of all saints,
Queen conceived without
  original sin,
Queen of the most holy rosary,
Queen of peace.
Pray for us, Holy Mother of God.

All: That we may be made worthy of the promises of Christ.

Time for Reflection

Choose one of the titles of Mary used in the litany prayer. Think about how it can help you to live as Jesus' disciple today.

Title _____

I will live as a disciple of Jesus by

_____

_____

_____

Closing Hymn

"Sing of Mary"

A Way of the Cross

Act One: Arrest and Sentencing

All: *Sing an appropriate song.*

Leader: A reading from the holy gospel according to Mark. (Read Mark 14:43–46.)

First Station

Reader: The next day Pontius Pilate sentenced you, Jesus, to be crucified. You always did God's will and lived to bring about the reign of God. Help us when others make fun of us and ignore us for doing God's loving will.

All: We adore you, O Christ, and we praise you, because by your holy cross you have redeemed the world.

Second Station

Reader: Jesus, the soldiers made fun of you. They placed a crown of thorns on your head and laughed at you. Help us when others make fun of us because we are living the Law of Love.

All: *Repeat response "We adore you...."*

Third Station

Reader: Jesus, you are the Son of God and one of us. The cross became too heavy and you fell under it. Help us when others tempt us to disobey the Ten Commandments. (Response)

Think and Decide:

What will you do to show that you are proud to be a disciple of Jesus?

Act Two: Helpers Along the Way

All: *Sing an appropriate song.*

Leader: A reading from the holy gospel according to Luke. (Read Luke 23:26–27.)

Fourth Station

Reader: Jesus, your mother, Mary, sees and shares in your pain and suffering. Help us turn to Mary, our mother, for strength to live as your disciples. (Response)

Fifth Station

Reader: Jesus, the soldiers order Simon to help you carry your cross. Help us to bring freedom to those suffering from injustice. (Response)

Sixth Station

Reader: Jesus, Veronica wipes the blood and sweat from your face. Help us to live the Works of Mercy. (Response)

Seventh Station

Reader: Jesus, the weight of the cross causes you to fall a second time. May the Holy Spirit help us to live your Law of Love. (Response)

Eighth Station

Reader: Jesus, you tell a group of women from Jerusalem to have hope in your promises. Help us to trust in all God's promises. (Response)

Think and Decide:

What will you do to show that you are proud to be a disciple of Jesus?

Act Three: Darkness Over the Earth

All: *Sing an appropriate song.*

Leader: A reading from the holy gospel according to Luke. (Read Luke 23:32–34.)

Ninth Station

Reader: Jesus, you fall a third and final time on your way to Calvary. Give us strength in the Eucharist. (Response)

Tenth Station

Reader: Jesus, the soldiers stripped you and divided your clothes among themselves. Help us to forgive those who hurt us. (Response)

Eleventh Station

Reader: Jesus, the soldiers crucified you like a criminal. You asked the Father to forgive them. Help us to appreciate your love for us. (Response)

Twelfth Station

Leader: A reading from the holy gospel according to Luke. (Read Luke 23:44–46.)

Reader: Kneel and ask yourself: "How do I feel about Jesus dying out of love for me?"

Think and Decide:

What will you do to show that you are proud to be a disciple of Jesus?

Act Four: From Death to Life

Thirteenth Station

Reader: Jesus, your disciples must have felt their dreams were shattered when Joseph of Arimathea took your lifeless body down from the cross. Help us to see the signs of God's life around us. (Response)

Fourteenth Station

Reader: Jesus, as they buried your body, the disciples must have felt that their hopes were being buried, too. Help us to see the signs of God's love around us. (Response)

Leader: A reading from the holy gospel according to John. (Read John 20:11–18.)

Think and Decide:

What will you do to be a sign of God's life and love?

All: *Sing an appropriate Easter song.*

Jesus Christ Reveals God

Jesus Christ is truly human. Jesus was like us in every way except that he never sinned. Jesus Christ is also truly divine. Jesus is God the Father's own Son. Jesus revealed by his words and deeds that "God is love" (1 John 4:8). Today, God works through us and other people to show his love in the world.

Jesus Christ and the Kingdom of God

Jesus showed by his words and actions that he was the Messiah. Jesus announced the good news of the kingdom, or reign, of God. The good news is that God loves us and will always be with us.

By his words and actions Jesus brought about the reign of God. Jesus showed us how to live for the reign of God by loving God, our neighbor, and ourselves.

Jesus Christ Blesses Our Lives

Jesus Christ invited everyone to live for the reign of God. Jesus forgave people their sins. By his words and actions Jesus lived his whole life helping and serving others. We live for the reign of God by following the example of Jesus.

The Church Carries on Jesus' Mission

After Jesus' ascension into heaven, the Holy Spirit came to Jesus' disciples and filled them with gifts to preach the good news to everyone. The Holy Spirit continues to help the Church to carry on the mission of Jesus to all people.

The Church welcomes all people to believe in Jesus and to follow him. The Church forgives and heals, as Jesus did. Every member of the Church is called to carry on Jesus' mission by serving others.

The Sacraments and the Church

There are many signs of God's love in our everyday life. The Church is the sacrament of Jesus. The most effective signs of God's presence in the Church are the seven sacraments.

Baptism, Confirmation, and Eucharist are called sacraments of initiation. Through these sacraments the Church welcomes all people into the community of the Church.

Reconciliation and the Anointing of the Sick are sacraments of healing. Through these sacraments the Church brings us God's forgiveness when we sin, and strengthens us when we are sick.

Matrimony and Holy Orders are sacraments of service. Through these sacraments the Church continues Jesus' mission of service through married couples and through our ordained ministers: bishops, priests, and deacons.

Circle the letter beside the correct answer.

1. By the incarnation we mean that the Son of God
   a. is not really like us.
   b. became an angel of God.
   c. became one of us.
   d. stopped being God.

2. Jesus revealed to us that God
   a. prefers rich people.
   b. cares for all people.
   c. cares only for good people.
   d. rejects sinners.

3. Jesus began his public ministry by
   a. being born in Bethlehem.
   b. announcing God's reign.
   c. dying on the cross.
   d. sending the Holy Spirit.

4. Jesus offered forgiveness of sins
   a. only to good people.
   b. only to sick people.
   c. only to wealthy people.
   d. to all people.

5. The most effective signs of Jesus' presence in the Church are the
   a. parish churches.
   b. priests.
   c. pope and bishops.
   d. seven sacraments.

Complete the following statements.

6. Baptism, Confirmation, and the Eucharist are called sacraments of initiation because

   _____

   _____

7. Reconciliation and Anointing of the Sick are called sacraments of healing because

   _____

   _____

8. Matrimony and Holy Orders are called sacraments of service because

   _____

   _____

9. By the reign of God we mean

   _____

   _____

10. We can show that we live for God's reign by

   _____

   _____

Think and Decide: Tell how you can live one of the sacraments today.

_____

_____

Name _____

Your fifth grader has just completed Unit 1. Take time now to evaluate how he or she is growing in understanding and living the faith. Check and return this page to your son's or daughter's teacher.

_____ My son/daughter needs help understanding the part of the Review I have underlined.

_____ I would like to speak with you. My phone number is _____.

Signature: _____

Jesus Christ Brings Us Life (Baptism)

Baptism is a sacrament of initiation. In Baptism we are born again through water and the Holy Spirit. We share in God's life, or grace, and begin our initiation into the Church, the body of Christ. A priest or deacon pours water on the head of the person being baptized saying, "*Name*, I baptize you in the name of the Father, and of the Son, and of the Holy Spirit." Our Baptism calls us to live for the reign of God.

Jesus Christ Strengthens Us (Confirmation)

Confirmation is a sacrament of initiation. In Confirmation the Holy Spirit fills us with the gifts we need to give witness to our Catholic faith.

The bishop extends his hands over the heads of those to be confirmed. He prays that they will receive the gifts of the Holy Spirit. He then anoints them, saying, "*Name*, be sealed with the Gift of the Holy Spirit." The gifts of the Holy Spirit help us to live as responsible witnesses to the good news of Jesus today.

Jesus Christ Feeds Us (Eucharist)

Jesus is the Bread of Life. The food that Jesus gives us in the Eucharist is his own Body and Blood. In the Eucharist we remember what Jesus asked us to do at the Last Supper. In this meal and sacrifice, ordinary bread and wine become the Body and Blood of Christ.

The Eucharist is a sacrament of initiation. The Eucharist nourishes us to live our new life with God. In the Eucharist, Jesus is really present. Through the Eucharist we become a living sacrifice of praise.

Our Church Celebrates the Eucharist (The Mass)

At Mass we thank God the Father for the gift of his Son Jesus Christ. The major parts of the Mass are the *Liturgy of the Word* and the *Liturgy of the Eucharist*.

The *Introductory Rites* prepare us to listen to God's word and celebrate the Eucharist. In the *Liturgy of the Word*, we listen and respond to God's word. In the *Liturgy of the Eucharist* we join with Christ to praise God for all the great things he has done. We offer ourselves with Jesus to his Father. In the *Concluding Rite* we are blessed and sent forth to love and serve God and people.

The Church Remembers (The Liturgical Year)

In the liturgical year, we celebrate and enter into the life, death, and resurrection of Jesus. The liturgical year helps us to live as Christ's followers and to live in the presence of God. The liturgical seasons are Advent, Christmas, Lent, the Easter Triduum, Easter, and Ordinary Time. During the liturgical year, we also honor Mary and the saints.

Match each feast with the correct date.

1. Immaculate Conception

2. Christmas

3. Saint Joseph

4. All Saints

5. Assumption

_____ August 15

_____ March 19

_____ November 1

_____ December 8

_____ February 2

_____ December 25

Define the following words.

6. Confirmation

_____

_____

_____

7. Eucharist

_____

_____

_____

8. Liturgy

_____

_____

_____

9. Blessed Sacrament

_____

_____

_____

10. Mass

_____

_____

_____

Think and Decide: How will you share Jesus, our Bread of Life, with others?

_____

_____

_____

Name _____

Your fifth grader has just completed Unit 2. Take time now to evaluate how he or she is growing in understanding and living the faith. Check and return this page to your son's or daughter's teacher.

_____ My son/daughter needs help understanding the part of the Review I have underlined.

_____ I would like to speak with you. My phone number is _____.

Signature: _____

31 FIRST SEMESTER · REVIEW

Chapter 1—Jesus Christ Reveals God

- Jesus Christ is both human and divine.
- Jesus showed us that "God is love" by the things he said and did.
- God works through us and others to show his love in the world.

Chapter 2—Jesus Christ and the Kingdom of God

- Jesus announced the good news of the kingdom, or reign, of God. The good news is that God loves us and will always love us.
- The reign of God is the power of God's life and love in the world.
- Jesus lived his whole life for the reign of God and calls us to do the same.

Chapter 3—Jesus Christ Blesses Our Lives

- Jesus invited everyone to live for the reign of God.
- Forgiveness heals the separation from God and from others that sin causes.
- Like Jesus, we try to forgive those who hurt us, no matter how great the hurt.

Chapter 4—The Church Carries on Jesus' Mission

- The Holy Spirit helps the Church carry on the mission of Jesus to all people.
- Jesus is the head of the Church, his body, and we are its members.
- The Church serves people, continuing Jesus' mission of healing and forgiveness.

Chapter 5—The Sacraments and the Church

- A sacrament is an effective sign through which Jesus Christ shares God's life and love with us.
- There are seven sacraments: Baptism, Confirmation, Eucharist, Reconciliation, Anointing of the Sick, Matrimony, and Holy Orders.
- We receive God's grace in the sacraments.

Chapter 8—Jesus Christ Brings Us Life (Baptism)

- We receive new life at Baptism when we are reborn of water and the Holy Spirit.

- At Baptism we are initiated into, or begin to become members of the Church, the body of Christ.

- Our Baptism calls us to decide to live for the reign of God.

Chapter 9—Jesus Christ Strengthens Us (Confirmation)

- Confirmation is the sacrament in which we are sealed with the Gift of the Holy Spirit and strengthened to give witness to the good news of Jesus Christ.

- In Confirmation the Holy Spirit fills us with the gifts that we need to live our Christian faith.

- We live our Confirmation when we become witnesses to the reign of God in the world.

Chapter 10—Jesus Christ Feeds Us (Eucharist)

- The Eucharist is the sacrament of the Body and Blood of Christ.

- Jesus is the Bread of Life. The food that Jesus gives us is His own Body and Blood.

- We respond to the gift of the Eucharist by living for the reign of God.

Chapter 11—Our Church Celebrates the Eucharist (The Mass)

- The two major parts of the Mass are the Liturgy of the Word and the Liturgy of the Eucharist.

- During the Liturgy of the Word, we listen to God's word from the Bible.

- During the Liturgy of the Eucharist, our gifts of bread and wine become the Body and Blood of Christ.

Chapter 12—The Church Remembers (The Liturgical Year)

- The liturgical seasons of the Church year are Advent, Christmas, Lent, the Easter Triduum, Easter, and Ordinary Time.

- During the liturgical year we also honor and pray to Mary and the other saints.

- The liturgical year reminds us that we always live in the presence of God.

Circle the letter beside the correct answer.

1. Jesus is like us in every way except that
  a. he never laughed.
  b. he never got angry.
  c. he never sinned.
  d. he never died.

2. Jesus is divine because
  a. he is the Son of God.
  b. he is loving.
  c. he is kind and merciful.
  d. he is Mary's son.

3. Jesus is human because
  a. he is the Son of God.
  b. he is the son of Mary.
  c. he is the second Person of the Blessed Trinity.
  d. he quieted the storm at sea.

4. Sacraments are
  a. powerful signs of Jesus' presence.
  b. Spiritual Works of Mercy.
  c. seasons of the Church year.
  d. Beatitudes in action.

5. When we celebrate the Eucharist, we
  a. share in the one sacrifice of Christ.
  b. are given a new white garment.
  c. are reborn of water and the Spirit.
  d. are anointed with holy oil.

Define the following words.

6. Liturgy

_____

_____

_____

7. Reconciliation

_____

_____

_____

8. grace

_____

_____

_____

9. incarnation

_____

_____

_____

10. ascension

_____

_____

_____

31 FIRST SEMESTER · TEST

Read each sentence. Cross out the word or words that are *incorrect*.

11. To live our new life of grace, we receive in Baptism (the help of the Holy Spirit/holy water).

12. In Confirmation the Holy Spirit gives us gifts that help us live and witness to (our faith/our citizenship).

13. After Mass, the Blessed Sacrament is kept (in the tabernacle/on the altar).

14. The Fruits of the Holy Spirit are signs that we (are living/need help to live) as witnesses to our faith.

15. The food that Jesus gives us as our Bread of Life is (ordinary bread and wine/Jesus' own Body and Blood).

16. Mary is the patroness of the United States of America under the title of (the Immaculate Conception/Our Lady of Guadalupe).

17. Jesus first gave us the gift of his Body and Blood at (his ascension into heaven/ the Last Supper).

18. We prepare for Easter during the liturgical season of (Christmas/Lent).

19. The Easter Triduum begins on (Ash Wednesday/Holy Thursday).

20. The Church remembers and celebrates the resurrection of Jesus on (Good Friday/ Easter Sunday).

Think and Decide: Explain how the sacrament of Baptism makes a difference in your life.

_____

_____

_____

Jesus Christ Forgives Us (Reconciliation)

The Church celebrates all the sacraments by the power of the Holy Spirit. In the sacrament of Reconciliation Jesus Christ shares God's forgiveness of our sins. Reconciliation is one of the sacraments of healing.

Reconciliation, or Penance, may be celebrated individually or communally. In both rites, or forms of celebration, we confess our sins to a priest in private.

Examination of conscience, confession, contrition, penance, and absolution are important parts of Reconciliation.

Jesus Christ Helps Us in Sickness and Death (Anointing of the Sick)

In the sacrament of Anointing of the Sick, the Church carries on Jesus' mission of bringing God's healing power to the sick and dying. Anointing is one of the sacraments of healing. The two most important signs of this sacrament are the laying on of hands and anointing with oil.

We also carry on Jesus' mission of healing when we take care of and respect our bodies and when we support our Church's efforts to eliminate disease and suffering in our world.

Jesus Christ Helps Us to Love (Matrimony)

Matrimony is a sacrament of service. It is a powerful sign of God's love and faithfulness. In Matrimony a bride and groom enter into a lifelong marriage covenant. They promise to love each other and serve the Church. We can prepare for Matrimony by being faithful in our friendships and practicing unselfish love.

Jesus Christ Calls Us to Serve (Holy Orders)

Jesus Christ chose twelve apostles to lead his Church. In time, the Church chose other leaders called bishops, priests, and deacons.

Holy Orders is a sacrament of service. Our bishops, priests, and deacons are ordained in the sacrament of Holy Orders to lead our Church in service and worship. The pope is the leader of the whole Church. We support our ordained leaders by praying for them and helping them.

We Share Jesus Christ's Priesthood (Ministry)

Through Baptism every Christian shares in Jesus' priestly mission and ministry and is called to serve the Church. Each person has a vocation, or call, to serve others. There are many vocations: married, ordained, religious, and single persons. Our preparation for a life of service begins now.

Circle the letter beside the correct answer.

1. The sign of God's forgiveness in Reconciliation is the
   a. Act of Contrition.
   b. absolution.
   c. penance.
   d. examination of conscience.

2. Anointing of the Sick and Reconciliation are sacraments of
   a. initiation.
   b. service.
   c. healing.
   d. good news.

3. Through Baptism, all Christians share in
   a. ordained priesthood.
   b. original sin.
   c. the seal of confession.
   d. the priesthood of the faithful.

4. The servant-leader of the whole Church is the
   a. deacon.
   b. pope.
   c. lector.
   d. priest.

5. Holy Orders and Matrimony are sacraments of
   a. initiation.
   b. service.
   c. healing.
   d. good news.

6. The sacrament that brings God's special blessing to the sick, elderly, or dying is
   a. Holy Orders.
   b. Confirmation.
   c. Anointing of the Sick.
   d. Eucharist.

Answer the following:

7. Name the ministers of Matrimony.

   _____

   _____

8. Name two ways of celebrating Reconciliation.

   _____

   _____

9. How does the Church continue Jesus' mission of healing?

   _____

   _____

10. Explain how your parish priest serves the Church.

   _____

   _____

Think and Decide: How can you prepare for your vocation in life ?

   _____

   _____

Name _____

Your fifth grader has just completed Unit 3. Take time now to evaluate how he or she is growing in understanding and living the faith. Check and return this page to your son's or daughter's teacher.

_____ My son/daughter needs help understanding the part of the Review I have underlined.

_____ I would like to speak with you. My phone number is _____.

Signature: _____

Becoming a Catholic (Marks of the Church)

The Church is one, holy, catholic, and apostolic. These are marks, or qualities, that let people know the kind of community we are.

That the Church is one means we are united in faith and love. That the Church is holy means we share in God's own life. That the Church is catholic means the Church goes to everyone and all people are welcome. That the Church is apostolic means that we carry on the mission Jesus gave to the apostles. We are called to live the four marks of the Church.

All People Are God's People

All people are created in God's image and likeness. Catholics respect all people who are different in color, sex, religion, or in any way. We have a special relationship with the Jewish people, who are still God's chosen people. We share many beliefs and traditions with them.

We respect and seek unity with those Christians who are not members of the Catholic Church. Today there are many Christian Churches. We pray for the success of the ecumenical movement, the search for the union of all Christian Churches.

We Believe in God

The virtues of faith, hope, and love are gifts from God. Faith is a virtue that enables us to trust and believe in God, to accept what he has revealed, and to live according to his loving will.

Creeds are prayers that summarize what we believe. We will never fully understand the mysteries of our faith. We believe and trust God and our Church even when we do not understand. We practice our faith by living it.

God Fills Us with Hope

Hope is the virtue that enables us to trust that God will be with us in every situation. The resurrection of Jesus is our source of hope. Mary is a special sign of hope for us. Celebrating the sacraments and praying help us to act as hopeful people to change our world.

The Gift of God's Love

Love is a virtue that enables us to love God, our neighbor, and ourselves. Saint Paul said that of the three virtues of faith, hope, and love, the greatest is love. We practice love by what we say and do. The Corporal and Spiritual Works of Mercy show us how to practice love.

33 UNIT 4 ▪ TEST

Circle the letter beside the correct answer.

1. The marks of the Church are
   a. Baptism, Eucharist, and Confirmation.
   b. bishops, deacons, and priests.
   c. one, holy, catholic, and apostolic.
   d. apostles and disciples.

2. The ecumenical movement is
   a. the search for the reunion of all Christians.
   b. a religious group.
   c. a Protestant Church.
   d. a group separated from the Church.

3. Faith, hope, and love are the
   a. mysteries of the faith.
   b. sacraments of the Church.
   c. works of mercy.
   d. theological virtues.

4. The beliefs of the Church are summarized in
   a. songs.
   b. creeds.
   c. news stories.
   d. psalms.

5. The Church teaches that Mary
   a. died in Nazareth.
   b. died a martyr's death.
   c. was buried in Jerusalem.
   d. was brought body and soul to heaven.

Answer the following questions.

6. What is prejudice?

   _____

   _____

7. What does it mean to say that the Church is one?

   _____

   _____

8. What does it mean to say that the Church is holy?

   _____

   _____

9. What does it mean to say that the Church is catholic?

   _____

   _____

10. What does it mean to say that the Church is apostolic?

   _____

   _____

   _____

Think and Decide: Choose one Spiritual or Corporal Work of Mercy.
Tell how you can practice it.

_____

_____

_____

Chapter 15—Jesus Christ Forgives Us (Reconciliation)

- Reconciliation is the sacrament in which we are forgiven by God and the Church for our sins.

- Examination of conscience, contrition, confession, penance, and absolution are important steps in the celebration of Reconciliation.

- In Reconciliation we receive God's help to do his loving will, to avoid sin, and to live as his people.

Chapter 16—Jesus Christ Helps Us in Sickness and Death (Anointing of the Sick)

- The sacrament of Anointing of the Sick brings God's special blessings to those who are sick, elderly, or dying.

- Anointing of the Sick is one of the two sacraments of healing.

- We must respect our bodies by caring for them. We must work to eliminate sickness and evil from the world.

Chapter 17—Jesus Christ Helps Us to Love (Matrimony)

- The sacrament of Matrimony is a powerful and effective sign of Christ's presence that joins a man and woman together for life.

- Married couples promise to serve each other and the whole Church. Matrimony is a sacrament of service.

- We can prepare now for Matrimony by trying to love others as God loves us.

Chapter 18—Jesus Christ Calls Us to Serve (Holy Orders)

- Jesus chose twelve apostles to lead our Church in teaching and worship.

- Bishops, priests, and deacons are ordained in the sacrament of Holy Orders.

- Our ordained ministers lead us in building up the Christian community.

Chapter 19—We Share Jesus Christ's Priesthood (Ministry)

- Jesus calls each of us to a specific vocation to carry on his priestly mission.

- Evangelization means spreading the good news of Jesus Christ and sharing our faith by our words and deeds.

- There are many vocations—married, ordained, religious, and single life. We are called to carry on Jesus' mission.

Chapter 22—Becoming a Catholic (Marks of the Church)

- The marks of the Church are one, holy, catholic, and apostolic.

- The Church of Jesus Christ shows it is one and holy when we are united in faith and live holy lives.

- The Church of Jesus Christ shows it is catholic and apostolic by welcoming all and being faithful to the mission and beliefs Jesus gave to the apostles.

Chapter 23—All People Are God's People

- As Catholics we must fight against prejudice in our lives.

- We respect those who worship God in other religions.

- We have a special bond with the Jewish people. We seek unity with all Christians.

Chapter 24—We Believe in God

- The virtues of faith, hope, and love are gifts from God.

- Faith is a virtue that enables us to trust and believe in God, to accept what he has revealed, and to live according to his will.

- The creeds of our Church summarize what we believe.

Chapter 25—God Fills Us With Hope

- Hope is the virtue that enables us to trust that God will be with us in every situation.

- Jesus is our greatest source of hope.

- Mary, the Mother of the Church, is a sign of hope for us.

Chapter 26—The Gift of God's Love

- Love is a virtue that enables us to love God, our neighbor, and ourselves.

- The Corporal and Spiritual Works of Mercy are some very specific ways to practice the virtue of love.

- Saint Paul tells us that love is the greatest Christian virtue.

Circle the letter beside the correct answer.

1. The sacraments of initiation are
   a. Holy Orders, Anointing of the Sick, Baptism.
   b. Confirmation, Matrimony, Holy Orders.
   c. Baptism, Confirmation, Eucharist.
   d. Confirmation, Matrimony, Eucharist.

2. God's life and love in us is called
   a. worship.
   b. action.
   c. grace.
   d. respect.

3. We celebrate God's forgiveness in
   a. Holy Orders.
   b. Confirmation.
   c. Matrimony.
   d. Reconciliation.

4. The Eucharist is a sign of
   a. unity.
   b. division.
   c. healing.
   d. liturgy.

5. The successors of the apostles are the
   a. religious.
   b. priests.
   c. bishops.
   d. deacons.

6. The love of married couples is
   a. not celebrated in a special sacrament.
   b. a sign of Jesus' love for the Church.
   c. not meant to last forever.
   d. meant only for them.

7. The sacrament that confers the ordained ministry of bishops, priests, and deacons is
   a. Baptism.
   b. Matrimony.
   c. Confirmation.
   d. Holy Orders.

8. The Church is one means
   a. we received the good news from the apostles.
   b. we welcome all people to our Church.
   c. all baptized persons are united together with Jesus Christ.
   d. we share in God's own life.

9. The virtues of faith, hope, and love are
   a. gifts from God which help us to believe, trust, and love.
   b. sacraments of the Church.
   c. values we learn.
   d. prayers to say.

10. Our most important source of hope is
    a. our vocation.
    b. our bishops, priests, and deacons.
    c. our knowledge.
    d. the resurrection of Jesus Christ.

34 SECOND SEMESTER • TEST

Define the following words.

11. Holy Orders

12. Baptism

13. Reconciliation

14. grace

15. Liturgy

16. Confirmation

17. Anointing of the Sick

18. Matrimony

19. Eucharist

20. How can you continue Jesus' mission of healing in the world?

DAY OF RETREAT

Theme: Living the Law of Love

◀ OPENING ACTIVITY ▶

During your retreat this year, you will think about who you are and how you want to live your life as a disciple of Jesus. Imagine you could be anyone or anything for one day.

For example:

- an animal
- a star athlete
- a famous entertainer
- other _____

- a musical instrument
- a world leader
- a leader of our Church
- an automobile

_____

Who or what would you choose to be? Write it here and explain why._____

_____

_____

_____

On a piece of paper:

- draw or write what you would look like.
- describe what you would like to do.

After all have finished, fold your papers and place them in a container. Each member of the group takes a paper from the container, shows it to the group, and tries to guess the identity of the person described on it. Then have the person share with the group responses to the following questions:

- Why did you pick that person or thing?
- What does your choice tell others about you?

◀ JOURNAL ▶

Find a quiet place.
Think about the following questions:

- What importance or value do I see in my choice?
- What can I discover about myself from my choice?

Write your responses in the space below.

◄ SCRIPTURE REFLECTION ►

Sometimes you might wonder what God really wants you to be and to do in your life. In the gospel, Jesus teaches that everything we do and say must show that we are trying to live the Law of Love. Listen carefully to what Jesus says.

Reader: A teacher of the Law tried to trap Jesus with a question. "Teacher," he asked, "which commandment in the law is the greatest?"

Jesus answered, "You shall love the Lord, your God, with all your heart, with all your soul, and with all your mind. This is the greatest and the first commandment. The second is like it: You shall love your neighbor as yourself."

Based on Matthew 22:34–40

Imagine that you are one of Jesus' disciples. Later that evening you and the other disciples gather to discuss Jesus' response to the teacher of the Law. What might you say?

Take a few moments to think about the following:

- What does the Law of Love mean to me?
- What people do I know who are living the Law of Love? Tell how.
- What are the talents or the things that I do best?
- How can I use my talents to live the Law of Love?

◄ JOURNAL ►

Reflect briefly on your responses in the group discussion.

Write your reflections here.

◄ GROUP DISCUSSION ►

Divide into small groups and discuss your responses. Then choose a group leader to share your group's discussion with the larger group.

AUDIO-VISUAL ACTIVITY ◀ ▶

On the day of your Baptism, your parents and godparents promised to help you to live the Law of Love. Now you are taking more responsibility for living that promise. After watching a videotape or filmstrip on the sacrament of Baptism, take a few minutes to reflect individually on the following:

- How does the videotape or filmstrip help me to understand my Baptism?
- How does the Law of Love guide me to live the new life I received in Baptism?
- How does the Law of Love guide me to live as a member of the body of Christ, the Church?
- Share your reflections with your group.

◀ LIVING THE LAW OF LOVE ▶

Divide into three groups. Each group will do one of the following projects.

- Create a word collage depicting the Law of Love.
- Illustrate a mural showing how you will live the Law of Love.
- Role-play a TV spot reporting on the Law of Love.

Each group will present its completed project during the closing prayer service.

279

◀ PRAYER SERVICE ▶

Opening Hymn

"They Will Know We Are Christians by Our Love" (or another appropriate hymn)

Scripture Reading

Reader: A reading from the holy gospel according to John.

Jesus said to his disciples, "This is my commandment: love one another as I love you. No one has greater love than this, to lay down one's life for one's friends. . . . I chose you and appointed you to go and bear fruit that will remain. . . . This I command you: love one another."

John 15:12–13,16–17

Presentation of Projects

Each group presents and explains its project on the Law of Love.

Prayer of the Faithful

Leader: When we live our Baptism by following the Law of Love, we become signs of God's love and help bring about the reign of God. Today, we pray for the coming of the reign of God.

Prayer leader 1: For our pope, our bishop, our priests, and all who lead our Church in service and worship, we pray to the Lord.

All: Thy kingdom come; thy will be done. (Repeat this response after each petition.)

Prayer leader 2: For the leaders of our world, our nation, our state, and our communities, we pray to the Lord. (Response)

Prayer leader 3: For ourselves, that we may reach out to help the hungry, the homeless, those suffering from injustice, oppression, illness, or addiction, and for all those with special needs, we pray to the Lord. (Response)

Prayer leader 4: For the needs of those in our parish and neighborhood, especially...(Response)

Now quietly pray this prayer.

† Holy Spirit, help me to live my Baptism and follow the Law of Love by

_____

_____

_____ .

_____

Amen.

◀ BLESSING ▶

Turn to a partner and trace a cross on her or his forehead, saying:

† As Christ was faithful in following his Father's will, so may you always live the Law of Love and bring about the reign of God.

Closing Hymn

"They Will Know We Are Christians by Our Love" (or another appropriate hymn)

SHARING OUR FAITH AS CATHOLICS

God is close to us at all times and in all places, calling us and helping us in coming to faith. When a person is baptized and welcomed into the faith community of the Church, everyone present stands with family and other members of the parish. We hear the words, "This is our faith. This is the faith of the Church. We are proud to profess it in Christ Jesus, our Lord." And we joyfully answer, "Amen"—"Yes, God, I believe."

The Catholic Church is our home in the Christian community. We are proud to be Catholics, living as disciples of Jesus Christ in our world. Each day we are called to share our faith with everyone we meet, helping to build up the reign of God.

What is the faith we want to live and to share? Where does the gift of faith come from? How do we celebrate it and worship God? How do we live it? How do we pray to God? In these pages, you will find a special faith guide written just for you. It can help you as a fifth grader to grow in your Catholic faith and to share it with your family and with others, too.

Following the Church's teachings and what God has told us in the Bible, we can outline some of our most important beliefs and practices in four ways:

WHAT WE BELIEVE—CREED

HOW WE CELEBRATE—SACRAMENTS

HOW WE LIVE—MORALITY

HOW WE PRAY—PRAYER

CATHOLICS BELIEVE...

THERE IS ONE GOD IN THREE DIVINE PERSONS: Father, Son, and Holy Spirit. One God in three divine Persons is called the Blessed Trinity. This is the central teaching of the Christian religion.

GOD THE FATHER is the creator of all things.

GOD THE SON took on human flesh and became one of us. This is called the incarnation. Our Lord Jesus Christ, who is the Son of God born of the Virgin Mary, proclaimed the reign of God. Jesus gave us the new commandment of love and taught us the way of the Beatitudes. We believe that by his sacrifice on the cross, he died to save us from the power of sin—original sin and our personal sins. He was buried and rose from the dead on the third day. Through his resurrection we share in the divine life, which we call grace. Jesus, the Christ, is our Messiah. He ascended into heaven and will come again to judge the living and the dead.

GOD THE HOLY SPIRIT is the third Person of the Blessed Trinity, adored together with the Father and Son. The action of the Holy Spirit in our lives enables us to respond to the call of Jesus to live as faithful disciples.

We believe in **ONE, HOLY, CATHOLIC, AND APOSTOLIC CHURCH** founded by Jesus on the "rock," which is Peter, and the other apostles.

As Catholics, **WE SHARE A COMMON FAITH.** We believe and respect what the Church teaches: everything that is contained in the word of God, both written and handed down to us.

We believe in **THE COMMUNION OF SAINTS** and that we are to live forever with God.

I have also learned this year that
to believe as a Catholic means

_____

_____

_____

CATHOLICS CELEBRATE...

S
A
C
R
A
M
E
N
T
S

THE CHURCH, THE BODY OF CHRIST, continues the mission of Jesus Christ throughout human history. Through the sacraments and by the power of the Holy Spirit, the Church enters into the mystery of the death and resurrection of the Savior and the life of grace.

THE SEVEN SACRAMENTS are Baptism, Confirmation, Eucharist, Holy Orders, Matrimony, Reconciliation, and Anointing of the Sick. Through the sacraments, we share in God's grace so that we may live as disciples of Jesus.

THE SACRAMENTS ARE EFFECTIVE SIGNS through which Jesus Christ shares God's life and love with us. Through the power of the Holy Spirit, the sacraments actually bring about what they promise.

The Church carries on Jesus' mission of welcoming members into the body of Christ when we celebrate Baptism, Confirmation, and Eucharist. We call these the sacraments of initiation.

The Church forgives and heals as Jesus did by celebrating Reconciliation and Anointing of the Sick. We call these the sacraments of healing.

The Church serves others and is a special sign of God's love by celebrating and living the sacraments of Matrimony and Holy Orders. We call these the sacraments of service.

IN THE SACRAMENTS, WE RECEIVE GOD'S GRACE: a sharing in the divine life of the Father, Son, and the Holy Spirit which Jesus shares with the Church through the power of the Holy Spirit. We are called to respond by living as disciples of Jesus.

By celebrating the sacraments, the Church worships and praises God. In celebrating the sacraments, the Church becomes a powerful sign of God's presence and reign in our world.

CATHOLICS CELEBRATE...

By participating in the celebration of the sacraments, Catholics grow in holiness and in living as disciples of Jesus. Freed from sin by Baptism and strengthened by Confirmation, we are nourished by Christ himself in the Eucharist. We also share in God's mercy and love in the sacrament of Reconciliation.

CATHOLICS CELEBRATE THE EUCHARIST AT MASS.
They do this together with a priest. The priest has received the sacrament of Holy Orders and acts in the person of Christ, our High Priest. The Mass is both a meal and a sacrifice. It is a meal because in the Mass, Jesus, the Bread of Life, gives us himself to be our food. Jesus is really present in the Eucharist. The Mass is a sacrifice, too, because we remember all that Jesus did for us to save us from sin and to bring us new life. In this great sacrifice of praise, we offer ourselves with Jesus to God.

THE EUCHARIST IS THE SACRAMENT OF JESUS' BODY AND BLOOD. It is the high point of Catholic worship. It is a great privilege to take part weekly in the celebration of the Mass with our parish community.

I have also learned this year that
to celebrate as a Catholic means

_____

_____

_____

_____

_____

Catholics Live...

WE ARE MADE IN THE IMAGE AND LIKENESS OF GOD and are called to live as disciples of Jesus Christ. Jesus said to us, "Love one another as I have loved you."

When we live the way Jesus showed us and follow his teachings, we can be truly happy and live in real freedom.

To help us live as Jesus' disciples, we are guided by **THE LAW OF LOVE, THE BEATITUDES, AND THE TEN COMMANDMENTS.** The Works of Mercy and the Laws of the Church also show us how to grow in living as Jesus' disciples.

AS MEMBERS OF THE CHURCH, THE BODY OF CHRIST, we are guided by the Church's teachings that help us to form our conscience. These teachings have come down to us from the time of Jesus and the apostles and have been lived by God's people throughout history. We share them with millions of Catholics throughout the world.

THROUGH PRAYER AND THE SACRAMENTS, especially Eucharist and Reconciliation, we are strengthened to live as Jesus asked us to live. In faith, hope, and love, we as Catholic Christians are called not just to follow rules. We are called to live a whole new way of life as disciples of Jesus Christ.

In living as Jesus' disciples, we are challenged each day to choose between right and wrong. Even when we are tempted to make wrong choices, the Holy Spirit is always present to help us make the right choices. Like Jesus, we are to live for God's reign. Doing all this means that we live a Christian moral life. As Christians we are always called to follow the way of Jesus.

I have also learned this year that
to live as a Catholic means

_____

_____

_____

CATHOLICS PRAY...

Prayer is talking and listening to God. We pray prayers of thanksgiving and sorrow; we praise God, and we ask him for what we need as well as for the needs of others.

We can pray in many ways and at any time. We can pray using our own words, words from the Bible, or just by being quiet in God's presence. We can also pray with song or dance or movement.

We also pray the prayers of our Catholic family that have come down to us over many centuries. Some of these prayers are the Our Father, the Hail Mary, the Glory to the Father, the Apostles' Creed, the Angelus, the Hail Holy Queen, and Acts of Faith, Hope, Love, and Contrition. Catholics also pray the rosary while meditating on events in the lives of Jesus and Mary.

As members of the Catholic community, we participate in the great liturgical prayer of the Church, the Mass. We also pray with the Church during the liturgical seasons of the Church year—Advent, Christmas, Lent, the Triduum, Easter, and Ordinary Time.

In prayer, we are joined with the whole communion of saints in praising and honoring God.

I have also learned this year that
to pray as a Catholic means

_____

_____

_____

_____

PRAYER

By this time, you should know many of these prayers and practices by heart.

Sign of the Cross

In the name of the Father,
and of the Son,
and of the Holy Spirit. Amen.

Glory to the Father

Glory to the Father,
and to the Son,
and to the Holy Spirit:
as it was in the beginning,
is now, and will be for ever. Amen.

Our Father

Our Father, who art in heaven,
hallowed be thy name;
thy kingdom come;
thy will be done on earth
as it is in heaven.
Give us this day our daily bread;
and forgive us our trespasses
as we forgive those
who trespass against us;
and lead us not into temptation,
but deliver us from evil. Amen.

Hail Mary

Hail Mary, full of grace,
the Lord is with you;
blessed are you among women,
and blessed is the fruit
of your womb, Jesus.
Holy Mary, Mother of God,
pray for us sinners now
and at the hour of our death. Amen.

Morning Offering

My God, I offer you all my prayers, works, and sufferings of this day for all the intentions of your most Sacred Heart. Amen.

Evening Prayer

Dear God,
before I sleep
I want to thank you for this day,
so full of your kindness
and your joy.
I close my eyes to rest
safe in your loving care.

Grace Before Meals

Bless us, O Lord,
and these your gifts
which we are about to receive
from your bounty,
through Christ our Lord. Amen.

Grace After Meals

We give you thanks, almighty God,
for these and all your gifts
which we have received
through Christ our Lord. Amen.

Memorare

Remember, O most gracious Virgin Mary, that never was it known that anyone who fled to your protection, implored your help, or sought your intercession was left unaided. Inspired with this confidence, we fly unto you, O Virgin of virgins, our Mother. To you we come, before you we kneel, sinful and sorrowful. O Mother of the Word made flesh, do not despise our petitions, but in your mercy hear and answer them. Amen.

Apostles' Creed

I believe in God, the Father almighty,
creator of heaven and earth.

I believe in Jesus Christ,
his only Son, our Lord.
He was conceived by the power
of the Holy Spirit
and born of the Virgin Mary.
He suffered under Pontius Pilate,
was crucified, died, and was buried.
He descended to the dead.
On the third day he rose again.
He ascended into heaven,
and is seated at the right hand
of the Father.
He will come again to judge
the living and the dead.

I believe in the Holy Spirit,
the holy catholic Church,
the communion of saints,
the forgiveness of sins,
the resurrection of the body,
and the life everlasting. Amen.

Prayer to the Holy Spirit

Come, Holy Spirit,
fill the hearts of your faithful
and enkindle in them
the fire of your love.
Send forth your Spirit and
they shall be created, and
you shall renew the face of
the earth.

Nicene Creed

We believe in one God,
the Father, the Almighty,
maker of heaven and earth,
of all that is seen and unseen.

We believe in one Lord, Jesus Christ,
the only Son of God,
eternally begotten of the Father,
God from God, Light from Light,
true God from true God,
begotten, not made,
one in Being with the Father.
Through him all things were made.
For us men and for our salvation
he came down from heaven:
by the power of the Holy Spirit
he was born of the Virgin Mary,
and became man.

For our sake he was crucified
under Pontius Pilate;
he suffered, died, and was buried.
On the third day he rose again
in fulfillment of the Scriptures;
he ascended into heaven and is seated
at the right hand of the Father.
He will come again in glory
to judge the living and the dead,
and his kingdom will have no end.

We believe in the Holy Spirit,
the Lord, the giver of life,
who proceeds from the Father
and the Son.
With the Father and the Son
he is worshiped and glorified.
He has spoken through the Prophets.

We believe in one holy catholic
and apostolic Church.
We acknowledge one baptism
for the forgiveness of sins.
We look for the resurrection of the dead,
and the life of the world to come. Amen.

Act of Contrition

My God,
I am sorry for my sins with all my heart.
In choosing to do wrong
and failing to do good,
I have sinned against you
whom I should love above all things.
I firmly intend, with your help,
to do penance,
to sin no more,
and to avoid whatever leads me to sin.
Our Savior Jesus Christ
suffered and died for us.
In his name, my God, have mercy.

Prayer for My Vocation

Dear God,
You have a great and loving plan
for our world and for me.
I wish to share in that plan fully,
faithfully, and joyfully.

Help me to understand what it is
you wish me to do with my life.
Help me to be attentive to the signs
that you give me about preparing for
the future.

Help me to learn to be a sign
of the kingdom, or reign, of
God whether I'm called to the
priesthood or religious life,
the single or married life.

And once I have heard and understood
your call, give me the strength
and the grace to follow it
with generosity and love. Amen.

The Angelus

The angel of the Lord declared to Mary
and she conceived by the Holy Spirit.
Hail Mary....

Behold the handmaid of the Lord,
be it done to me according to your word.
Hail Mary....

And the Word was made Flesh
and dwelled among us.
Hail Mary....

Pray for us, O Holy Mother of God,
That we may be worthy of the promises of
Christ.
Let us pray:
Pour forth, we beseech you, O Lord,
your grace into our hearts
that we to whom the incarnation of
Christ your Son was made known by the
message of an angel may,
by his passion and cross,
be brought to the glory of his resurrection,
through Christ Our Lord. Amen.

Prayer of Saint Francis

Lord, make me an instrument of your peace:
where there is hatred, let me sow love;
where there is injury, pardon;
where there is doubt, faith;
where there is despair, hope;
where there is darkness, light;
where there is sadness, joy.
O Divine Master, grant that I may not
so much seek
to be consoled as to console,
to be understood as to understand,
to be loved as to love.
For it is in giving that we receive,
it is in pardoning that we are pardoned,
and it is in dying that we are born
to eternal life.

The Stations of the Cross

1. Jesus is condemned to die.
2. Jesus takes up his cross.
3. Jesus falls the first time.
4. Jesus meets his Mother.
5. Simon helps Jesus carry his cross.
6. Veronica wipes the face of Jesus.
7. Jesus falls the second time.
8. Jesus meets the women of Jerusalem.
9. Jesus falls the third time.
10. Jesus is stripped of his garments.
11. Jesus is nailed to the cross.
12. Jesus dies on the cross.
13. Jesus is taken down from the cross.
14. Jesus is laid in the tomb.

Hail, Holy Queen

Hail, Holy Queen, Mother of Mercy;
hail, our life, our sweetness,
and our hope! To you do we cry,
poor banished children of Eve;
to you do we send up our sighs,
mourning and weeping in this valley of tears.

Turn, then, most gracious advocate,
your eyes of mercy toward us;
and after this our exile, show unto us
the blessed fruit of your womb, Jesus,
O clement, O loving, O sweet Virgin Mary!

The Rosary

A rosary has a cross, followed by one large bead and three small ones. Then there is a circle with five "decades." Each decade consists of one large bead followed by ten smaller beads. Begin the rosary with the sign of the cross. Recite the Apostles' Creed. Then pray one Our Father, three Hail Marys, and one Glory to the Father.

To recite each decade, say one Our Father on the large bead and ten Hail Marys on the ten smaller beads. After each decade, pray the Glory to the Father. As you pray each decade, think of the appropriate joyful, sorrowful, or glorious mystery, or a special event in the life of Jesus and Mary. Pray the Hail, Holy Queen as the last prayer of the rosary.

The Five Joyful Mysteries (by custom, used on Mondays, Thursdays, and the Sundays of Advent)

1. The annunciation
2. The visitation
3. The birth of Jesus
4. The presentation of Jesus in the Temple
5. The finding of Jesus in the Temple

The Five Sorrowful Mysteries
(by custom, used on Tuesdays, Fridays, and the Sundays of Lent)

1. The agony in the garden
2. The scourging at the pillar
3. The crowning with thorns
4. The carrying of the cross
5. The crucifixion and death of Jesus

The Five Glorious Mysteries
(by custom, used on Wednesdays, Saturdays, and the remaining Sundays of the year)

1. The resurrection
2. The ascension
3. The Holy Spirit comes upon the apostles
4. The assumption of Mary into heaven
5. The coronation of Mary in heaven

Prayer of Inner Stillness

Choose a time when you can be alone. Sit in a comfortable position and relax by breathing deeply. Try to shut out all the sights and sounds around you so that you feel the peaceful rhythm of your breathing in and out.

Slowly repeat a short prayer such as "Come, Lord Jesus" or perhaps just the name Jesus.

A Scripture Meditation

1. Pray for inner stillness.
2. Read one of your favorite stories about Jesus.
3. Close your eyes and imagine you are with Jesus.
4. Talk to Jesus about what the reading means to you.

The Storm at Sea

Quiet your mind and body as you breathe deeply.
Pray, "Jesus, be with me."

Listen to God's Word

One day Jesus got into a boat with his disciples. As they were sailing, Jesus fell asleep. Suddenly a strong wind came up, and the boat began to fill with water. They woke Jesus, saying, "Master, master, we are perishing!"

Jesus got up and gave an order to the wind and to the stormy water. They quieted down, and there was great calm.
Based on Luke 8:22–24

Imagine you are in the boat with Jesus. What do you say to the other disciples when you first see the storm? What do you say to Jesus?

What do you say to yourself after Jesus calms the storm?

What are things that can cause storms in your life right now? Imagine Jesus is standing in front of you. Talk to Jesus about how you can become calm.

Decide how you can help others through stormy times.

Pray in these words or your own

Jesus, when a storm comes up in
   my life, calm my fears.

When I am afraid to do what I know
   is right, give me courage.

When I am afraid to try something
   new because I might fail,
   give me hope.

When I have a problem that is too
   big to handle alone, give me trust
   in you and in those who can
   help me.

The Ten Commandments

1. I am the LORD your God: you shall not have strange gods before me.

2. You shall not take the name of the LORD your God in vain.

3. Remember to keep holy the LORD's day.

4. Honor your father and your mother.

5. You shall not kill.

6. You shall not commit adultery.

7. You shall not steal.

8. You shall not bear false witness against your neighbor.

9. You shall not covet your neighbor's wife.

10. You shall not covet your neighbor's goods.

The Beatitudes

Blessed are the poor in spirit,
   for theirs is the kingdom of heaven.

Blessed are they who mourn,
   for they will be comforted.

Blessed are the meek,
   for they will inherit the land.

Blessed are they who hunger and
   thirst for righteousness,
   for they will be satisfied.

Blessed are the merciful,
   for they will be shown mercy.

Blessed are the clean of heart,
   for they will see God.

Blessed are the peacemakers,
   for they will be called children of God.

Blessed are they who are persecuted for
   the sake of righteousness,
   for theirs is the kingdom of heaven.

The Laws of the Church

1. Celebrate Christ's resurrection every Sunday (or Saturday evening) and on holy days of obligation by taking part in Mass and avoiding unnecessary work.

2. Lead a sacramental life. Receive Holy Communion frequently and the sacrament of Penance, or Reconciliation, regularly. We must receive Holy Communion at least once a year at Lent-Easter. We must confess within a year, if we have committed serious, or mortal, sin.

3. Study Catholic teaching throughout life, especially in preparing for the sacraments.

4. Observe the marriage laws of the Catholic Church and give religious training to one's children.

5. Strengthen and support the Church: one's own parish, the worldwide Church, and the Holy Father.

6. Do penance, including not eating meat and fasting from food on certain days.

7. Join in the missionary work of the Church.

Holy Days of Obligation

On these days Catholics must celebrate the Eucharist just as on Sunday.

1. Solemnity of Mary, Mother of God (Jan. 1)
2. Ascension (During the Easter season)
3. Assumption of Mary (August 15)
4. All Saints Day (November 1)
5. Immaculate Conception (December 8)
6. Christmas (December 25)

Corporal and Spiritual Works of Mercy (see page 246)

CLOSING PRAYER SERVICE

Leader: As we gather together for the last time this year, let us pause to give thanks to God for all that we have shared. Let us give thanks in the name of Jesus, whom we have come to know even more through our study of the sacraments. Finally, let us call upon the Holy Spirit to guide us in the way of love.

(Pause for quiet prayer. Instrumental music may be playing in the background.)

Reader 1: Before we go our separate ways, let us listen again to the words of Saint Paul that we heard at the beginning of our time together.

As the Scripture says, "Everyone who calls on the name of the Lord will be saved." But how can they call on him in whom they have not believed? And how can they believe in him of whom they have not heard? And how can they hear without someone to preach? And how can the people preach unless they are sent? As it is written, "How beautiful are the feet of those who bring [the] good news!'"

Romans 10:13–15

Leader: After all we have learned this year, we should be ready to be sent out as informed messengers of the good news, ready to proclaim the love of Jesus Christ to the world. Let us join in giving thanks to God.

Reader 2: We thank you, God, for the sacraments of initiation: Baptism, Confirmation, and Eucharist. We can help the Church carry on Jesus' mission of welcoming members into the body of Christ by . . . . (Anyone who wishes may share ways of being welcoming signs of God's love.)

All: O God, help us to be your evangelizers and carry on the work of your Son.

Reader 3: We thank you for the sacraments of healing: Reconciliation and Anointing of the Sick. We can bring Jesus' healing love to others by . . . . (Anyone who wishes may share ways of being signs of Jesus' healing love.)

All: O God, help us to be your evangelizers and carry on the work of your Son.

Reader 4: We thank you for the sacraments of service: Matrimony and Holy Orders, which are gifts to the Church in the service of all. We can serve others by . . . . (Anyone who wishes may share ways of being signs of love and service.)

All: O God, help us to be your evangelizers and carry on the work of your Son.

Leader: Let us share with one another a sign of peace.

(After the sign of peace is exchanged, the final prayer is shared by all.)

All: Loving God, we thank you for all the blessings you have given to us this year. Each time we looked at our religion books, we were reminded of our membership in the Church and the wonder of the sacraments. Send forth your Spirit upon us that we may grow into the best of messengers. We ask this through our Lord Jesus Christ who lives and reigns with you and the Holy Spirit, one God, forever and ever. Amen.

GLOSSARY

Absolution (page 142)

Absolution is the prayer the priest says asking forgiveness of our sins.

Anointing of the Sick (page 153)

The sacrament of Anointing of the Sick brings God's special blessings to those who are sick, elderly, or dying.

Apostles (page 170)

The apostles were the twelve special helpers chosen by Jesus to lead the early Church.

Ascension (page 47)

The ascension is the event in which Jesus Christ was taken into heaven after the resurrection.

Baptism (page 81)

Baptism is the sacrament of our new life with God and the beginning of our initiation into the Church. Through this sacrament we are freed from sin, become children of God, and are welcomed as members of the Church.

Beatitudes (page 293)

The Beatitudes are ways of living that Jesus gave us so that we can be truly happy.

Bethlehem (page 136)

The town in which Jesus was born.

Blessed Sacrament (page 101)

Another name for the Eucharist. Jesus is really present in the Blessed Sacrament.

Catholic (page 47)

The Church welcomes all people and has the message of God's good news for all people.

Confirmation (page 91)

Confirmation is the sacrament in which we are sealed with the gift of the Holy Spirit and are strengthened to give witness to the good news of Jesus.

Conscience (page 66)

Conscience is the ability we have to decide whether a thought, word, or deed is right or wrong. We form our conscience according to the teachings of the Church.

Consecration (page 110)

The consecration is that part of the Mass in which the bread and wine become Jesus' own Body and Blood through the power of the Holy Spirit and the words and actions of the priest.

Corporal Works of Mercy (page 246)

The Corporal Works of Mercy are ways we care for one another's physical needs.

Disciple (page 19)

A disciple is one who learns from and follows Jesus Christ.

Divine (page 16)

A word that means having the nature of God.

Eucharist (page 99)

The Eucharist is the sacrament of Jesus' Body and Blood. Jesus is really present in the Eucharist. Our gifts of bread and wine become the Body and Blood of Christ at Mass.

Evangelization (page 181)

Evangelization means spreading the good news of Jesus Christ and sharing our faith by our words and actions.

Faith (page 223)

Faith is a virtue that enables us to trust and believe in God, to accept what he has revealed, and to live according to his loving will.

Fruits of the Holy Spirit (page 67)

The Fruits of the Holy Spirit are the good results people can see in us when we use the gifts of the Holy Spirit. They are love, joy, peace, patience, kindness, goodness, faithfulness, humility, and self-control.

Gifts of the Holy Spirit (page 89)

The seven gifts of the Holy Spirit are: wisdom, understanding, right judgment, courage, knowledge, reverence, and wonder and awe. They help us to live and witness to our Catholic faith.

Grace (page 59)

Grace is a sharing in the divine life, in God's very life and love.

Holy Orders (page 173)

Holy Orders is the sacrament that confers the ordained ministry of bishops, priests, and deacons.

Hope (page 233)

Hope is a virtue that enables us to trust that God will be with us in every situation.

Incarnation (page 17)

The incarnation is the mystery of God "becoming flesh," or becoming one of us in Jesus Christ.

Kingdom of Heaven (page 37)

The kingdom of heaven is another way of saying kingdom, or reign, of God in Matthew's gospel.

Laity (page 182)

The laity are single or married people who belong to the Church. Lay people serve the Church in many ways.

Law of Love (page 30)

Love the Lord your God with all your heart, with all your soul, with all your strength, and with all your mind. Love your neighbor as you love yourself.

Liturgical Year (pages 118–119)

Advent, Christmas, Lent, the Easter Triduum, Easter, and Ordinary Time make up the seasons, or times, of the liturgical year. Our Church celebrates the liturgical year to help us remember the whole story of the life, death, and resurrection of Jesus Christ.

Liturgy (page 77)

Liturgy is the official public worship of the Church. The Liturgy includes the ways we celebrate the Mass and the other sacraments.

Liturgy of the Eucharist (page 76)

The Liturgy of the Eucharist is one of the two major parts of the Mass. It is made up of the Presentation and Preparation of the Gifts, the Eucharistic Prayer, and Holy Communion.

Liturgy of the Word (page 76)

The Liturgy of the Word is one of the two major parts of the Mass. It is made up of readings from the Old and New Testaments, Responsorial Psalm, Gospel, Homily, Creed, and Prayer of the Faithful.

Love (page 173)

Love is a virtue that enables us to love God, our neighbor, and ourselves.

Marks of the Church (page 148)

The marks of the Church are: one, holy, catholic, and apostolic. These are four great identifying qualities that let people know the kind of community Jesus began and calls us to be.

Mass (page 76)

The Mass is our celebration of the Eucharist. The two major parts of the Mass are the Liturgy of the Word and the Liturgy of the Eucharist.

Matrimony (page 117)

The sacrament of Matrimony is a powerful and effective sign of Christ's presence that joins a man and woman together for life.

Messiah (page 88)

"Messiah" refers to the savior and liberator promised to the people in the Old Testament. Jesus is the Messiah.

Original Sin (page 61)

Original sin is the sinful condition into which all human beings are born. It is the loss of grace passed on from our first parents to all generations

Passover (page 70)

Passover is a feast in which Jews celebrate God's deliverance of their ancestors from slavery in Egypt.

Penance (page 105)

The penance we receive from the priest in the sacrament of Reconciliation helps to make up for the hurt caused by our sins and helps us to avoid sin in the future. Our penance can be a prayer or good deed.

Pope (page 149)

The pope is the bishop of Rome. He is the successor of Saint Peter and the leader of the whole Catholic Church.

Prayer (page 202)

Prayer is directing one's heart and mind to God. In prayer we talk and listen to God.

Priesthood of the Faithful (page 180)

The priesthood of the faithful is the priesthood of Jesus in which all baptized people share through Baptism and the anointing of the Holy Spirit.

Racism (page 213)

Racism is a sin of prejudice against a person because of race.

Reconciliation (page 142)

Reconciliation is the sacrament in which we are forgiven by God and the Church for our sins.

Reign of God (Kingdom of God) (page 27)

The reign, or kingdom, of God is the saving power of his life and love in the world.

Sacrament (page 57)

A sacrament is an effective sign through which Jesus Christ shares God's life and love with us. The sacraments cause to happen the very things they stand for. There are seven sacraments.

Sacramental (page 252)

A sacramental is a blessing, an action, or an object that helps us remember God, Jesus, Mary, or the saints.

Sin (page 141)

Sin is freely choosing to do what we know is wrong. When we sin, we disobey God's law on purpose.

Spiritual Works of Mercy (page 246)

The Spiritual Works of Mercy are ways we care for one another's spiritual needs.

Ten Commandments (page 293)

The Ten Commandments are laws given to us by God to help us live as God's people. God gave the Ten Commandments to Moses on Mount Sinai.

Viaticum (page 153)

When Holy Communion is given to a dying person, it is called Viaticum. Viaticum means "food for the journey." Viaticum is often received along with the sacrament of Anointing of the Sick.

Vocation (page 180)

A vocation is our call to live holy lives of service in our Church and in our world.

Worship (page 59)

Worship is praise and thanks to God in signs, words, and actions.

INDEX

*Bold-faced pages indicate chapters

† *Italics* refer to definitions

*Bold-faced pages indicate chapters

†*Italics* refer to definitions

Acknowledgments

Grateful acknowledgment is due the following for their work on the *Coming to Faith Program*:

Kathleen Hlavacek, Editor
Tresse De Lorenzo, Manager: Production/Art
Joe Svadlenka, Art Director
Stuart Vance, Manager: Electronic Art/Production
Barbara Berger, Design Director
Eileen Elterman and Ana Jouvin, Designers
Jim Saylor, Photo Editor
Mary Kate Coudal, Photo Research

Scripture selections are taken from the *New American Bible* copyright © 1991, 1986, 1970 by the Confraternity of Christian Doctrine, Washington D. C. and are used by permission. All rights reserved. Excerpts from the English translation of *Rite of Marriage* © 1969, International Committee on English in the Liturgy, Inc. (ICEL); excerpts from the English translation of *Rite of Baptism for Children* © 1969, ICEL; excerpts from the English translation of *The Roman Missal* © 1973, ICEL; excerpts from the English translation of *Rite of Penance* © 1974, ICEL; excerpts from the English translation of *Rite of Confirmation*, Second Edition © 1975, ICEL; excerpts from the English translation of *Pastoral Care of the Sick: Rites of Anointing and Viaticum* © 1982, ICEL. All rights reserved.English translation of the Lord's Prayer, the Apostle's Creed, Gloria Patria and the Nicene Creed by the International Consultation on English Texts.

Cover Photos

Myrleen Cate: *insets*.
H. Armstrong Roberts: *background and nature insets*.

Photo Credits

Diane J. Ali: 36/37 *background*, 83, 116 *top right*, 116 *center right*, 227.
Art Resource: 21, 56, 57, 204, 222/223, 52, 60, 66, 67, 72, 73; Erich Lessing: 98/99; Giraudon: 99; Scala: 120, 234.
Dennis Barnes: 152.
Myrleen Cate: 9 *top*, 9 *bottom*, 12, 14, 15, 20 *bottom*, 36/37 *inset*, 41, 46, 46/47, 49, 52, 60, 66, 67, 72, 73, 84, 91, 102, 103, 108, 111, 114 *bottom*, 116 *bottom*, 116 *center left*, 127 *center right*, 127 *center left*, 127 *top left*, 127 *bottom left*, 143, 148, 159 *center top left*, 159 *bottom left*, 159 *top right*, 159 *center top right*, 159 *center right bottom*, 159 *bottom right*, 164 *center*, 164 *top*, 168, 174 *bottom*, 182 *left*, 184, 188 *top*, 200 *top*, 200 *right*, 201, 210, 224/225, 226, 230 *bottom*, 234 *top right*, 248, 252.
Catholic Near East Welfare

Association/Arturo Mari: 216 *top*.
Catholic News Service: 171; Arturo Mari: 202/203, 205.
Catholic Relief Services: 47.
Bill Coleman: 215 *right*.
Contact Press/David Burnet: 247.
CROSIERS/Gene Plaisted, OSC: 90, 109, 134, 144, 145, 153, 172, 173 *right*, 174 *top*, 183, 197 *center*, 202, 206, 242, 250, 254.
Kathy Ferguson: 30, 45, 51, 65, 87, 117 *bottom*.
FPG International/Color Box: 77, 231 *background*; Laurence Aiuppy: 122 *background*; Ron Chapple: 149; Travel Pix: 180; Mike Malyszko: 189 *top*; O'Brien and Mayor: 189 *center*.
Christopher Talbot Frank: 76 *bottom*.
The Granger Collection: 88/89.
Marcia W. Griffin/Animals Animals: 76 *left*.
Impact Visuals/Jeff Scott: 185 *right*; Jack Kurtz: 207; Rick Reinhard: 243 *bottom*.
Josephite Archives: 175.
Anna Jouvin: 159 *top left*, 159 *center left bottom*.
Ken Karp: 182 *right*, 221, 225, 241.
Elfie Kluck/Stock Imagery: 195.
P. LeSegretian/SYGMA: 189 *bottom*.
LIAISON International/Bob Rina, Jr.: 127 *bottom right*; Eric Brissaud: 185 *top*; John Chiasson: 243 *top*.
Mark Mittleman: 173 *left*.
Aline Monoukian/Black Star: 117 *top*.
Mitzi Moorman: 162.
Francis Roberts: 154 *top*.
H. Armstrong Roberts: 127 *top right*, 138, 163 *top*, 197 *top*, 197 *bottom*, 235 *insets*.
Allen Russell/Profiles West: 200 *left*.
James L. Shaffer: 113, 117 *bottom left*, 203.
Nancy Sheehan: 80, 94, 110, 114 *top*, 196.
Chris Sheridan: 50, 183 *bottom*, 231 *inset*.
Harry Sieplinga/The Image Bank: 216 *bottom*.
The Stock Market/Paul Barton: 9 *bottom*; Peter Beck: 20 *top*, 166, 188 *bottom*; Elizabeth Hathon: 117 *center bottom left*; Michael Keller: 117 *center bottom right*; Paul Chauncey: 76 *top*; Jean Miele: 128/129; Anthony Edgeworth: 158; Gerald Zanetti: 165.
Tony Stone Images/Chris Thomaidis: 31; Lawrence Migdale: 71; Bruce Forster: 82; Rosemary Weller: 116 *top left*; Bob Torrez: 154 *bottom*; Dale Durfee: 163; Arthur Tilley: 164 *bottom*; Bill Aron: 214; David H. Endersbee: 230 *background*; David Olsen: 235 *background*.
Alex Webb/Magnum Photos: 236.
H. Mark Wiedman: 215 *left*.
Xavier University, New Orleans, LA: 217.

Illustrators

Blaine Martin: Cover, Digital Imaging
Wendy Pierson:Cover, Logo Rendering
Diane Ali: 165.
Skip Baker: 238.
Jim Baldwin: 176.
David Barber: 136.
David Barnett: 10–11, 26–27, 28–29, 140–141, 181.
Karen Bell: 68, 130, 198.
Eric Berendt: 46–47.
Menny Borovski: 87.
Kevin Butler: 30–31, 50–51, 185, 188, 191, 224–225, 246–247.
Pam Carroll: 97.
Robert Casilla: 150–151.
Antonio Castro: 18–19, 38–39, 40, 160–161, 232–233.
Young Sook Cho: 120–121.
Pat DeWitt: 256, 257.
Cathy Diefendorf: 106, 134–135, 218.
Victor Durango: 124.
Len Ebert: 58–59.
Eileen Elterman: 93, 102, 211, 231.
Yvonne Gilbert: 126.
Byron Gin: 20.
Adam Gordon: 42, 48–49, 52, 60, 114, 116–117, 127, 136, 152–153, 154, 166, 169, 171, 174, 175, 200, 201, 240, 241, 252–253.
Brad Hamann: 248.
John Haysom: 16–17, 100–101, 212–213.
Icon Graphics: 214–215.
W.B. Johnston: 118–119.
Ana Jouvin: 56, 71, 142–143, 250.
Al Leiner: 170–171.
Judy Love: 34–35, 54–55, 146, 148.
Steve Marchesi: 78–79.
Blaine Martin: 97, 140–141, 164, 192, 195, 228.
Shelly Matheis: 240.
David Scott Meier: 88–89.
Verlin Miller: 208.
Andrew Muonio: 155, 237.
Patricia Murphy: 107.
Cheryl Kirk Noll: 156.
Olivia: 236.
Julie Pace: 258–259.
Julie Peterson: 73.
Rodica Prato: 138–139.
Fernando Rangel: 61.
Alan Reingold: 22.
Dorothy Reinhardt: 110–111, 162–163.
Frank Riccio: 86.
Margaret Sanfilippo: 48–49, 132–133, 178–179, 186, 194.
Joanne Scribner: 64.
R. J. Shay: 112.
Bob Shein: 24–25, 74.
Mark Sparacio: 158.
Tom Sperling: 44–45, 70, 190–191, 220.
Matt Straub: 92.
Gregg Valley: 32, 134–135, 251.
Jenny Williams: 62, 104
Michael Woo: 21, 81, 90–91, 99, 181, 221, 244–245.